D1599768

RECOVERING THE PRAIRIE

RECOVERING

The University of Wisconsin Press

THE PRAIRIE

Edited by
Robert F. Sayre

The University of Wisconsin Press
2537 Daniels Street
Madison, Wisconsin 53718

3 Henrietta Street
London WC2E 8LU, England

Printed in the United States of America

Library of Congress Cataloging-in-Publication Data

Recovering the prairie / edited by Robert F. Sayre.
    266 pp.   cm.
    Essays contributed to a symposium held September 20–22, 1996.
    Includes bibliographical references and index.
    ISBN 0-299-16460-8 (cloth: alk. paper)
    1. Prairie conservation.   2. Prairies.   3. Prairies Pictorial works.   I. Sayre,
Robert F.
    QH75.R432   1999
    333.74'16—dc21   99-25650

CONTENTS

Contents

ACKNOWLEDGMENTS

In August 1996, a very unusual exhibit, "Plain Pictures: Images of the American Prairie," opened at the University of Iowa Museum of Art. Curated by Joni Kinsey of the Department of Art and Art History, it was the first major survey ever assembled of the landscapes of the American prairies and plains, a subject that has been neglected by American museums and art historians. It covered the period from the 1830s to the present, and included nearly a hundred paintings and photographs. After closing in November 1996, it moved to the Amon Carter Museum in Fort Worth and the Joslyn Museum of Art in Omaha.

In 1993, when Professor Kinsey first told me of her plans for "Plain Pictures," we both realized that it was a splendid opportunity to explore relationships between how the prairie has been seen—not only by artists, but also by writers, explorers, and settlers—and how it has been used. Accordingly, she and I and Rebecca Roberts of the Department of Geography applied for and received an interdisciplinary grant from the Obermann Center for Advanced Studies at the University of Iowa to study the relationships. Our work resulted in the paper "Prairie Prospects: The Aesthetics of Plainness," which was published in *Prospects: An Annual of American Cultural Studies*. I also undertook to organize the public symposium "Images and Functions of the American Prairie," which would be held shortly after the exhibit opened. The ideas and insights of Professors Kinsey and Roberts, as well as their friendship and counsel, have been essential to this project.

It is also a pleasure to thank Jay Semel and Lorna Olsen of the Obermann Center for their constant support and Jack Salzman of *Prospects* and Cambridge University Press for permission to reprint "Prairie Prospects."

The symposium was held on September 20–22, 1996, with participants representing environmental history, landscape architecture, biology, literature, political history, agriculture, and ecology. There were also talks by four of the artists whose work was exhibited in "Plain Pictures": Fred Easker, Terry Evans, Keith Jacobshagen, and Genie Patrick; a performance by Baxter Black; and a visit to Rochester Cemetery, a prairie–savanna east of Iowa City, for poetry readings and a performance of Lincoln's speeches by Michael Krebs.

Most of the chapters in *Recovering the Prairie* began as contributions to the symposium, and I am grateful to their authors—Ed Folsom, Tom Lutz, Shelton Stromquist, Robert Grese, Curt Meine, Pauline Drobney, and Wes Jackson—for permission to print them. I thank them, too, for carefully and in some cases substantially revising them for this volume.

But filling out *Recovering the Prairie* are other pieces written especially for it. Jane Simonsen's "On Level Ground: Alexander Gardner's Photographs of the Kansas Prairies" has been adapted from work done for a Walt Whitman seminar with Ed Folsom. Lance Foster's "*Tanji na Che:* Recovering the Landscape of the Ioway" has been adapted from his research at Iowa State University and his knowledge of Ioway language and traditions. A third and very appropriate contributor, Aldo Leopold, comes back to be with us thanks to Curt Meine, who found Leopold's manuscript "Prairie: The Forgotten Flora," written in 1942, in the Aldo Leopold Papers. It is a great pleasure to be able to print it for the first time, and I am grateful to Curt Meine, the Leopold family, and the Leopold Foundation (from which we also have some of the Leopold photographs).

"Sizing Up the Country" is based on a survey of the artists represented in "Plain Pictures," and I thank the artists who generously responded. I also invited them to send one or two other examples of their work, in order to assemble a visual essay especially for this volume. These are gathered in the color insert. Thanks to each of the artists—Robert Adams, Lee Allen, James Butler, Fred Easker, Terry Evans, Harold Gregor, Walter Hatke, Stan Herd, Harold Holoun, Gary Irving, Keith Jacobshagen, Stuart Klipper, Genie Patrick, David Plowden, and James Winn—and to the Phyllis Kind Gallery, which supplied photographs of the paintings of the late Roger Brown. Thanks, too, to Jon Van Allen, who took the aerial photograph of Stan Herd's crop art.

The sponsors of "Plain Pictures: Images of the American Prairie" and the symposium "Images and Functions of the American Prairie" were The National Endowment for the Humanities; Land O' Lakes, Inc.; The Iowa Arts Council; University of Iowa Office of the Provost; University of Iowa Cultural Affairs Council; The Iowa Humanities Board; University of Iowa Departments of Art and Art History, English, and History; University of Iowa Obermann Center for Advanced Studies; University of Iowa Lecture Committee; and University of Iowa Museum of Art. I thank them not only for myself and the contributors to this volume, but for everyone who attended the symposium and visited the exhibition.

Finally, it is a pleasure to acknowledge the support of the staff of the University of Iowa Museum of Art, particularly Stephen S. Prokopoff, Jo Jones, Emily Vermillion, and Pamela White Trimpe; Gayle Sand of the Department of English; and many other members of the faculty and staff of the university, especially Sam Becker and Stephen Foster.

RECOVERING THE PRAIRIE

1 Introduction

Robert F. Sayre

Americans in ever increasing numbers are rediscovering the prairie. They are searching out remnants of original native prairie along old railroad rights-of-way and county roads, in old parks, and even in abandoned army bases and ordinance plants. They are buying and collecting rare seeds of prairie plants and grasses and are planting them in new parks and on their farms and suburban acreages. And they are forming clubs and volunteer organizations to continue this work and to protect the restoration projects that have been started. In the 1930s, when this work had its modest beginnings, it was done by only a few university ecologists, such as John E. Weaver at the University of Nebraska and Aldo Leopold at the University of Wisconsin.[1] But in the past ten years, the protecting and replanting of prairie has become a broad, regional movement, from Oklahoma and Texas into Canada, from Illinois to the High Plains.

As this recovery effort has grown, it has engaged many more kinds of people, with many perspectives. Although the movement still has strong environmental purposes, such as the preservation of native species and prevention of soil erosion, it now includes painters, photographers, historians, art historians, geographers, writers, farmers, schoolchildren, and ethnic groups. The prairie appeals to them all, in a variety of ways and for a wide variety of reasons. It is, one could say, like an emerging lost continent—not a lost Atlantis but a lost America. Buried for a hundred years, it has not been forgotten. It has endured not only in physical remnants but also in the memories of settlers and their families, the books of prairie authors, and the work of prairie artists. As the grass returns, the shock waves of recognition ripple through it; and the more that returns, the wider the waves and the more numerous the perspectives.

This book illustrates some of these new perspectives, although there are so many that it is impossible to include them all. It is also difficult to classify them, for they overlap and are interdependent. To recover the prairie as it was in the days before Euro-American settlement requires, as Curt Meine says, imagination, for there is no one living who saw it as it was then. Indeed, he notes, quoting Aldo Leopold, we will never again see it as it was: "What a thousand acres of Silphiums [compass plants] looked like when they tickled the bellies of the buffalo is a question never again to be answered, and perhaps not even asked."[2] Imagination can be aided by referring to historical documents like letters, travel accounts, and the autobiographies of pioneers; by looking at early artists' representations; and by learning from the modern restoration ecologists. It can also be richly stimulated by reference to the traditions, stories, and language of American Indians, as Lance Foster demonstrates here. All this research is interdependent, and each activity benefits the others. The early surveyors' records of the plants that were growing in a certain place help the restoration ecologist, and the ecologist, in turn, can help the reader of the documents to identify and actually see the plants and animals named in them. Thus does the slow and yet exciting process of imagination and recovery go on. It may be true in the end, as Leopold said, that the question cannot be answered. But as he also said, unless we try, we will not be able even to ask the question. The plants will become extinct, and the names in the books will become meaningless, just fading ink on crumbling pages.

Further benefits from this recovery of the prairie are the recoveries of our social and economic and political history, in which the prairie played such an enormous role. The Iowa novelist and historian Herbert Quick wrote of the enormous impact of the prairies:

[They] gave the railways something on which to live, placed a great population far in the interior where it is dependent on railways, killed our seamanship and turned us from a nation of sailors to one of landsmen, broke the backs of the farmers of the Eastern States and of Great Britain and Europe generally, and [were] felt by almost every people from the rice eaters of Asia to the sugar planters of the West Indies.[3]

But not only did their vast size and fertility draw millions west; at the same time, their lack of trees to supply lumber, fuel, fencing, sugar, nuts, honey, and fruit made the settlers directly dependent on the national market economy.[4] They could not be independent subsistence farmers. They needed cash crops, such as wheat and corn, and to grow them they needed the continually developing farm machinery—plows, seeders, cultivators, reapers, thrashers, and tractors—that was being made in cities. This, in turn, made the settlers further dependent on railroads, banks, and capital. Thus the legendary fertility of the prairie and its legendary remoteness and barrenness of trees and other amenities were equally important to the development of American agrarian capitalism. The one made prairie farmers great producers. The other made them consumers and debtors, and the two went hand in hand in later political and economic history.

The recovery of the prairie is also an opportunity, therefore, to reassess this history, rehear our poets and novelists, and look again at prairie artists. It is an opportunity to read Walt Whitman, Willa Cather, and Hamlin Garland in something closer to their early context and to see the interrelationships between how the prairie was used and how it was represented in literature and art. How land is seen and how it is used are, of course, integrally connected. But in the case of the prairies, as in much of the American West, the artists and photographers like Alexander Gardner were actually working for the railroads and developers. The aesthetics and economics of the prairies, the artistic representations and economic promotions, were managed together. So recovery of the prairie is a challenge and an opportunity to art history and literature as well as to restoration biology. It is one of those occasions when the study of environmental history and political and economic history really come together.

From another perspective, prairie recovery and restoration give us the means of critiquing our present systems of land use and developing better ones. Natural systems agriculture, such as Wes Jackson advocates, is based on prairie ecology. It follows the pioneer ecologists like John Weaver and Aldo Leopold in regarding the native prairie as the ideal form of vegetation with which to cover the soil and prevent wind and water erosion. Using "nature as measure" means letting the prairie set the standard. Measure the success of agriculture not just by bushels raised and dollars in the bank but by how the land's health and fertility are maintained, the soil preserved. Then try to make agriculture mimic the prairie.

Employing these diverse and yet related perspectives, the chapters in this book start by looking at the prairie as it was seen by the early Euro-American artists and writers who documented it, because it was through their eyes that the prairie was first interpreted for other Americans and because their visions had such a lasting impact. In "Prairie Prospects: The Aesthetics of Plainness," Joni L. Kinsey, Rebecca Roberts, and I propose that the prairies were an aesthetic problem, not just a physical or an economic or a military one, as is usually assumed. Nineteenth-century landscape artists had difficulty painting the prairies because they had no "prospects"—no pleasing views framed by trees or glens, with mountains in the background, and no elevated positions, like the conventional "prospect points," from which to look out. Instead, the prairies were just vast space, with a seemingly changeless and monotonous "sea of grass." They were, therefore, treated as a blank slate, a tabula rasa, on which settlers and farmers and the agents of American civilization could write their own character and destiny. They ordered the vast space into square-mile sections, divided it into farms and cities, and made the desert bloom. Ironically, what they thought was desert was actually a diverse and complex ecosystem composed of scores of grasses and hundreds of flowers, of which they knew the names of only a few. It was much less monotonous than the monocultures of wheat and corn with which they replaced it. But the process of that transformation, requiring years of labor and sacrifice,

produced the wealth and comfort of what we know today as the Middle West. This labor and achievement also became integral to modern Midwesterners' identity, as illustrated in the celebration of it in pioneer literature and county histories as well as the objections, in places like O'Brien County, Iowa, to prairie reconstruction. Why bring back what required blood, sweat, and tears to change? Why sacrifice the wealth—the new prospects—that the prairie has given us or that we have wrested from it?

These are questions that the subsequent chapters directly and indirectly try to answer. Walt Whitman was one of the earliest admirers of the prairie, celebrating both its past and its destiny. As Ed Folsom pointedly reminds us in "Walt Whitman's Prairie Paradise," the grass of *Leaves of Grass* was not a lawn. It was grass that had leaves, "usually broad leaves and firm long stems," and that meant, especially in the mid-nineteenth century, prairie grasses. Those were the grasses that were strong, thick, hardy, native, varied, and, as Whitman liked to say, "manly," and that supplied his basic metaphor for American democracy. That Whitman did not know them as well as he knew the calamus grass of Long Island—he seems, like most other Americans then and now, not to have known even their names—did not stop him from being a "prairie-wanna-be," as Folsom calls him. He identified with the prairies and prairie people, and he saw them as "a newer garden of creation. . . . Dense, joyous, modern, populous" that would "justify the past." They were not an Eden, a Garden for two, but a garden for "millions," the one that would fulfill the democratic dream. In addition, Folsom cleverly notes, the prairies supplied Whitman with a "style—flat and rolling—where it is easy to get lost because the conventional landmarks (the syntactical pathways we are accustomed to) are absent." It's a style with many nouns and adjectives, prepositional phrases and gerunds or infinitives ("dead verbs") but very few verbs, so it becomes, like a prairie, a giant "jagged, jarring" aggregate of many parts. Thus one of the reasons for restoring prairie—one of incalculable value, for it is spiritual and ideological rather than financial—is simply to understand Whitman's vision of American democracy. To understand the metaphor, we need the fact.

One of the shapers of Whitman's vision of the prairie was Alexander Gardner, the former Civil War photographer who in 1867 and 1868 had produced a series of stereographs entitled *Across the Continent on the Kansas-Pacific Railway, Eastern Division,* discussed in Jane E. Simonsen's "On Level Ground: Alexander Gardner's Photographs of the Kansas Prairies." Whitman had seen Gardner's work before his own visit to the prairies in 1879, so it may have supplied him with the images of vastness, fecundity, and egalitarian uniformity that later made the prairies so attractive to him. Gardner's focus on the railroad as the new organizer of the prairies could also lie behind Whitman's description of them as "with iron interlaced"—held together by rails and the other manufactured goods, like reapers and barbed wire, that the railroads brought in. The railroad, as Gardner represented it, spanned the prairies. It bridged its rivers and connected its new cities and towns, just as Whitman wanted to span the continent with his poetry. It could then carry farm produce to cities and manufactured goods to farms—the very economic exchange its backers sought. As a railroad photographer, Gardner made these relationships visual, encouraging investors and settlers and appealing to the national sense of manifest destiny. By using stereographs, he also rendered the prairie in three dimensions.

A more ambivalent view of the prairie and the railroads came from the later regional writers, such as Hamlin Garland and Willa Cather, and the political leaders like William Jennings Bryan, who expressed the discontent of the settlers. As Garland showed in "Under the Lion's Paw" and his other early stories, they were not always the beneficiaries of agrarian capitalism. They were mainly its victims. The harder they worked and the more the land produced, the less they were paid, so they had to borrow more money and work still harder. Improved communication also made the comforts of urban life more visible, without necessarily making them more accessible, thus adding to the farmers' own discomforts and sense of inequality. The differences between city and country were not reduced but increased, and the "barrenness" of the prairie, which once referred to the absence of trees and mountains and visual diversity, now referred to the absence of human culture and pleasure. According to Garland, the farther "Up the Cooley" or down the "Branch Road" one went, the harsher the drudgery and the greater the crudity of people who had no time for beauty and manners.

The conditions of prairie life, therefore, required careful interpretation. They could not be described adequately from either the inside or the outside, a rural or an urban point of view. They required what Tom Lutz calls "Cosmopolitan Vistas," in a chapter that takes issue with the views of many fans of Garland, Cather, and other prairie regionalists. To Lutz, I think it is fair to say, the prairie regionalists were essentially like all other regional writers—New England, southern, and so on—in being writers first and last and in appealing to a mainly metropolitan audience. They did not have a lifelong bond with their region, as proved by the choice that most made to live elsewhere. Thus they were interpreters of the prairie more than champions of it, and their cosmopolitan vistas, like those of other regionalists, established a moral and aesthetic position from which they could both sympathize and criticize, siding at some points with the plight of the prairie characters and at others with the sophistication of the outsider. They, like their readers, wanted to be citizens of the world, and regional writing was, paradoxically, a means to that end, not an end in itself.

Lutz thus raises basic questions about the relations in the United States between region and nation. Are the prairies and their residents very different from other regions and their inhabitants, or are they basically the same? Is the Midwest the epitome of the nation, a "heartland"? Or is it, as others would say, the "boondocks"? And what have the prairies to do with these radically different images?

The questions are of further interest because the recovery of the prairies is, in addition, a recovery of a word and a name, the older name for the region. The word "prairie," it is generally believed, derives from *praerie,* the Old French word for "meadow," and was the name given to the rolling, grassy, and generally treeless midsection of the country by the first French explorers. "Middle West," the geographer James Shortridge has determined, was a term first used in 1827 to refer to Tennessee. The journalist Timothy Flint wished to distinguish between the Northwest (Ohio and Indiana) and the Southwest (Alabama and Mississippi). In the ensuing conflict between North and South, the term did not catch on, but it was used again in the 1880s by a Kansas journalist, Charles Harger, to distinguish Kansas and Nebraska from the new Southwest of Texas and Oklahoma and the new Northwest of the Dakotas. (Harger also was using a north–south axis.) Not until the early twentieth century did the designation "Middle West" come to refer to the broad band of states between the Appalachians and the Rockies, between the East and the West. The Indiana novelist Booth Tarkington, in an article in *Harper's Weekly* in 1902,

wrote of his home as being in the center of a "Middle West that extended from Omaha to Buffalo."[5] This usage rapidly caught on, and articles followed in other magazines defining this region and its character in very positive terms.[6] Whereas the East was old and industrial and the West still young and uncivilized, the Middle West was mature and stable, with vital, democratic, pastoral roots. As such, these writers said, it was the real America, and the term "Middle West" largely replaced such earlier regional names as "the Old Northwest," "the great interior region" (Lincoln), "central states," and "prairies."

One of the reasons for the popularity of the term "Middle West," Shortridge says, is that it suddenly formed a *middle,* a resolution to political and social conflicts of the early twentieth century, as well as a reassuring sense of the permanence of traditional American values. Indeed, the cultural work that the newly denominated "Middle West" performed was even greater, comparable to that suddenly performed in the 1970s and 1980s by the terms "middle voter" and "middle America."[7] Between the apparent extremes of East and West—wealth and poverty, city and country, capital and labor, immigration and nativism, conservatism and populism—the Middle West struck a balance. But it was clearly a political and cultural descriptor rather than a biological and environmental one. Whereas "prairie" had referred to the land and its vegetation, "Middle West" referred to a region between two other regions, without reference to the landform or the plants that grew there. It even suppressed the users' sense of landforms and vegetation and, in the process, suppressed a sense of the region's political ferment. The discontents and frustrated hopes of prairie farmers—their anger over railroad rates, plagues of grasshoppers, high mortgages, and low wheat prices, along with their democratic optimism and idealism, all those forces that had inspired prairie populism and given rise to William Jennings Bryan—were covered over with a new term that was to become synonymous first with moderation and later with complacency.

Historically, however, anger and optimism, optimism and anger had been the moods of millions of prairie settlers. The anger and sense of injustice, as Shelton Stromquist shows in "Prairie Politics and the Landscape of Reform," arose from the experiences of farmers and small-town merchants at the "encroachment of railroads and banks and the new aggregations of corporate power," which threatened their individual and community livelihood and independence. Sometimes bringing prairie people together and uniting them across class and ethnic boundaries, sometimes dividing them along those boundaries, the anger fueled their demands for reform. Yet their reform programs also expressed their sense of optimism, which grew in part from the productivity of the soil and the new chance in life that the prairies gave them. Thus prairie imagery infused both politics and poetry, in the speeches of Bryan and Robert La Follette, the work of Jane Addams, and certainly Carl Sandburg's biographies of Abraham Lincoln.

Another proud celebration of prairie bounty and hope came in the work of the Danish-born landscape architect Jens Jensen.[8] Although no longer so well known, Jensen was once as famous as his contemporary Frank Lloyd Wright. Robert Grese, who has been instrumental in reviving his reputation, celebrates his work in "The Landscape Art of Jens Jensen." Jensen's designs for Chicago parks, as well as for gardens, college campuses, and other parks throughout the old prairie states, used native plants and trees, rather than the imported ones then in fashion. Jensen, unlike other landscapers of the period, also saw the aesthetic potential of prairie landforms.[9] He planted the native species in order to develop patterns of light and shade and

rhythms of open and enclosed space that would enhance the viewer's perception of the land and pleasure in it. He also founded groups that publicized places of special historic and geologic significance and that recommended them as sites for state parks. In his designs, he set aside spaces for pageants and community gatherings, and he devised an adaptation of the American Indian council ring as an egalitarian meeting point. In Jensen's work, the aesthetic and the social and political were inseparable. He had a Jeffersonian and Whitmanian vision of the prairie as a democratic garden, but he also had a greater appreciation than Whitman for the native species in that garden and the need to help people value them. Appreciation of the aesthetics of the prairie would reinforce, and be reinforced by, respect for democracy. Jensen implicitly associated appreciation of diversity in nature with tolerance of diversity in society. Today, the recovery of respect for the prairie and the revival of the reputation of Jensen are not mere coincidence. The renewed appreciation of the land, the landscape artist, and his vision are interrelated.

Whether Aldo Leopold and Jens Jensen knew each other personally I have not been able to determine. In their concern for prairie preservation and love of native landscape, they had a lot in common. But where Jensen the architect designed, trying to create an artificial landscape on natural principles, Leopold the ecologist tried to restore and re-create. As Curt Meine's chapter "Reimagining the Prairie: Aldo Leopold and the Origins of Prairie Restoration" shows, Leopold was also much more concerned with trying to repair the damages in the American rural landscape that by the 1930s had become a national disaster. Not that Jensen was unresponsive to this need. His masterpiece, the Lincoln Memorial Gardens in Springfield, Illinois, was planted on a worn-out cornfield. But Leopold's restorations at his "shack" along the Wisconsin River and at the University of Wisconsin Arboretum in Madison were less concerned with beauty in a conventional sense than with what he came to call his "land ethic." Land, for Leopold, was beautiful in proportion to its overall health—its integrity, stability, diversity, and capacity to regenerate itself. He took an ecological approach to aesthetics. And yet his frequent linkage of his terms "land ethic" and "land aesthetic" indicates that he was constantly aware of their interaction. People value land in proportion to the beauty they find in it, and find it beautiful in proportion to the value they place on it. Making it beautiful, whether by landscaping it or by painting or photographing it, is also a way of physically and emotionally taking possession of it. But custom, social pressure, and economics also sway aesthetic judgments. Thus to Leopold, it was vitally important that we be as self-conscious and critical of our aesthetics as of our ethics and economics, so he sought a new environmental aesthetic along with an environmental ethic.

Leopold's own short manuscript "Prairie: The Forgotten Flora," the earliest known proposal for a prairie restoration at a historic site, also argues for the importance of prairie in understanding American history. The restorers of the Agency House in Portage, Wisconsin, had "restored, at great pains, the architecture and furniture of an 1830 household" but left it "in a landscape monopolized by stowaways." This "incongruity" could happen and not offend because no one knew where prairie was—or even what it was. "Prairie, to most Americans, is a flat place once dotted with covered wagons," Leopold wrote sardonically. Americans defined prairie, as most of us still do, by the form of the land and by a picture-book concept of history rather than by the plants and animals that made it up. As well define a forest as a mountainside with loggers on it. Leopold's definition of prairie was

also partially cultural and moral, but it was primarily ecological: "a community of plants and animals so organized as to build, through the centuries, the rich soil which now feeds us."

The prairie–savanna restorations that Pauline Drobney describes in "The Phoenix People of Sod Corn Country" are clearly in the Leopold tradition. They further the work begun in the 1930s by Weaver in Nebraska and Leopold in Wisconsin, only now much more is known about both the techniques and the underlying science of restoration. Drobney emphasizes the necessity of species diversity, the preservation of local ecotypes, and the importance of large-scale restorations like the 8,000-acre Neal Smith National Wildlife Refuge, east of Des Moines. But as someone who grew up on an Iowa farm, she also loves agriculture and honors the memories of her Bohemian ancestors who pioneered in Pocahontas County. Thus she writes personally as well as scientifically, describing her associations with her grandfather's "single-bottom, horse-drawn plow" and the Shawnee story that illustrates what it means to be one of the "True People." Prairie restoration, or recovery, for her is, therefore, a matter of work and a matter of love, a means by which she and others can make themselves whole. Furthermore, it is a highly communal enterprise, as it was for Jensen and his associates. The projects at Neal Smith and elsewhere have required the assistance of many volunteers, the collection of nearby seeds, and even the participation of schoolchildren, who will grow up with the trees and grasses and flowers they have planted, just as the scout troops of Springfield, Illinois, grew up with the oaks they planted sixty some years ago. I might add that a large-scale restoration like the Neal Smith National Wildlife Refuge also raises problems in design and landscape aesthetics, to which Jensen's work is also relevant. The designers of prairie–savanna restorations need, like him, to go beyond the traditions of the baroque and the picturesque, which have dominated landscape architecture, and to explore the aesthetics of plain-ness.

For Lance Foster, author of "*Tanji na Che:* Recovering the Landscape of the Ioway," the restoration at the Neal Smith refuge has yet another dimension. As an Ioway Indian, he is interested in the landscape as it was when his ancestors left Iowa in the early nineteenth century, so he went to the refuge, hoping to see the small herd of buffalo that had been introduced and the prairie "returning to life." In addition, however, he has been independently engaged in his own effort at landscape recovery. For several years, Foster has been imaginatively recovering the prairie by putting together the recorded history of the Ioway, the findings of modern archaeology, and the Ioway language, legends, and traditions. The process is complex, requiring many kinds of research and expertise, but it is also highly rewarding. It is significant that the Ioway and their neighbors lived mainly in river valleys, using the prairies for hunting and crossing them in their travels, but well aware of the difficulties and dangers they presented. The Ioway language had specific words for different kinds of walking in grass, brush, and on and off trails. Ioway tales recount many traditions about trees—proof of the widespread presence of wooded valleys and savannas. Yet other stories and traditions, as well as the Ioway names for the months of the year, document the people's great dependence on buffalo and prairie animals. Foster not only has "recovered" the landscape of the Ioway, but has assembled information that is of great importance to a modern environmental historian.

Lance Foster's Native American perspective on the prairie and Wes Jackson's agricultural one, as presented in "Natural Systems Agriculture: The Truly Radical Alternative," are also surprisingly compatible. Jackson is fond of quoting Wendell Berry's comment on the American pioneers: "They came with vision but no sight." They therefore destroyed Indian land-stewardship practices before they really saw what they were or understood the reasons for them. But whereas Foster hopes to learn more about those Indian practices, Jackson seeks a new agriculture, operating on natural systems. It must preserve land and soil. It must use sunlight for all its power, directly or indirectly. And the plants must fertilize one another and protect one another from insects and weeds. In essence, it is a marriage of agriculture and ecology, and Jackson has become a compelling advocate for this union. With scientific studies for his texts and warnings of environmental apocalypse for his message, he is also in the full sense a modern prairie prophet, even though, as he says, he resists that label. At the same time, his research fits within the themes of this book because of its relevance to our cognition of the prairie. Our prospects of the prairie, Jackson would agree, have been primarily economic, with aesthetic and ecological ones largely ignored.

The last chapter in this book returns to the aesthetic prospect. "Sizing Up the Country: Contemporary Artists' Perspectives on the Prairie" is based on questions sent to exhibiting artists, asking about their work: how they felt about the prairie as a subject, why they painted or photographed it, what challenges it presented, how they felt about such issues as regionalism and environmentalism, and how they wanted their work to be interpreted. The answers were extremely interesting, and all the more so in reference to the examples of their work included in the exhibition "Plain Pictures."[10]

It is also very interesting, and in a sense more just, to see and study these exhibiting artists' work without the benefit or bias of their verbal comments. As visual artists, they express themselves in pictures rather than words. And so a "visual essay" color insert, which I assembled from images they sent me, is presented without direct reference to their responses to my questionnaire and with minimal comment. It says to the viewer-reader, "Here, look. See. See for yourself." It follows page 160.

And yet I cannot resist observing that these pictures make a stunning contrast to the nineteenth-century landscapes shown in "Prairie Prospects." The beneficiaries of modern technology—including color photography, acrylic paints, aerial photography, and panoramic cameras—and of liberating modernist movements in the arts, these twentieth-century artists can see and represent the prairies in ways that nineteenth-century artists could not. In all this, I think, they have been as inventive and enterprising as prairie farmers, architects, and mechanics. Inevitably, they also show us, for better and worse, the visual markers of 150 years or more of Euro-American settlement—roads, railroads, fences, plowed fields, houses, and barns—and convey both the human and the environmental history that they symbolize. The beneficiaries, too, of modern biological and ecological study of the prairies, they have a much wider range of interests and perspectives than their predecessors. As a result, they can help others see the prairie more clearly and carefully, too—its desolation and consolations, its grandeur, its romance, its sublimity, and its many other moods and forms. As Terry Evans notes, "Artists do not necessarily see it better than anyone else, although at least we start with the intention of seeing it." But they are more successful in representing what they see and so helping others to see. In their images, these artists show how the prairie, past and present, has affected them and how our agro-industrial civilization has affected it. Giving their own responses, they, in turn, help us discover and express our own. If we continue to regard the prairie as a great American

desert, we should not blame our artists. And if we both see and treat it as a desert, we may transform it into one.

Collectively, then, all the chapters in this book testify to the difficulty of representing the prairie—in pictures and texts, in fiction and history, and even in biology and landscape design—and yet the urgency of trying. The chapters, like the pictures and the site restorations, also testify to a serious concern for and love of the prairie. As both landform and ecosystem, the prairie was and is so big, even in its remnants, while our eyes and hands and voices and science are so small. We are all like the proverbial blind men trying to describe the elephant. Or as Wes Jackson puts it, we are just "ignorant," so ignorant that we should give up our pretensions to "a knowledge-based worldview" and "go with our long suit." Each discipline can represent only those aspects of the prairie that it is equipped to represent. Each, moreover, has its conscious and unconscious historical biases. All the while, the thing itself, the vegetation, is nearly gone. Ninety-nine percent of it has been plowed or grazed or seeded in other plants and made into something else, from fields and woods to cities and shopping malls. The great prairies are gone, as extinct, Drake Hokanson has said, as the passenger pigeon.[11] Even if large areas, even larger than the Neal Smith refuge, could be reconstructed, they would still lack species like the passenger pigeon that were once a part of them. So we are left with the impossibility of recovering the prairie as it "really was" and the deep metaphysical question—for philosophers as well as historians, artists, and biologists—of whether we can ever represent what does not exist.

This being the case, why do we try? Is our effort ultimately just nostalgic and antiquarian? The answer, as demonstrated so vigorously in this book, is that it is not. While we all agree that the prairie is gone, the contributors show us that it has also become like a huge missing piece in a puzzle. We can see its magnificent and intriguing outlines by the edges of the pieces next to it. From them, we can go on to imagine its color, pattern, and texture, and thus theorize further what the piece looked like. With such theories, we can go back to the adjacent pieces and the whole picture. Economies, politics, history, agriculture, ecology, and literature were all built on and drawn from the now-vanished prairie. We need it to better understand them, and them to reimagine it. Therefore, even if we cannot recover the continent in the full sense of recovering the whole plains in grass and flowers, we can still imaginatively recover our history and the roots of our culture. That is what this book begins to do.

Finally, as Wes Jackson and others show, we have to recover some knowledge of the prairie, especially its ecology, in order to make our contemporary culture and agriculture more sustainable. Prairie not only is great cover, protecting soil, but also builds soil, while supporting life and offering protection to thousands of species. In physical restorations of prairie, we thus build examples of conservation systems against which to measure others. They are representations of the prairie that become a new laboratory and serve as models for future systems. But to build these laboratories, we need information from many sources, from plains and prairie Indians, artists, historians, and the other groups included here. Meanwhile, as we recover the environment of our past, we will also serve our environmental future.

Notes

1. John E. Weaver, *North American Prairie* (Lincoln, Neb.: Johnsen, 1954); John E. Weaver, *Grass-lands of the Great Plains: Their Nature and Use* (Lincoln, Neb.: Johnsen, 1956); Aldo Leopold, *A Sand County Almanac and Sketches Here and There* (New York: Oxford University Press, 1949); Curt Meine, *Aldo Leopold: His Life and Work* (Madison: University of Wisconsin Press, 1988), esp. 328–39; Cornelia Mutel, *The Tallgrass Restoration Handbook: For Prairies, Savannas, and Woodlands* (Washington, D.C.: Island Press, 1997).

2. Leopold, "Prairie Birthday," in *Sand County Almanac*, 45.

3. Herbert Quick, *One Man's Life* (Indianapolis: Bobbs-Merrill, 1925), 202.

4. For a dramatic illustration of this, see the beginning of Hamlin Garland's story "Among the Corn Rows" in *Main-Travelled Roads* (1891). The hero, a homesteader on the South Dakota prairie, is eating sardines, crackers, and peaches—all brought in by railroad.

5. Quoted in James Shortridge, *The Middle West: Its Meaning in American Culture* (Lawrence: University Press of Kansas, 1989), 22. Shortridge's full history of the term is instructive (13–41).

6. Ibid., 24. Two major series of articles were Edward Alsworth Ross, "The Middle West, Being Studies of Its People in Comparison with Those of the East," *Century*, February–May 1912, (vol. 83) 609–15, 686–92, 874–80, (vol. 84) 142–48, and Meredith Nicholson, "The Valley of Democracy," *Scribner's Magazine*, January–June 1918, 1–17, 137–62, 257–76, 385–404, 543–58, 654–65. Nicholson's articles were also published as a book, *The Valley of Democracy* (New York: Scribner, 1919).

7. The terms were defined by Richard M. Scammon and Ben J. Wattenberg, *The Real Majority* (New York: Coward-McCann, 1970). I have commented on their relation to the Middle West in "Rethinking Midwestern Regionalism," *North Dakota Quarterly Review* 62 (1994–1995): 114–31.

8. For more on Jens Jensen, see Robert Grese, *Jens Jensen: Maker of Natural Parks and Gardens* (Baltimore: Johns Hopkins University Press, 1992), and Leonard K. Eaton, *Landscape Artist in America: The Life and Work of Jens Jensen* (Chicago: University of Chicago Press, 1964).

9. One early Chicago landscape architect, Horace

William Shaler Cleveland, wrote to Frederick Law Olmsted that the land that became Chicago's Washington Park had the "dismal monotony of the original prairie and swamp" (quoted in Grese, *Jens Jensen,* 31).

10. The artworks are reproduced in Joni L. Kinsey, *Plain Pictures: Images of the American Prairie* (Washington, D.C.: Smithsonian Institution Press, 1996).

11. Drake Hokanson, letter to the author, 16 January 1997.

2 Prairie Prospects: The Aesthetics of Plainness

Joni L. Kinsey, Rebecca Roberts, and Robert F. Sayre

> Geographical studies of landscapes until very recently denied the existence of common ground between the object of their investigations and the sensibility implied by the artistic usage of landscape. In fact they are intimately connected both historically and in terms of a common way of appropriating the world.
> —Denis E. Cosgrove, *Social Formation and Symbolic Landscape*

The ways the American prairie landscapes have been used and understood, since the first Euro-American encounters with them in the early nineteenth century, are inseparable from how they have been *seen* and *described*. The converse is no less true for pictorial depictions and verbal accounts. Far from being disassociated, the differing actions of perception and utilization are interdependent, which has had far-reaching consequences for human interaction with the prairie landscape itself and for the subject of prairies as it is presented in literature and art. Although it is not often acknowledged, aesthetics lie at the heart of any discussion of the landform, even in policy debates over agricultural practices and proposals to restore a tract of na-

tive grasses. And just as critical, the land's use (or disuse) directly informs its representation in written or visual portrayals, whether they concern virgin territory or cultivated terrain.

Although similar assertions could be made for other types of landscapes, prairies are an especially rewarding focus for exploring the relationships between perception and utilization, aesthetics and application.[1] They are one of the few landforms that in their virgin state are considered featureless and monotonous by all but the most knowledgeable, but are in fact highly complex ecosystems. The cultivated prairie, by contrast, appears natural, but is actually a virtual monoculture, reduced to a few basic crops where hundreds of species had grown before.[2]

Furthermore, alterations to the prairie landscape have been dramatic and rapid both visually and economically, occurring during a period when attitudes toward land and its potential experienced unprecedented change. Finally, prairies are among the least analyzed types of landscape, especially in fields such as art history, which boasts voluminous literature on landscape images of other sorts, but also in geography and literature, where studies too often ignore the subject's interdisciplinary nature.[3] And perhaps most important, prairies are the focus today of some of the more bitter debates over land use and preservation that go to the heart of the way landscape is perceived.

In this chapter we survey some of the ways prairies have been *seen* by artists, *described* by writers, and examine some examples of how they have been *used* and discussed in a typical county in northwestern Iowa. These different processes—perception, description, and use—are, of course, related, and they are further complicated by the relationships between aesthetic theory and representation, by historical and economic changes, by changes in taste and artistic and literary methods, and by many other factors. The processes of vision, description, and use are in practice so related that they are difficult to sort out. Yet it is this very complexity that justifies and even necessitates interdisciplinary approaches.

The Prospect Problem

In their original state, the grasslands received many characterizations, but one of the most compelling was that they were a kind of tabula rasa, an apparently empty landscape that seemed almost entirely without promise or infinitely malleable to human aspiration. Although the concept of emptiness has persisted (primarily among coastal and mountain residents), in many ways the latter notion became a reality: the prairie region today, a vast territory encompassing much of central North America, is one of the most intensively developed and cultivated parts of the continent, containing both crowded cities and spacious and productive farmland, factories, suburbs, and small towns. And so prairies have been and continue to be among the most paradoxical of landscapes, considered to contain both nothing and everything, the repository of our culture's rejected past and its cherished ideals—a provincial backwater and sacred heartland. It is a landscape that receives its identity from the ideas and aspirations of its inhabitants (and other Americans) as much as from its own characteristics and, as a result, is a place of competing representations.

A key concept in considering the paradoxes is the issue of prospect. Relevant to landscapes of any sort but particularly germane to understanding the problem of prairies, the term is multivalent, connoting at once (1) a point of view or vantage from which something, especially a landscape, can be ascertained, (2) the scene itself, (3) a pictorial representation of that scene, (4) the concept of promise or an expectation of fulfillment, (5) the concept of futurity, or a mental looking forward in time, (6) an account, a description, or a survey, usually written, and (7) a reference to economic potential through mining the land.[4] Each of these meanings has specific applications in the disciplines that inform this study, but common among the definitions is the implication that landscape, whether an actual tract of property or its representation in a work of art or literature, is a cultural construction as much as a physical reality or the product of nature.[5] Focusing on the "prospects" of a particular landscape underscores human agency in relationship to it and facilitates understanding the land's history from a variety of perspectives and methodologies.

One of the earliest complaints about the vast American prairies before their development was that they seemed to have no prospects. As early as 1810, Zebulon Pike, who had traversed the Great Plains in 1806 and 1807, referred to them as "those internal deserts" and warned of their limited potential for settlement. More famous was Major Stephen Long's assessment in 1820 that the central United States was "almost wholly unfit for cultivation" and his designation on maps that the region was a "Great American Desert."[6] The only benefit that such a large, desolate region could offer the United States, they both argued in their federal reports, would be as a barrier to overexpansion and to protect the nation from invasion.[7] Their perception of the plains as a barren wilderness was a characterization that would persist until at least the Civil War, although it has lingering influence today in pejorative cultural references by coastal inhabitants.

Although changes had begun before 1860, prairie prospects improved considerably after the Civil War. As Henry Nash Smith and others have explained, with increased access by rail, new agricultural technology that facilitated cultivation (for example, windmills, sod-breaking plows, mechanized harvesters, and hybrid seeds), better ownership potential through the Homestead Act of 1862, and enthusiastic boosterism, the prevailing conception of a prairie desert was replaced by that of a garden paradise, a mythic concept that both accommodated and encouraged settlement.[8] To compensate for the prairies' lack of definition and to alter the landscape to fit their notion of a garden, as well as for a variety of practical and sometimes impractical reasons, new inhabitants began filling the landscape with everything from houses, barns, trees, and towns to carefully ordered fields and roads that followed the government-ordained, rectilinear section lines.[9] One important result of

this process, in addition to the transformation of the prairie landscape into one of the most domesticated, productive regions of the world, was the endowment of the prairie with prospects. It now had a future, economically, industrially, and conceptually, and it was newly provided with landmarks that offered focal points and vantages with which to assimilate the landscape visually.

By the 1930s, the process was complete, at least in the sense that most of the land had been settled, fenced, and cultivated to a high degree. At the same time, however, the prairie-as-garden concept was seriously challenged: drought, overproduction, poor soil conservation, and changing economic conditions prompted new awareness of the land's limitations and new solutions for more efficient and sustainable productivity. Added to this more recently is the recognition that little "wilderness" prairie remains and that increasing industrialization of the land has had a profound and often deleterious impact on the larger environment. Such contrasting perceptions of the prairie and its potential give the region, once considered to have no prospects, too many.

The Visual Prospect

Prairie prospects, from an artistic perspective, follow similar configurations, although the term has more specific aesthetic connotations that further reveal the complex human relationship to the grasslands. Central to the history of landscape painting is what is frequently referred to as "prospect." This, according to seventeenth- and eighteenth-century theories that established the form in the hierarchical art world, referred to the viewpoint from which a picture would be constructed, but it also included scenic elements that were to be arranged according to preconceived theories rather than literally recorded as a mirror of nature. In a proper or "classic" landscape, typology superseded topography. The typological theories concerned balance, which most often was conveyed through framing devices such as large trees, rocks, or ruins on both sides that kept the viewer's gaze contained and focused; a logical progression into space, which was conducted by a winding path or stream that meandered into the distance; clear proportional relationships, which usually were suggested by figures or animals throughout the scene; and a defined horizon that acted as the ultimate focal point for the entire picture. Although there was some room for variation, no successful landscape painting lacked many of these essential features. Thus the search for a good "prospect" became the quest not only for a location that offered a perspective, but also for a site that would live up to its name by presenting a combination of the required elements and thus promise a satisfying view.[10]

As landscape theorists Stephen Daniels and Albert Boime have discussed, prospect painting originated in the Renaissance, but was formally codified in the eighteenth century. At first it was used to portray the vast property of the European landed gentry, but during the nineteenth century the framed-vista format was appropriated to suggest American futurity:[11] "The very term prospect meant a view into the future as well as the distance, with the realization of improvements in progress as well as the promise of more."[12] The elevated viewpoint implied ownership, a type of visual claiming, and in this way many images of the West (those with the requisite prospects) served an important function in facilitating the incorporation of unfamiliar landscapes into the psyche.[13]

Although this process of visual appropriation would have been useful for making the plains psychologically accessible during the expansionist era, quite obviously the empty prairies did not fit artistic or cultural preconceptions, either topographically or typologically. They literally had no prospects, no vantage points from which to survey a scene, no landmarks with which to construct a "view," and this deficiency implied as well, of course, the region's diminished promise as an artistic subject. As the twentieth-century Canadian painter Fredelle Maynard has observed, "There were no 'prospects' on the prairies—only one prospect, the absolute uncompromising monotony of those two parallel infinities, earth and sky."[14] Such a significant lack of subject matter required artists drastically to reorient their approach to landscape, invent solutions to the problem, or avoid depicting prairies altogether.

Although one of the earliest artists of the Great Plains, George Catlin (1796–1872), consistently referred to prairies as "beautiful," "sublime," and "picturesque" (all terms with specific artistic connotations more commonly used to describe conventional landscape forms), these descriptions were usually in regard to views from bluffs, riverbanks, or the summits of rolling terrain. When he experienced a prairie from within, his reactions were remarkably different:

For two or three of the first days, the scenery was monotonous, and became exceeding painful from the fact that we were (to use the phrase of the country) "out of sight of land," i.e. out of sight of anything rising above the horizon, which was a perfect straight line around us, like that of the blue and boundless ocean. The pedestrian over such a discouraging sea of green, without a landmark before or behind him; without a beacon to lead him on, or define his progress, feels weak and overcome when night falls; and he stretches his exhausted limbs, apparently on the same spot where he has slept the night before, with the same *prospect* before and behind him; the same canopy over his head, and the same cheerless sea of green to start upon in the morning. It is difficult to describe the simple beauty and serenity of these

Figure 2.1. George Catlin, *Nishnabottana Bluffs, Upper Missouri* (1832). Oil on canvas, 11 × 14⅜ inches. (National Museum of American Art, Washington, D.C./Art Resource, N.Y.)

scenes of solitude, or the feelings of feeble man, whose limbs are toiling to carry him through them—without a hill or tree to mark his progress, and convince him that he is not, like a squirrel in his cage, after all his toil, standing still. One commences on peregrinations like these with a light heart, and a nimble foot, and spirit is as buoyant as the very air that floats along by the side of him; but his spirit soon tires, and he lags on the way that is rendered more tedious and intolerable by the tantalizing *mirage* that opens before him beautiful lakes, and lawns, and copses; or by the *looming* of the prairie ahead of him, that seems to rise like a parapet, and decked with its varied flowers, phantom-like, flies and move along before him. . . . I at length felt like giving up the jour-ney, and throwing myself upon the ground in hopeless despair.[15]

The sameness of view, instead of being "sublime," was almost beyond endurance, and as compensation the artist fantasized about landscapes with better prospects.

Catlin was unique, however, in his occasional willingness to render the prairie as simple bands of blue and green, a result perhaps of his relative lack of traditional artistic training and his commitment to documentation (Figure 2.1). Until modernism validated such abstraction in the twentieth century, almost all other artists who

Figure 2.2. John Mix Stanley (1814–1872), *Herd of Bison Near Lake Jessie* (ca. 1853). Color lithograph. (From Isaac I. Stevens, *Explorations and Surveys for a Railroad Route from the Mississippi River to the Pacific Ocean. War Department. Route Near Forty Seven and Forty Ninth Parallels, Explored by Isaac I. Stevens, Governor of Washington Territory, in 1853–5*, H. Misc. Doc., 36th Cong., 1st sess., 1860, facing p. 59. University of Iowa Libraries, Iowa City)

encountered the prairies either avoided depicting them or filled their compositions with something, anything, to compensate for the aesthetic void. Their efforts were not unlike those of the "classic" landscapists in that they usually composed their views with elements—figures, animals, wagons, locomotives, or even gravestones—that convey as much about cultural attitudes toward the landscape as about the appearance of the land itself. Even the emptiest views contain some locating elements to define the space and provide it with identity and meaning. In John Mix Stanley's *Herd of Bison near Lake Jesse* (ca. 1853), for example, sketched on Isaac Stevens's survey of possible routes for the transcontinental railroad, the sprawling landscape is enlivened by the countless bison that identify it as a North American scene at the same time as they provide it with discernable scale (Figure 2.2). The figure in W. D. Johnson's photograph *Man Sitting by a Sink Hole (Kansas)* (1897) functions similarly, even though the work even more strongly emphasizes human alienation amid the expansive surroundings and the unusual geologic feature (Figure 2.3). Confronted with such vacancy and wildness, new settlers filled their homesteads with as many vertical elements as possible; the trees and crops they planted not only offered visual relief to the unending sameness, but also eventually changed the appearance of the prairies over a wide area. As a more immediate benefit, these efforts also

Figure 2.3. W. D. Johnson (active 1890s), *Man Sitting by a Sink Hole (Kansas)* (1897). Silver gelatin print, 4¾ × 6⅓ inches. (Openlands Project, Chicago, from a negative at the United States Geological Survey)

maximized harvests, as we see in Nebraska photographer Solomon Butcher's *Using all the Farm for Crops, Plowing Corn in the Dooryard, Custer County Nebraska* (1888) (Figure 2.4).

As if to validate such domestication of American land and incorporate its representation into art theory, critics after 1870 increasingly called for artists to avoid uncultivated nature in their work, even that which had been "improved" and manipulated according to classic conventions, in favor of settled countryside:

The artists' business is not . . . to portray the commonplace or the merely natural. No skill in depicting even the grandest scenes will suffice for art. It is the artist's business to lay hold of and to present a kind of beauty which does not exist in mere natural scenery—a beauty which is the result of human influence. . . . Nothing so much contributes to the production of what may be called a smiling landscape as a generous system of agriculture; and the districts where such agriculture exists will offer the most material for the beautiful landscape art.[16]

The few prairie artists who ignored this advice, such as Nebraskan Elizabeth Holsman (1873–1856) in her painting *Still Waters* (1914) (Figure 2.5), were the exception. The influence of traditional art theory which decreed that landscape pictures be carefully composed of certain elements, the development of the prairies themselves into cultivated terrain, and the shift in taste away from views of wilderness that had dominated mid-nineteenth-century painting combined to discourage artists from portraying landscapes that did not conform to the prevailing perception of human harmony with the land.

This trend came to fulfillment in what has become known as regionalism, the artistic movement of the late 1920s and 1930s that empha-

Figure 2.4. Solomon Butcher (1856–1927), *Using All the Farm for Crops, Plowing Corn in the Dooryard, Custer County Nebraska* (1888). Photograph. (Nebraska State Historical Society, Lincoln)

sized the American scene, often through rural idylls. Best remembered from the work of Midwesterners—Grant Wood (1882–1942) of Iowa, Thomas Hart Benton (1889–1975) of Missouri, and John Steuart Curry (1897–1946) of Kansas—the movement was actually wide ranging and characterized by a variety of styles and subjects. But while figurative compositions such as Wood's famous *American Gothic* (1932) have become the archetype of Depression-era regionalism, landscapes also offer insight into the paradoxes of the period, frequently contrasting nostalgic or idealized pastoral scenes with more contemporary views of dust-bowl– or Depression-wrought devastation. Curry's *Spring Shower, Western Kansas Landscape* (1931) is a "smiling landscape" that, from a lofty prospect, looks over a peaceful ranch set amid a rolling western

prairie (Figure 2.6). From this perspective, any evidence of toil or poverty is subsumed in the epic sweep of the verdant, rolling grassland and the appeal of its promising prospect. As late as the 1950s, Benton was still recalling these ideals in works, such as *Open Country* (1952), that harken back to an earlier age of the open range (Figure 2.7). Such views indicate not only a fondness for such anachronistic scenes in an age of increasing industrialism, but also perhaps a new appreciation for the prairies in their original form.

More indicative of the changes of the 1930s, although no less powerful, is Joe Jones's (1909–1963) *Men and Wheat* (1936), a mural study for the Seneca, Kansas, post office, produced as part of a New Deal program that supported artists and decorated new government buildings (Fig-

Figure 2.5. Elizabeth Holsman, *Still Waters* (1914). Oil on canvas, 27 × 32 inches. (Joslyn Art Museum, Omaha)

ure 2.8).[17] In this homage to Kansas's most cherished and, at the time, most threatened activities, Jones appealed to his audience's identification with the land as they had developed it. "Aside from the importance of wheat to Kansas," he commented about his subject, "my interest was in portraying man at work—his job before him—and how he goes about it with his tools—man creating."[18] At a time when the prairie states were suffering as never before, such heroic portrayals offered reminders of the dreams that had transformed the region less than a cen-

tury before. The alternative was all too evident, as photographs such as Wright Morris's *Abandoned Farm* (1941) from the Farm Security Administration (FSA) emphasize (Figure 2.9). Written about in everything from John Steinbeck's *Grapes of Wrath* (1939) to *An American Exodus: A Record of Human Erosion* (1939), a book by FSA photographer Dorothea Lange and her husband, economics professor Paul Schuster Taylor, this mass migration represented a major shift in the demographics of the United States and in the American relationship to the land,

Figure 2.6. John Steuart Curry, *Spring Shower, Western Kansas Landscape* (1931). Oil on canvas, 29⅞ × 43⅞ inches. (The Metropolitan Museum of Art, New York, Arthur H. Hearn Fund, 1932)

Figure 2.7. Thomas Hart Benton, *Open Country* (1952). Tempera with oil on canvas mounted on panel, 27¼ × 35¼ inches. (Nelson-Atkins Museum of Art, Kansas City, Kans., © T. H. Benton and R. P. Benton Testamentary Trusts/Licensed by VAGA, New York)

Figure 2.8. Joe Jones, *Men and Wheat* (1936). Mural study for Seneca, Kansas, post office. Oil on canvas, 15½ × 35¼ inches. (National Museum of American Art, Washington, D.C./Art Resource, N.Y.)

Figure 2.9. Wright Morris (b. 1910), *Abandoned Farm* (1941). Silver gelatin print, 16 × 30 inches. (Josephine Morris)

one that threatened to reverse the very settlement patterns that had originally peopled the prairies. As Taylor wrote laconically of Oklahoma in 1938, "The treeless landscape is strewn with empty houses."[19] The prairies' prospects once again seemed in doubt, but with the new awareness of the limitations that the Depression era prompted—they were not an infinite resource that would yield indefinitely to human manipulation—came new appreciation, at least some, for their innate characteristics. The new understanding that recognizes the prairie as a unique ecosystem and the ability of contemporary painters to be comfortable with the land-

scape's minimalist offerings had brought a rebirth in prairie art. As Iowan Genie Hudson Patrick and countless other artists today are discovering through works such as *A Season Turning* (1955), the prairies are not so plain (Figure 2.10). It is this recognition that forms the basis for contemporary struggles over prairie use, preservation, and representation.

Literary Prospects

The problems confronting the prairie painter—a vast, featureless, horizontal land, with no be-

Figure 2.10. Genie Hudson Patrick (b. 1938), *A Season Turning* (1995). Oil on canvas, 47 × 80 inches. (Collection of the artist)

ginning, middle, or end, and no prospects from which to view it or with which to enhance it—also confronted the prairie writer. Early explorers, pioneers, travelers, and novelists all made the same complaint (as have contemporary motorists): the land may be rich and at moments beautiful, but it is mostly flat and boring. They were nearly as desperate as Francis Chardon, who wrote in his *Fort Clark Journal* (1839), "Having nothing else to do, I set fire to the Prairies."[20]

Herman Melville also recognized the problem of this vastness and sameness when in *Moby-Dick* he described the gigantic blank forehead of the sperm whale as being like a prairie. It had no eyes, nose, mouth, or other features on it—as the great grassy prairie had none of the familiar features of a landscape, "a spire, cupola, monument, or tower."[21] Confronted with the prairie, the viewer was as lost and disoriented as Ish-

mael before the head of the whale. The prairie was all one vast plain of inscrutable plainness.

Yet as the verbal inventiveness of Melville demonstrates, it is generally easier for a writer than a painter to fill a blank space. There have also been more writers than visual artists if we count all the housewives, immigrants, and farmers, the diarists, letter writers, and memoirists. Thus the written text has been the overwhelming means by which the prairie has been described, its tabula rasa metaphorically filled. Moreover, the writer can more easily supply the prospects of past and future, as William Cullen Bryant did in his very popular poem "The Prairies," in which he evoked the distant past of "a race that long has passed away" (the Mississippian mound builders), then the recent past of "roaming hunter tribes, warlike and fierce," and finally a future of children, maidens, and "Sab-

26

bath worshippers."[22] To writers of Bryant's generation, the prairie's lack of visual prospects was an invitation to supply prophetic ones—to dream about the past and look into the future.

The investment of a blank present with a glorious future has always been a strategy of American writers. But the prairies were a landscape with no European equivalent, except possibly the Rhône delta of France. They were initially called not just the West, but the Great West. By means of the Northwest Ordinance and the Louisiana Purchase, they also became a part of the United States at the very time when the new nation was struggling to identify itself, so that they were appropriated as the stage on which the national character and destiny would display themselves. "'The Far West' is the right name for these verdant deserts," wrote Ralph Waldo Emerson, after a trip up the Mississippi. "On the shores, interminable silent forest. If you land there is prairie behind prairie, forest behind forest, sites of nations, no nations. The raw bullion of nature; what we call 'moral' value not yet stamped on it."[23] The prospect for the prairies, then, was to become the epitome of America.

Linking the character of the land to the future character of the people and nation was, in a way, to avoid one question by posing another, to turn from the "raw bullion of nature" to the raw and untested, unstamped *Homo americanus*. But it was also a way to answer both questions at once. The most obvious features of the land—that it was broad, level, fertile, blessed with a generally benign climate, and rich in promise—were made metaphors of egalitarian democracy, expansiveness, beneficence, health, and optimism. This was the land for Americans, and Americans were the people for this land. Moreover, once this equation was accepted, it could also be reversed: the pioneer farmers, railroad builders, journalists, merchants, and governors could put their stamp, their imprint, on the land. They

would not only "claim" it, but also "tame" it, "civilize," and "domesticate" it, by giving it the "'moral' value" it had lacked. It would be known by them.

Such metaphors of taming and civilizing were, of course, already familiar. The Puritans had had their errands in the wilderness. Jefferson had envisioned American yeomen building republics in the forests. But the immense expanse of the prairies and the short span of years in which they were settled (roughly, from the Black Hawk War of 1832 to the "closing of the frontier" in 1890) meant that this process of metaphoric identification was rapidly broadened and elaborated. Meanwhile, other powerful influences—such as the building of railroads, the Civil War, immigration, and industrialization—supplied other means and metaphors for changing the land and defining it and its prospects.

Still another contributing factor was the growth of magazine journalism. Magazines such as *Harper's Monthly* (founded in 1850) and *Harper's Weekly* (1857) sought a broad national audience, and articles and illustrations celebrating the American landscape and its prospects had wide appeal. At the same time, more refined regional magazines such as the *Atlantic Monthly* (founded in 1857) sought to unite the interests of New England and the Great West, especially as sectional conflict with the South intensified. Articles in the *Atlantic* celebrated the West as the "daughter of the East," the "new New England," and a land fervently opposed to slavery and secession. All these qualities, *Atlantic* writers asserted, corresponded to the West's expansiveness, breadth, and beneficence.[24]

But the magazine with the most to gain from promoting the prairies was the *Western Monthly,* which began publication in Chicago in 1869 as a western imitation of the *Atlantic.* Defending western interests like low tariffs, it also proclaimed the virtues of western land and the western man. It did this in an especially revealing way in a series of biographical profiles or "sketches" of prominent men of the Great West, including state governors, railroad builders, lumber barons, judges, and congressmen. The series began with the first issue in January 1869 and continued for over a year, each sketch generally opening each issue and accompanied by a full-page engraved portrait of the man (Figure 2.11).[25] Highlighting the men as symbols of the land, such treatment said, in effect, that Illinois, Iowa, Wisconsin, and Indiana *were* the men, and that the men were important as the representatives of these states. All fifteen men in the profiles had actually been born in the East, but it was the West to which the writers assigned most influence. It was the West that allowed their character to emerge, their native genius to bloom.

The first sketch in the series, of William B. Ogden, "the Railway King of the West," set the pattern.[26] Born in Delaware County, New York, Ogden took over his father's affairs when his father died and became a "partner in a mercantile firm." But this "did not satisfy his young ambition," so "he determined to turn his attention westward." In June 1835, he moved to Chicago, which he foresaw would become "one of the leading cities of the West," and began to buy, manage, and sell real estate. By laying out streets and building bridges, he "literally made the rough places smooth and the crooked ways straight in Chicago"—the sort of biblical echo the *Western Monthly* used approvingly. He was also "a contractor upon the Illinois and Michigan Canal," before becoming president or director of railroads that connected Chicago with the North, Northwest, West, and East. At the same time, he served as a trustee of universities and learned societies, gaining a reputation for benevolence, energy, and sound financial judgment.

Sometimes a sketch opens with a direct celebration of the West and its specific virtues. "It accords with the genius of the West to honor the

worker," begins the profile of David Atwood.[27] "Untold wealth lies locked in the storehouse of Nature, and the work has been to possess ourselves of her treasures." Those who extracted these treasures, therefore, were "men of foresight and will, content to lead a life of deprivation." Such "wonderful resources" of character, matching and mastering the resources of the land, "distinguish the people of the West." The writer thereby makes Atwood and the other men not only agents but embodiments of the West's transformation: "Those who have caused nature to blossom and to fruit, become imbued with the beauty they have created." Sketching on—and stretching on from figure to figure—the writer finally turns to a quotation from Oliver Wendell Holmes, at that time America's favorite literary doctor: "The prairies of the West are the lungs of the continent, and upon reaching them men take a long breath, which makes them more largely human than they ever were before." Prairie-as-lung saves the writer from describing prairie-as-prairie, while also promoting the connection between prairie and person. Prairie-as-lung becomes enlarged human lung; enlarged lung becomes expanded, "more largely human" person; and person embodies prairie.

The character of David Atwood seems to justify these elaborate, celebratory tropes of work, war, cultivation, and lungs because he was a hardworking printer and then for two years a farmer near Freeport, Illinois; next a newspaper editor in Madison, Wisconsin; and finally a major general in the Wisconsin militia. Moreover, his two years of farming had also brought "brawny development" and "served to restore [his] health," a note that was inserted, perhaps, to show that the prairies did not bring on just ague and consumption, as was often said, but also their cure. Atwood's prairie cure made him all the more a personification of the prairie.

The sketches in the *Western Monthly* do not attribute all their subjects' virtues to the influence of the prairies and the West. Many had served in the Union Army, acquiring or displaying such traits as decisiveness and leadership. John Palmer of Illinois had been a delegate to the Peace Convention in Washington in early 1861, but when war came "he drew his sword and threw away the scabbard."[28] A number of the *Western Monthly* men, like Palmer, had early associations with abolitionism, the founding of the Republican Party, or Abraham Lincoln—a connection the magazine emphasized. William B. Allison of Iowa, for example, as a delegate to the National Republican Convention in Chicago, "labored modestly but heartily for the nomination of Abraham Lincoln."[29] Yet this celebration of the Union, abolition, and Lincoln, who was already recognized as the highest ideal of the western man, also had the effect of making these causes and memories themselves into aspects of prairie character and destiny. Being a Republican and against the slave interests (a euphemism for the South) was something the Westerner shared with the Easterner, but in which he might now lead. Patriotism, common sense, practicality, and self-reliance are not unique to the prairie, the readers are told, but they do "flourish" there.

What also flourished on the prairie, these articles make abundantly clear, was agro-industrial capitalism. Only a few of these representative men of the prairie states began life as independent, subsistence farmers, and all eventually became bankers, railroad owners, lumbermen, lawyers, mining investors, and newspaper owners. (Even the politicians had such other interests.) Thus it was by transforming the land into industrial sites and material for investment that these men established their identities and gave the prairie its ultimate meaning and value.

This transformation of blank prairie prospect into an agro-industrial promise is starkly clear in the opening paragraph of the last sketch in the *Western Monthly* series. Discussing Samuel H. McCrea, president of the Chicago Board of Trade, the author begins an elaborate simile to explain the board's function (see Figure 2.11):

Society, in its subsistive aspect, may be compared to a steam engine; which is at once the grand result and the mighty agent of human effort to achieve progress in the reformation of Nature. The agricultural regions are the boiler of the vast structure, in which the motor power is generated; the avenues of transportation are the conducting pipes; the city is the cylinder, wherein the force finds expression; the capitalists are the fly-wheel, which equalizes and distributes the effective force, and stores up the temporary surplus of power for use when an extra amount of inertia needs to be overcome; the Board of Trade is the governor, which controls the ever-varying relations of supply to demand, and indexes them on its daily price lists. If we conceive a number of steam engines, connected in such a way as that all shall co-operate in driving one vast system of machinery, we shall complete an exponential idea of the enginery which moves the whole Aryan world.[30]

The comparison of a society to a steam engine must have seemed peculiarly appropriate to Chicago in 1870. Also dated and offensive, although very interesting, is the final celebration of "the whole Aryan world." The prairie capitalism of the time was only for white Euro-American Christians, who were incipiently imperialist in their outlook and were not agrarians or pastoralists. The prairie had been transformed into "the boiler of the vast structure," controlled by capitalists and the Board of Trade. Significantly, they are the only agents in the whole simile who are also in any way human. Everything else and everyone else are components of the machine. Yet the writer in no way indicates that his readers will object to this portrayal. Being a pipe or boiler or cylinder in such a "mighty agent . . . in the reformation of Nature" is an honor.

The recent work of William Cronon on Chicago and the growth of the Great West helps us

THE

WESTERN MONTHLY.

VOL. III.—JUNE, 1870.—No. 18.

THE CHICAGO BOARD OF TRADE.

SOCIETY, in its subsistive aspect, may be compared to a steam engine; which is at once the grand result and the mighty agent of human effort to achieve progress in the reformation of Nature. The agricultural regions are the boiler of the vast structure, in which the motor power is generated; the avenues of transportation are the conducting pipes; the city is the cylinder, wherein the force finds expression; the capitalists are the fly-wheel, which equalizes and distributes the effective force, and stores up the temporary surplus of power for use when an extra amount of inertia needs to be overcome; the Board of Trade is the governor, which controls the ever-varying relations of supply to demand, and indexes them on its daily price lists. If we conceive a number of steam engines, connected in such a way as that all shall co-operate in driving one vast system of machinery, we shall complete an exponential idea of the enginery which moves the whole Aryan world.

One of the greatest among the integral portions of such a system is comprised in what are still known as the Northwestern States—though our territorial expansion has, some time since, made that term a misnomer. Fully three hundred thousand square miles of this area is directly tributable to Chicago, and finds here the fly-wheel and governor which regulate the expression of its forces and increase or diminish the forces themselves.

The agricultural productions of the Northwest are its only primary convertible property, and their surplus forms the only original capital available for exchange for other kinds of property which it is desired to possess or use. The geographical position of Chicago—that of the neck of an hour-glass—constitutes it as the natural focus of both distribution and supply to this vast region. The produce of the farm is poured into this city along every rib of the immense fan which spreads out to the westward; it is here handled and massed and stored till required to be forwarded. These processes involve the employment of many men and much capital; and these, again, require buildings and food and clothing, which calls out more labor and capital. The number of workers and traders at the focal point is again

Figure 2.11. Opening page of profile and portrait of Samuel H. McCrea. (From "The Chicago Board of Trade," *Western Monthly*, June 1870)

to see, as well, that the Chicago Board of Trade by the 1870s had established procedures that made the stream of wheat and other grains from the prairies seem like an endless stream of money. Systems of classification abolished the differences between one farmer's grain and another's: "Farmers or shippers took their wheat or corn to an elevator operator as if they were taking gold or silver to a banker. After depositing the grain in a bin, the original owner accepted a receipt that could be redeemed for grain in much the same way that a check or a banknote could be redeemed for precious metal." These receipts became interchangeable themselves and were traded on the floor of the mercantile exchange, thus "obscuring [the] physical identity" of the wheat or corn as food and "displacing it into the symbolic world of capital."[31]

The added advantage of grain, as compared with other products of the new West, like lumber and ore, was that it was a renewable resource. Barring floods, fires, and droughts, it would never stop coming, and it was grown over such a vast area that such risks were spread. The number of farmers in the prairie states now rendered the individual farmer more like an industrial laborer.

This, then, was the prospect for the prairie by the 1870s—to find its representative being in the American capitalist and its function in the steam engine of American capitalism. Appreciation of the prairie as a natural world, as something unique and beautiful in itself, did not, for the most part, come from prairie writers until after the landscape had been transformed into something else.

A good example of this retrospective appreciation is in Hamlin Garland's *Boy Life on the Prairie* (1899). Debuted in the late 1880s as a series of reminiscences for magazines, this fictionalized autobiography reveals the nostalgia of a

son of the sodbusters. Garland, born in West Salem, Wisconsin, in 1860, had moved to a farm near Osage, Iowa, in 1868. While the *Western Monthly* was celebrating the leaders of the Great West, Garland's father was out in the "boiler," breaking sod and supplying the "motor power." Prairie to him and his fellow pioneer farmers was useful only as "wild meadows" for pasture and haying, until it could be plowed up and planted with crops or domestic grasses. The life was hard, although at moments heroic or poetic, and Lincoln Stewart (the Garland character) was glad to leave. By the age of twenty-four, however, when he returns, it was a changed world:

Where the cattle had roamed and the boys had raced the prairie wolves, fields of corn and oats waved. No open prairie could be found. Every quarter section, every acre was ploughed. The wild flowers were gone. Tumbleweed, smartweed, pigweed, mayflower, and all the other plants of semi-cultivation had taken the place of the wild asters, pea-vines, crow's-foot, sunflowers, snake-weed, sweet-williams, and tiger-lilies. The very air seemed tamed and set to work at the windmills which rose high above every barn, like great sunflowers.[32]

But nostalgia alone does not make the prairie beautiful. Nostalgia depends on former familiarity, knowledge of the names of plants and animals, and memories of past encounters with them. The first pioneer farmers, like the first travelers and painters, had had none of these advantages. To them, the prairie had been merely a landscape or "scene" in the dramatic sense: a time and place and action, where nature changed and people lived and worked.

"A working country is hardly ever a landscape," wrote Raymond Williams. "The very idea of landscape implies separation and observation."[33] The early prairie farmers, like the politicians and businessmen celebrated by the *Western Monthly*, were working the land; they were not separated or detached enough to observe it as "landscape." Their prospects on it were functional and economic. It was beautiful to them because of what it could produce. As they put themselves into it, they made it produce and left their mark on it.

Yet as fundamental as Williams's point is, it fails to recognize or account for the ways in which "working country" such as the tallgrass prairie, past and present, did become a "landscape" in the more conventional aesthetic senses—beautiful in its own right, with more than monetary value. As Garland's passage indicates, it acquired this attribute over time, primarily for the sons and daughters of those who had transformed it. Contact and familiarity, followed by memory and nostalgia, created a new knowledge of it and a new distance from which to view it. These, in turn, provided a new perspective that gave the land new prospects, in terms of both a vantage point and a sense of its past and future, its value and beauty. Further evidence of this transformation is that by the turn of the century, "prairie" had become a very favorable and even fashionable word in the American vocabulary, as evidenced by the emergence of the terms "prairie house" and "Prairie School" to designate the latest, native trends in American architecture. At the same time, midwestern writers and painters, led by those of the Chicago Renaissance, were taking pride in their own "prairie roots" and building a new "prairie" poetry and art.[34]

One of these writers was Herbert Quick, who had been born on a farm in north-central Iowa in 1861 but did not become a professional writer until 1905, by which time he had a much more optimistic outlook than Garland. Whereas Garland had rebelled against the conditions of pioneer farming and turned back to the prairie from a sense of loss, Quick celebrated both the original prairie and the agricultural landscape that succeeded it. He also stood above Sinclair Lewis's and Sherwood Anderson's bitterness over small-town paralysis and provincialism. His characters are aware of all these hardships, dangers, and limitations, but they manage to surmount them by combinations of pluck, irony, gratitude, and sometimes dumb luck.

"Cow" Vandemark of Quick's *Vandemark's Folly* (1922) is such a character, and his first-person descriptions of the prairie are correspondingly loving, elegiac, realistic, and convincing. Vandemark is an Iowa-Dutch pioneer farmer who makes mistakes and often seems like a fool, but has an instinct for loyalty, persistence, and survival. He got the nickname "Cow" because he used milk cows to pull his immigrant wagon, moving him slowly but surely and well supplied with milk along the way. He had been a factory hand and next a crewman on the Erie Canal, and then had gone to Madison, Wisconsin, looking for his dying mother. There he acquired his land, sight unseen, as a settlement from his evil stepfather, and it became a "folly" because it was half swampland. But when he eventually drains it and discovers the best soil in the county, the term becomes ironic. Vandemark's representations of the prairie are rich in detail and infused with a sense of wonder at its vastness and power. As he reaches the top of a bluff above Dubuque (a favorable lofty prospect), Iowa, he sees it "sweeping away as far as the eye could see" and pulls off the road to look more carefully, "as a man appraises one with whom he must live—as a friend or an enemy." Two long paragraphs list the wildflowers and the huge flocks of waterfowl: "It was sublime! . . . the immense expanse of sunny prairie, swelling up into undulations like a woman's breast turgid with milk for a hungry race." The sight makes him cry, and he thinks of his dead mother, which further emphasizes the identification of prairie as fertile woman, as mother earth.[35]

The breaking of the prairie is a "wedding-day—the marriage morning of the plow and the sod," and Quick describes it with sexual imagery that is at once tender and violent. The plow is "long, low and yacht-like in form; a curved blade of polished steel." Its point is "long and tapering, like the prow of a clipper." As it slices through the "bosom of earth," Vandemark hears "a curious thrilling sound . . . a sort of murmuring as of protest at this violation." When the plow hits a root, the jolt is like a ship hitting a rock. Yet there are no rocks in this vast, fertile, oceanic mother, so a man can plow in a day what would take a summer to clear of rocks and trees in the East. And all this makes him feel proud, potent, and hopeful: "Surely, this was a world in which a man with the will to do might make something of himself. No waiting for the long processes by which the forests were reclaimed; but a new world with new processes, new neighbors, new ideas, new opportunities, new victories easily gained."[36]

Yet Vandemark is also aware of the sadness and tragedy: "Breaking prairie was the most beautiful, the most epochal, and most hopeful, and as I look back at it, in one way the most pathetic thing man ever did, for in it, one of the loveliest things ever created began to come to its predestined end."[37] In passages like these, Quick describes the beauty and tragedy of the transformation of the prairie as have only a few other writers, such as Willa Cather. In so doing, he implicitly recognizes the transformation now of the prairie into a third state, a landscape of competing representations and contested prospects.

Preserving Prairies

Cultural debates over the meaning of landscapes are an integral component of political struggles over the uses of land. The ambiguities and paradoxes inherent in the prospects attributed to the prairies have been continually renegotiated in conflicts over agricultural commodity production, soil conservation and wetland preservation, and the protection of prairie parklands. By tracing the development of narratives that define the meaning of the prairie landscape in a northwestern Iowa county, political struggles over the proposed designation of a prairie preserve in the county become more understandable and more meaningful. The aesthetic perceptions and economic uses of the prairie cannot be separated, and any attempt to do so deprives an analysis of the conflict of meanings that motivate political participation. The same paradoxical metaphors expressed in art and regional literature are bound into the everyday experiences by which prairie people and communities construct their identities and assert their interests: wilderness/garden, empty/full, progress/nostalgia, location/dislocation.

Iowa, the quintessential prairie state, has acted very cautiously compared with its neighbors in designating open space and parkland and in preserving existing prairie as part of the public heritage. The Open Spaces Act of 1987 and the Resource Enhancement and Protection Act (REAP) of 1989, passed during a period of very active environmental legislation in Iowa, provided goals, planning procedures, and funding mechanisms to remedy this situation.[38] The Open Spaces Act anticipated protecting up to 10 percent of Iowa's area, but not necessarily through acquisition; REAP provided funds both to protect open space and to reimburse local governments for tax shortfalls.

Armed with this mandate and recognizing that the northwestern corner of the state had very few state parks or preserves, the Department of Natural Resources (DNR) conducted an internal study to identify and assess potential sites for a prairie preserve of several thousand acres, large enough to convey the aesthetic of the open prairie and to maintain itself without intensive management. Without extensive consultation with local people, it recommended to the favorably disposed state Natural Resources Commission (NRC) the 4,700-acre Waterman Creek site in southeastern O'Brien County because of its extensive tracts of heavily grazed but still unplowed prairie with good species diversity.

The DNR was unprepared for the storm of local protest that its proposal generated. At an informational meeting in O'Brien County in late April 1991, it was apparent that the DNR had misread the politics and therefore mismanaged its approach to local residents. As a result, the NRC delayed its decision until the fall to give communities and the DNR the opportunity for further study.[39] Bowing to intense local opposition, the NRC finally approved a much-scaled-back project without defined boundaries and without timetables for land acquisition.[40]

Understanding the intense commitments on both sides that led to the fence-straddling decision by the NRC requires insight into both the economic and aesthetic roles of the prairie in people's lives from the first white settlement to the present. The paradoxes inherent in aesthetic apprehensions of the prairie emerge alongside economic considerations to supply the meanings distinguishing alternative positions in the conflict. The inability of the preserve proponents to prevail ultimately derived from their failure to engage local people in their aesthetic appreciation of native prairies. For many of those who live within it, the transformed prairie continues to be too closely entwined with the prospects of cultivated, plentiful garden and machine of progress that define not only livelihoods but also identity and moral character. To O'Brien County residents, a prairie emptied of settled occupants could not be made full, as it could for the park proponents. Instead, it embodied only the disquieting images of dislocation and lack of prospect that disturbed early Euro-American encounters with the prairie.

Early Prospects

The first Euro-American settlers in O'Brien County came to what they saw as an empty "virgin" landscape in the 1860s and were arriving in full force in the 1870s. That this empty landscape had been created by the forceful removal of Native Americans and the extinction of their title to the land did not detract from the paradoxical idea that the prairie represented a wilderness of nature. This perception, and the arrival of the railroad, justified conquest at the same time as it conditioned their understanding of their settlement.[41] After a few short years, the settlers had imposed a new order on the landscape and begun to supply the eastern and European markets with grains and livestock. The early equality imposed by hardship gave way rapidly as the fertile soil and its unequal acquisition brought prosperity and social stratification.

Change also offered the opportunity to remember the early days, as both fantasy and reality, and one common means in Iowa, as in other former prairie states, was through what might be called the "subscription history." O'Brien County could boast two historical accounts by 1914 (the first was published in 1897), and they provide direct insight into the process of mythologizing the landscape that formed the foundation for later debates on land use. Most striking in both volumes are the repetitive engravings of self-assured prosperous farmers and merchants wearing starched Sunday collars and standing alongside their imposing corn-belt houses (Figures 2.12 and 2.13). These men's subscriptions to the volumes brought them the right to be immortalized in the engravings, and the images in turn reiterated, as eloquently as did the biographical sketches of the politicians and captains of industry in the *Western Monthly*, their fruitful occupation and identity as owners of the landscape. The written texts, meanwhile, filled in the details of how the early set-

Figure 2.12. Portrait of Allen Crossan. (From D. A. W. Perkins, *History of O'Brien County, Iowa, from Its Organization to the Present Time* [Sioux Falls, S. Dak.: Brown and Saenger, 1897]. Photograph courtesy of the State Historical Society of Iowa, Iowa City)

Figure 2.13. O'Brien County farm residence. (From D. A. W. Perkins, *History of O'Brien County, Iowa, from Its Organization to the Present Time* [Sioux Falls, S. Dak.: Brown and Saenger, 1897]. Photograph courtesy of the State Historical Society of Iowa, Iowa City)

tlers' toil and hardships had turned a wilderness into a plentiful garden, replacing the disquieting horizontal expanses of prairie and sky with a settled prospect more attuned to European aesthetics.

The prairie had been disquieting; getting lost in it could be "irksome" and "more unpleasant than one could imagine." But disquiet could turn to danger: "No condition could inspire a more perfect idea of lonely desolation, of entire discomfort, of helplessness, and of dismal foreboding, than to find one's self lost in the snow-covered prairie, with no object in sight in any direction but the cold undulating snow wreaths." At other times, it was sublime, a "gruesome and awful sight . . . when this same great expanse of thousands of acres of waving grass was ripened and dead and the fires had burned it over, all looking much like the judgement day was at hand."[42]

Settlement transformed the troubling expanses into a much more agreeable prospect:

To one who drove these prairies some twenty years ago, the scenery now, in comparison, is beautiful and magnificent. Where stood the sod house and the usual 8 by 10 shack, there are now commodious and tasty residences, and groves, whose trees, dressed in their green and luxuriant foliage, add to the beauties of nature, and mark the landscape with a fascinating and dignified splendor. . . . The settlers of those early days and particularly in the first few years of grass-hoppers were decidedly hard up. When there was but little, if any income from crops, improvements to be made, and the family to be clothed and provided for, it was quite satisfactory if there was enough to eat. . . . But after all, there was a feeling of contentment and happiness, there was no social distinction, all were on a level, and all struggling for the same end.[43]

In a local repetition of the process by which the development of the prairie defined the midwestern region and its people, the displacement of the "blank" prairie with agricultural prospects not only gave the prairies meaning and value, but endowed the inhabitants with identity and moral character:

The toil of those farmers has made the farms increase in prices; made those improvements, planted orchards and fruit gardens, made roads and bridges, converted a wild country into a land of beauty, and made it the happy abode of intelligent men. All this had to be done to make these farms advance in price, and those who have done this, and raised and educated their families, have done well; and if the advance in the price of their farms has given them a competence, it is what they anticipated, and nothing but the most persevering industry and frugality would have accomplished it.[44]

Mrs. Roma Woods, one of the old settlers, summed it up more tangibly in 1914: "The Martins, Hills and Tripletts, three large families, are all settled in fine homes with autos. Waterman is a rich township, and I wish it were possible to speak of each and every one in it."[45]

The degree to which residents of O'Brien County, along with most other rural Iowans, continued to identify the prospects of the prairie with farms, towns, and business development is well demonstrated in the aerial photographs of the state taken by Vincent Mart from Spencer, which is also in northwestern Iowa. For approximately thirty years, from the 1960s to the early 1990s, Mart made his living by photographing

farmsteads, small towns, fairgrounds, grain elevators, lumberyards, and other features of the landscape, selling the images to farmers, business owners, and chambers of commerce. In 1991, he donated a collection of 10,000 of these photographs to the State Historical Society in Iowa City.[46] They are an extremely comprehensive and precise documentary record of the rural landscape of this period, yet they foreground—quite literally—the economic landmarks, leaving the rest of the countryside relegated to the distance, the fiscal and aesthetic margins. Farmers wanted aerial views of their houses and barns rather than the fields, and chambers of commerce wanted pictures of their towns, not the surrounding farms (Figure 2.14). Prairie, if it existed at all in this conception, was not deemed an interesting or a valuable subject. In this respect, Mart's stunningly bright and clear images are no different from artists' bird's-eye views from the turn of the century. More prairie remained intact at that time, but the modern aerial photographer surely had the better means for portraying what little remained. He had the elevated perspective that earlier artists could only imagine and a medium that could faithfully portray nuances of color—in prairie flowers, seasonal changes, and the patterns of cultivated fields and pastures. Such subjects had little appeal for his clients, however, either economically or aesthetically. His viewers did not see their prospects in the prairie except as they had altered it.[47]

Even with their satisfaction with their modifications of the landscape, early O'Brien County residents recognized that they had lost something with the disappearance of the prairie, and between the 1897 and 1914 histories, some of the conquest imagery gave way to nostalgia. Even as she praised the modern, mechanized farm, Roma Woods remembered looking up to the "overarching . . . starlit sky so beautiful" the

Figure 2.14. Vincent Mart, *Aerial Photograph of Paullina, Iowa*. Paullina is one of the two neighboring towns to the proposed Waterman Creek Prairie Preserve. (Vincent Mart Collection, State Historical Society of Iowa, Iowa City, no. IBC-141-34)

first night she and her husband occupied their claim.[48] Her memories of the early days of struggle were tempered by the "hue of the vast prairie, with its ever changing and mysterious beauty [that] gave a broadness to life."[49]

Nostalgia began to feed memory as the disappearance of the prairie receded into the past. Like Hamlin Garland, Willa Cather, and many other prairie writers of the generation, the authors of the 1914 volume eulogized the lost prairie in a passage that juxtaposes an acceptance of progress, an appreciation of the open landscape and the complexity of prairie communities, and a nostalgic reverie for heritage that can never be retrieved:

Iowa is a prairie state. O'Brien county was distinctly prairie. The grand sight of a broad prairie expanse is never to be witnessed again by O'Brien county

people. The now large groves, the fences, the long lines of trees along the road sides, the tilled lands, the buildings and farm yards, the straight and squared up roads, the builded towns, the lines of railroads and telegraph lines and poles, the rural telephone lines, and many other items have each contributed to eliminate much of the idea and appearance of the original prairie.

Twenty-five miles of continuous waving prairie grass, from eight inches to four feet, and even five feet in height, solid hay so to speak, was in fact the grand sight as the original old settler saw it. . . . Millions of sweet williams, tiger lilies and other prairie flowers were like diamonds in the grass. No sweeter tame strawberries ever grew than the wild prairie variety. No boy or girl ever paid or dropped a cent into a slot machine for purer, healthier or better tasting gum than that boy gathered on the big rozin weed stalks. . . . And the loss was irretrievable, because the prairie was an utter failure to propagate itself. It had no seed. It moved out and grew from the roots. When once a plat of prairie sod, whether a rod square or five hundred acres, was broken or plowed up it never reestablished itself. It was forever done. Like Io, the poor Indian, it could not stand civilization.[50]

Competing Prospects of Waterman Creek Prairie

By 1991, an increasingly numerous, urban, and environmentally conscious Iowa population was pressing harder on the few remaining open and natural spaces. The DNR's proposal to protect a 4,700-acre tract at Waterman Creek generated a widespread response that in many ways echoed the early mythologizing, with all its contradictions, as well as introduced the modern preservationist and agro-industrialist arguments. Some who were in favor of the proposal reiterated some of the old settlers' nostalgia for what had been lost: "I'm a family farmer and new father who would truly like my son to be able to see a chunk of the prairie that would illustrate what his great grandfather saw upon coming to Iowa."[51] For others, especially those from university towns, the prairie was an ecosystem to be appreciated on its own terms:

I believe the preservation of a place where a person can walk in peace and feel for a moment the power of the prairie landscape, feel for a moment the health and vigor of a working natural system, and feel the sheer joy of the beauty of this land, should be important enough to us to work out any problems it may present.[52]

Another testified that he "would like to be able to stand in the middle of 4,700 acres of Iowa tall grass prairie and not be able to see any works of mankind," and long passages in other letters to the DNR detailed the extraordinary diversity and complexity of the prairie ecosystem and the scientific and aesthetic value of preserving that biodiversity.[53]

These remarks recall the teachings of botanists and ecologists such as Ada Hayden and Aldo Leopold, who discovered that the prairies were not empty and plain, but possessed of a surprising diversity, complexity, and stability that could not be matched by the crop systems that were replacing it. They and other scientists, often the sons and daughters of the old settlers, tramped through and mapped surviving prairies, cataloguing species and investigating the complex relationships that support the prairie ecosystem. Their love of the grasslands was frequently nourished, as in Hayden's case, by having grown up on farms where patches of prairie remained, and they pursued the hope that some of these remnants might be acquired by the state and preserved as scientific laboratories and a celebration of the state's heritage.[54] As early as 1944, Hayden had warned, "The time for action is limited,"[55] and her remarks have been quoted ever since by preservationists:

[Prairie] is identified with open sky. . . . It is the unprotected battleground of wind and weather. For the impressions of its former vastness and endless expanse now replaced by grove-dotted, fence-rowed fields of checkered green. . . . Preserving the prairie will not only protect a natural laboratory but will serve as a "cathedral," a monument to the past . . . for your grandchildren and great-grandchildren to enjoy.[56]

The ghosts of Ada Hayden and Aldo Leopold loom over the shoulders of the supporters of Waterman Creek Prairie Preserve: "If the biota, in the course of aeons, has built something we like but do not understand, then who but a fool would discard seemingly useless parts."[57]

Local people, however, although favoring prairie preserves in the abstract, were strongly opposed to taking so much land out of production in so small an area; agricultural occupation of the land and rural prospects were too tightly linked.[58] The goals to accelerate the acquisition of Iowa public lands enunciated in the Open Spaces Act and REAP brought the statewide Cattleman's Association and Farm Bureau in on the opponents' side, and their arguments echoed the observations of the O'Brien County histories almost seventy years before:[59]

Land is the basis of wealth. This is especially true in agricultural Iowa. In O'Brien county it is especially true even with an Iowa measurement. Some other counties in Iowa have coal and lead and other items to give variety. In this county it is all exclusively farming. . . . All estimates and enterprises in the county must hark back to the land.[60]

What in 1914 had seemed a solid prospect of future progress and prosperity secured by the wealth of the land had proved fleeting by the 1990s. Human occupation was as vulnerable as the prairie to capitalist development. The sodbusting plow that had facilitated settlement gave way to the tractor, hybrid seeds, and fertilizers that effectively depopulated the land. The early prosperity of corn-belt farmers that allowed them to mechanize and adopt scientific-farming innovations throughout the twentieth century resulted in a bounty that ironically undermined that property. Real prices fell as costs rose; farms expanded, forcing people off the land. In O'-Brien County, the total number of farms, stable since 1900, began to fall precipitously in the mid-1950s to a 1992 figure only 58 percent of its 1950 figure.[61] Not only did the landscape change as fencerows and farmsteads were pulled down to make way for a cash grain monoculture, but the small rural towns and the communities based in them were seriously threatened. The O'Brien County population, stable since 1920, began to slide after 1960, reaching 80 percent of its 1940 peak by 1990.[62] The effect in the smaller rural towns, such as Paullina and Sutherland, those closest to the proposed prairie preserve,

was even more dramatic. To be sure, the smallest rural towns were affected as much as or more by highways, autos, and changing retailing patterns, but the loss of farms and population was entangled both in fact and in imagination in the loss of the aesthetic of a prairie way of life.

The local objections to the proposed Waterman Creek Prairie Preserve centered on the magnitude of the economic impact. Such impact would, in fact, be small. The proposal itself and the legislation on which it was based ensured that land would be acquired from only willing sellers and that county property taxes would be replaced by state funds, but some opponents continued to be suspicious, fearful of the threat to the local economy and the community. Some initial local calculations suggested that over $1 million of agricultural income might be at stake, and an earlier cost–benefit study of a similar proposal in a different area had forecast that seven to fourteen families might be displaced, thirty-five jobs would vanish, and several hundred thousand dollars of retail sales would be lost.[63] The studies on which these estimates were based were actually highly flawed and recognized as such; costs were exaggerated, potential tourism income minimized, and the benefits to the general public of preserving the prairie heritage ignored, but nevertheless the estimates provided a compelling focus for the opposition. Moreover, the DNR declined, as was its policy, to do a more accurate cost–benefit analysis, relying on a political rather than an analytical balancing process. Lacking better numbers, local opponents were left with their worst fears and supporters without tangible evidence.

The extensive public testimony provides revealing insights into perceptions of wrenching threats to the landscape's prospects and the community and personal identities that were defined by those prospects. The potential of losing 4,000 productive acres fed on the reality of loss and depopulation that was evident everywhere. Income losses would mean continuing decline in a region already experiencing serious farm and population losses. Small towns were becoming empty husks, and local schools were giving way to countywide consolidated districts. An owner of two local rest homes was concerned with his ability to continue to recruit employees from local farm families and to maintain his certification: "Even if only three families were to be displaced by this project, I feel my business would be affected."[64]

Others were concerned less with the magnitude of income loss than with the character of the potential income shift. Proponents of the preserve frequently pointed to the tourist income that would replace the lost agricultural base, often to the point that the DNR felt compelled to emphasize the proposal's "undeveloped" status[65] to avoid raising expectations of "some sort of prairie theme park replete with covered wagons [and] fake buffalo horn souvenirs."[66] The problem with tourism, whatever its magnitude, was that it would tend to provide low-wage service-sector jobs in place of the farming opportunities and agribusiness jobs that supported the community valued by O'Brien residents. The character as well as the size of the community was threatened:

The younger, less well-established farmers in the area, many of whom because of their youth and potential we most value for the future of our communities, happen to be the ones who are most put at risk by a project like this. To gain a toehold in the expensive business of farming, they need to be able to rent or buy land at a moderate price. As a practical matter, the kind of land available at a moderate price is likely to be the kind of land this project proposes to take. Its pastures tend to be steep, hence less moist and less supportive of lush grass, and its areas of crop land tend to occur in small, irregular shaped plots that are a nuisance to farm with larger equipment. . . . A small

beginning farmer is willing to put up with those disadvantages to get a start. So when we take such land out of circulation, we are losing not only the dollar productivity of the land, but its value as a "spawning ground" for beginning farmers.[67]

In sum, if the "spawning ground" for a new generation of farmers was taken away, income from "food, gas, etc. [tourists bought] in Sutherland or Peterson on their way to or from the prairie" would not compensate.[68] It is the connection of community with the transformation of the prairie into a developed agricultural landscape that provides meaning and prospects to prairie life.

The NRC chose to calm the waters agitated by the proposed Waterman Creek Prairie Preserve. The project was approved, but without boundaries, acreage, or timetables for acquisition. The first small pieces of land were bought in 1992, but the larger project remains indefinite, and the tension between an intense but local interest and the wider public good continues. The DNR was responding to its statewide responsibility to protect a prairie heritage for future generations in a way that it believed was relatively noncontroversial, and in this it had and continues to have wide but diffuse support. Supporters express perplexity over why Iowa has such difficulty protecting so little when all the surrounding states do better: "Almost all of Iowa's landscape has been converted to agriculture. . . . [W]hat Iowa lacks is what most other states already have—a protected, sustainable piece of our original pre-European-settlement landscape."[69] They reiterate the always compelling argument that the public good must be supported by private sacrifice by pointing out to the NRC: "If not now, when? If not this way, how? If not there, where? If not you, who?"[70]

If the stalemate is to be resolved, however, it will be more than just a question of private interest versus public gain. Implicit are confrontations with the paradoxical metaphors that embody and guide human interaction with a natural landscape. What *are* the prospects of the prairies? *Who* are the people who define, and are defined by, those prospects? In returning a few thousand acres to a natural state, the environmentalists seek to fill the prairie with an alternative vision of complexity, diversity, sustainability, even wildness, and argue that the positive gain balances the local losses. But to the descendants of O'Brien County settlers, a prairie preserve would empty the landscape—of fences, groves, farmsteads, but, above all, the people who created an occupying community. After all, aren't "humans, domestic animals and food-producing crops" also part of the prairie heritage?[71] The vehemence of the opposition emphasizes that not only does the filling of the landscape by agricultural occupation provide prospects to the prairie, but those prospects foster communities that define the identities of the people who compose them. Identity and human occupation become synonymous with prospects. A local doctor who described himself as a card-carrying environmentalist asked the NRC to consider the feelings of the people in the area: "We're asking them for the collective good of Iowa to give up part of their life.... I don't think we have to be in any hurry to ride over the sensibilities of the people living there."[72] The political problem facing the NRC, if it does not wish to ride roughshod over those sensibilities, is to find a way for the local people to become a part of the prospects of a prairie preserve without losing their identity.

Notes

Our research was conducted with funding from an Interdisciplinary Research Grant at the Obermann Center for Advanced Studies at the University of Iowa. We thank Jay Semel and Lorna Olson at the center for their support and encouragement, and Gail Hollander, University of Iowa Department of Geography, for her valuable assistance.

1. Similar assertions have been made for landscape generally, in a theoretical framework, by Denis E. Cosgrove, *Social Formation and Symbolic Landscape* (London: Croom Helm, 1984).

2. For more on this aesthetic, see Allen Carlson, "On Appreciating Agricultural Landscapes," *Journal of Aesthetics and Art Criticism* 43 (1985): 301–12. For a discussion of approaches to prairie ecology, see Ronald C. Tobey, *Saving the Prairies: The Life Cycle of the Founding School of American Plant Ecology, 1895–1955* (Berkeley: University of California Press, 1981).

3. In art history, the lack of studies focusing on prairie imagery is due in part to the historical preference for monographs on an artist's reproduction, or on stylistic or regional designations of a particular subject (that is, baroque landscape, English, and so on). Even in recent American art history, however, where methodologies have proliferated and landscape has been especially favored, prairie landscapes are either ignored or subsumed within discussions of western art. Most recent art historical treatments of prairie landscapes have been from Canadian sources, especially Ronald Rees, *New and Naked Land: Making the Prairies Home* (Saskatoon: Western Producer Prairie Books, 1988), although an exception is Joni L. Kinsey, *Plain Pictures: Images of the American Prairie* (Washington, D.C.: Smithsonian Institution Press, 1996). Literary and geographical studies of prairies include Robert Thacker, *The Great Prairie Fact and Literary Imagination* (Albuquerque: University of New Mexico Press, 1989); Steven Olson, *The Prairie in Nineteenth-Century American Poetry* (Norman: University of Oklahoma Press, 1994); John Madson, *Where the Sky Began: Land of the Tallgrass Prairie* (Boston: Houghton Mifflin, 1982); and Richard Manning, *Grassland: The History, Biography, Politics, and Promise of an American Prairie* (New York: Viking, 1995).

4. These definitions are paraphrased from the *Oxford English Dictionary* (Oxford: Oxford University Press, 1971).

5. In this chapter, the word "landscape" refers to the idea of land within human history and understanding, its depiction in both literature and visual art, and the actual land itself and the uses to which it is put.

6. Elliot Coues, ed., *The Expeditions of Zebulon Montgomery Pike* (1895; reprint, New York: Dover, 1987), 2:524; Stephen Long, "General Description of Country Traversed by the Exploring Expedition Between the Meridian of Council Bluffs and the Rocky Mountains," in Edwin James, *Account of an Expedition from Pittsburgh to the Rocky Mountains, Performed in the Years 1819 and '20,* in *Early Western Travels, 1748–1846,* ed. Reuben Gold Thwaites (Cleveland: Clark, 1904–1907), 17:147–48.

7. Ibid. The implications of these theories are discussed in Walter Prescott Webb, *The Great Plains* (1931; reprint, Lincoln: University of Nebraska Press, 1981), 155–57, and William Goetzmann, *Exploration and Empire: The Explorer and the Scientist and the Winning of the American West* (1967; reprint, Austin: Texas State Historical Association, 1993), 51, 62.

8. Henry Nash Smith, *Virgin Land: The American West as Symbol and Myth* (1950; reprint, Cambridge, Mass.: Harvard University Press, 1970), 175.

9. An example of the impractical reason would be the large-scale planting of trees throughout the prairies with the idea that such vegetation would alter the climate and general fertility of the land. This was promoted enthusiastically by the federal government, which allowed, through the Timber Culture Act of 1873, a settler to claim more than the normal 160 acres if he would plant and maintain a certain acreage of trees (Webb, *Great Plains,* 412).

10. For more on the "classic" landscape, see Kenneth Clark, *Landscape into Art,* rev. ed. (New York: Harper & Row, 1976).

11. Stephen Daniels, "Goodly Prospects: English Estate Portraiture, 1670–1730," in *Mapping the Landscape: Essays on Art and Cartography,* ed. Nicholas Alfrey and Stephen Daniels (Nottingham: University Art Gallery, Castle Museum, 1990), 9–17; Albert Boime, *The Magisterial Gaze: American Landscape Painting, 1830–1865* (Washington, D.C.: Smithsonian Institution Press, 1991). For a different perspective on visual claiming of the American landscape, see Angela Miller, *Empire of the Eye: Landscape Representation and American Cultural Politics, 1825–1875* (Ithaca, N.Y.: Cornell University Press, 1993).

12. Daniels, "Goodly Prospects," 9.

13. The issues are discussed in William Truettner, ed., *The West as America: Reinterpreting Images of the Frontier* (Washington, D.C.: Smithsonian Institution Press, 1991), especially in Patricia Hill, "Picturing Progress in the Era of Expansion," 97–147.

14. Fredelle Bruser Maynard, *Raisins and Almonds* (Toronto: Doubleday, 1972), 187.

15. George Catlin, *Letters and Notes on the Manners, Customs, and Conditions of the North American Indians* (1844; reprint, New York: Dover, 1973), 1:218. [Emphasis added]

16. Charles H. Moore, "Materials for Landscape Art in America," *Atlantic Monthly,* November 1889, 670–72.

17. Joe Jones began addressing the subject of wheat farming as early as 1934 when he included one work, *Wheat,* in the biennial exhibition at the Whitney Museum of American Art. Two years later, he exhibited an entire series at the Walker Gallery in New York City, and for a number of years was so well known for the subject that he jokingly called himself the "Professor of Wheat." When the Treasury Department began looking for artists in the wheat belt for their local commissions, Jones was a logical choice. From 1936 to 1941, he produced three murals of grain harvesting for post offices in Seneca and Anthony, Kansas, and in Charleston, Missouri, and the 905 liquor company in St. Louis commissioned him and another artist, James Barre Turnbull (1909–1976), to produce five murals entitled *The Story of the Grain* in a similar mode, for its stores. See Marlene Park and Gerald E. Markowitz, *Democratic Vistas: Post Offices and Public Art in the New Deal* (Philadelphia: Temple University Press, 1984), and Karal Ann Marling, *Wall to Wall America: A Cultural History of Post Office Murals in the Great Depression* (Minneapolis: University of Minnesota Press, 1982); "Joe Jones, Regionalist, Communist, Capitalist," *Journal of Decorative and Propaganda Arts, 1875–1940* 4 (1987): 46–58; and "Workers, Capitalists, and Booze: The Story of the 905 Murals," in *Joe Jones and J. B. Turnbull—Visions of the Midwest in the 1930's* (Milwaukee: Patrick and Beatrice Haggerty Museum of Art, 1987).

18. Joe Jones painted four post office murals altogether, including *Turning a Corner* in Anthony, Kansas, and *Harvest* in Charleston, Missouri (Jones to Watson, 17 August 1939, Anthony, Kansas, General

Services Administration, quoted in Park and Markowitz, *Democratic Vistas,* 49).

19. Dorothea Lange and Paul Schuster Taylor, *An American Exodus: A Record of Human Erosion,* rev. ed. (New Haven, Conn.: Yale University Press, 1969), 63. Taylor was labor economics professor at Berkeley in the 1930s. For more on his work, see Taylor, *On the Ground in the Thirties* (Salt Lake City: Peregrine, 1983).

20. Francis Chardon, *Fort Clark Journal* (1839), quoted in William Least Heat-Moon, *PrairyErth* (Boston: Houghton Mifflin, 1991), 62.

21. Herman Melville, *Moby-Dick* (New York: Penguin, 1992), 378.

22. William Cullen Bryant, "The Prairies" (1834), in *The Norton Anthology of American Literature,* 2nd ed., ed. Nina Baym et al. (New York: Norton, 1985), 1:814–17.

23. Ralph Waldo Emerson, *The Correspondence of Emerson and Carlyle,* ed. Joseph Slater (New York: Columbia University Press, 1964), 470.

24. See the following *Atlantic Monthly* articles: "Illinois in Spring-time," September 1858, 475–88; "The New World and the New Man," October 1858, 513–31; "The Prairie State," May 1861, 579–95; "Pioneering," April 1867, 403–16; and "How We Grow in the Great Northwest," April 1869, 438–48.

25. A full list of the *Western Monthly* individuals and articles follows: From volume 1: "William Ogden," January 1869, 1–7; "Lucius Fairchild," February 1869, 65–69; "Anson S. Miller," April 1869, 193–97; "Richard J. Oglesby," May 1869, 257–61; "William Bross," June 1869, 321–30; from volume 2: "Philetus Sawyer," July 1869, 1–5; "Samuel Merrill," August 1869, 69–74; "Schuyler Colfax," September 1869, 133–38; "David Atwood," October 1869, 213–16; "John M. Palmer," November 1869, 293–98; "William B. Allison," December 1869, 373–80; from volume 3: "John D. Caton," February 1870, 81–86; "Robert Kennicott," March 1870, 165–172; "Thaddeus C. Pound," April 1870, 245–48; "The Chicago Board of Trade [Samuel H. McCrea]," June 1870, 405–9. All the articles are unsigned. The *Western Monthly* later became the *Lakeside Monthly.*

26. "Ogden," 1–7.

27. "Atwood," 213–16.

28. "Palmer," 293–98.

29. "Allison," 373–80.

30. "Chicago Board of Trade," 405–9.

31. William Cronon, *Nature's Metropolis: Chicago and the Great West* (New York: Norton, 1991), 120.

32. Hamlin Garland, *Boy Life on the Prairie* (1899; reprint, Lincoln: University of Nebraska Press, 1961), 416.

33. Raymond Williams, *The Country and the City* (New York: Oxford University Press, 1973), 120.

34. There have been many studies on the Chicago Renaissance. Recent works that are especially useful for their insight into relationships among aesthetics, prairies, and economics are Robert C. Bray, *Rediscoveries: Literature and Place in Illinois* (Urbana: University of Illinois Press, 1982); J. Ronald Engel, *Sacred Sands: The Struggle for Community in the Indiana Dunes* (Middletown, Conn.: Wesleyan University Press, 1983); James Hurt, *Writing Illinois: The Prairie, Lincoln, and Chicago* (Urbana: University of Illinois Press, 1992); and Garry Wills, "Sons and Daughters of Chicago," *New York Review of Books,* 9 June 1994, 52–59.

35. Herbert Quick, *Vandemark's Folly* (1922; reprint, Iowa City: University of Iowa Press, 1992), 111–13.

36. Ibid., 228–29.

37. Ibid.

38. Iowa Department of Natural Resources, "What Is HF 620 and Iowa's Natural Beauty?" *Open Spaces,* April 1988, 3–4, and "REAP Act Means Brighter Future for Iowa's Diverse Environment" and "Iowa Open Spaces Protection Plan," *REAP,* September–October 1989.

39. Larry Stone, "Prairie's Economic Impact Eyed," *Des Moines Register* [Metro/Iowa], 10 May 1991, 5.

40. Larry Stone, "Prairie Protection Proposal Satisfies Few," *Des Moines Register* [Metro/Iowa], 4 October 1991, 5.

41. This issue is extensively discussed by the "New Western Historians," most notably Patricia Nelson Limerick, *The Legacy of Conquest: The Unbroken Past of the American West* (New York: North, 1987).

42. J. L. E. Peck, O. H. Montzheimer, and William J. Miller, *Past and Present of O'Brien and Osce-*

ola Counties, Iowa (Indianapolis: Bowen, 1914), 1:72, 178.

43. D. A. W. Perkins, *History of O'Brien County, Iowa, from Its Organization to the Present Time* (Sioux Falls, S. Dak.: Brown and Saenger, 1897), 96–97.

44. Ibid., 72.

45. Roma Wheeler Woods, "Reminiscences of Early Pioneer Days in O'Brien County," quoted in Peck, Montzheimer, and Miller, *Past and Present,* 1:221.

46. "Iowa from Above," *Des Moines Register,* 6 May 1991, sec. T, 1–2.

47. Mart's work can be compared with the aerial views of crops taken during the same period for the Department of Agriculture, but since they were taken from higher elevations, with no efforts at framing or selection, they do not have the same visual appeal. Moreover, their purpose was economic and administrative and emphasized the value of the land through its human habitation and cultivation. More recently, however, aerial photographs of farmland have been increasingly appreciated aesthetically, at least by photographers. See Georg Gerster, *Amber Waves of Grain: America's Farmlands from Above* (New York: Harper Weldon, Owen, 1990). See also the photographs by Terry Evans, this volume, color insert.

48. Woods, "Reminiscences," 1:207.

49. Ibid., 1:216.

50. Peck, Montzheimer, and Miller, *Past and Present,* 1:177–78.

51. George Taylor to Iowa Natural Resource Commission, updated, Waterman Prairie public comment file, Iowa Department of Natural Resources, Des Moines.

52. Scott Bryant to Iowa Natural Resource Commission, 22 September 1991, Waterman Prairie public comment file, Iowa Department of Natural Resources.

53. Bruce T. Stiles to Iowa Natural Resource Commission, 6 September 1991, Waterman Prairie public comment file, Iowa Department of Natural Resources.

54. Jan Lovell, "She Fought to Save Iowa's Prairies," *Iowan,* Winter 1987, 22–27, 56, 57; Ada Hayden, "State Parks and Preserves," *Proceedings of the Iowa Academy of Science* 51 (1944): 43–48.

55. Hayden, "State Parks," 48.

56. Quoted in Lovell, "She Fought," 48.

57. Aldo Leopold, *Round River, from the Journals of Aldo Leopold,* ed. Luna B. Leopold (New York: Oxford University Press, 1953), 146–47, quoted in Perry and De An Thostenson to Iowa Natural Resource Commission, 24 September 1991, Waterman Prairie public comment file, Iowa Department of Natural Resources.

58. Harrison Fisch, testimony before the Iowa Natural Resources Commission, Iowa Natural Resources Commission Minutes, May 1991, 45–49.

59. Gene Wiese, president of Iowa Cattleman's Association, to Richard C. Young, 18 September 1991, Waterman Prairie public comment file, Iowa Department of Natural Resources; Iowa Natural Resources Commission Minutes, October 1991.

60. Peck, Montzheimer, and Miller, *Past and Present,* 1:178.

61. U.S. Department of Commerce, Bureau of the Census, *United States Census of Agriculture,* part 15, various years.

62. Ibid.

63. Fisch testimony, 48; Daniel M. Otto, "Economic Impact of Creating a Wildlife Preserve in Emmet and Dickinson Counties" (Department of Economics, Iowa State University Ames, Typescript).

64. Tom V. Nelson to John D. Field, 16 September 1991, Waterman Prairie public comment file, Iowa Department of Natural Resources.

65. Sutherland Area Prairie Study Committee, letter to the editor, *Sutherland Courier,* 20 June 1991.

66. Fisch testimony, 48.

67. Ibid., 46–47.

68. Ibid., 48.

69. "Getting the Facts on Prairies" [editorial], *Des Moines Register,* 29 September 1991.

70. Cindy Hildebrand, testimony before the Iowa Natural Resource Commission, Iowa Natural Resources Commission Minutes, October 1991, 89.

71. Harrison Fisch, "Iowa's Prairies Heritage: Another View" [editorial], *Des Moines Register,* 8 September 1991, 3.

72. Stone, "Prairie's Economic Impact Eyed."

3 Walt Whitman's Prairie Paradise

Ed Folsom

Walt Whitman—a writer associated with Long Island, New York City, Washington, D.C., and New Jersey—was nonetheless, like many Americans who lived in the East during the mid-nineteenth century, a prairie wanna-be. "I am called a Western man," he proudly claimed in 1879. "Although born in New York, I am in sympathy and preference Western—better fitted for the Mississippi Valley."[1] Throughout Whitman's career, the prairies struck him as the emblematic heart of democratic America, and he was convinced that they would produce not only the nation's physical nutriment, but eventually its art, its capital city, and its essential character: "the prairie States will be the theater of our great future."[2]

From the time he got his first glimpse of the prairies, in the winter and spring of 1848 on his way to and from New Orleans (when he rode the steamer *Prairie Bird* up the Illinois River [*PW* 607]), he incorporated them into his writing in key ways—ways that critics in this century have often overlooked. Through the 1850s, 1860s, and 1870s, he continued to form impressions of the prairies as he clipped and saved newspaper and journal articles about the midwestern states, saw paintings of the prairies, and no doubt saw the photographs of the prairies by his friend Alexander Gardner. Gardner, whom

Whitman described as "mightily my friend" and "a real artist" who "saw farther than his camera—saw more,"[3] took these photos in 1867 to document and provide support for the continuing westward expansion of the Kansas Pacific Railroad. Exhibited back east in 1868, the series was entitled *Across the Continent on the Kansas-Pacific Railway, Eastern Division.*[4]

These visual and verbal representations of the prairies set the stage for Whitman's second and last trip to the prairies, in 1879, when he was able to test the representations against an extended encounter with the massive reality of the western landscape. Traveling across Indiana, Illinois, and Missouri, he then retraced Gardner's journey, riding the Kansas Pacific all the way from Kansas City to Denver.[5] During and just after the trip, he wrote powerful evocations of the landscape he traveled through, articulating some of the first possibilities for a powerful prairie art. At this time, he became so convinced that the prairies were the geographic soul of the nation that he even began to discover prairie roots in his Long Island childhood. In his autobiography, written soon after his return from the prairies, he described the Hempstead plains he grew up near as "quite prairie-like, open, uninhabited" (*PW* 11), and a few years later he was recalling "the flat plains of the middle of Long

Island ... with their prairie-like vistas" (*PW* 629). If he could not claim a prairie nativity, he could at least re-prairie the narrative of his own childhood.

Whitman was so taken with the prairies that he once toyed with the idea of compiling a "Western Edition" of his poetry, in which he would dedicate a poem to each western state (along with a "Poem of corn and meat"); he considered titles like "Prairie Psalms," "Prairie Spaces," "Prairie Babes," and (playing on the fact that "air" is literally the heart of the word "prairie") "Prairie Airs."[6] Like many of Whitman's proposed projects, this one never materialized, but the prairies nonetheless came to function for him as an emblematic landscape, and he loved to sound the prairie names in his poetry:

> Chants of the prairies,
> Chants of the long-running Mississippi, . . .
> Chants of Ohio, Indiana, Illinois, Iowa, Wisconsin
>   and Minnesota,
> Chants going forth from the centre from
>   Kansas. . . .[7]

In this chapter, I suggest the resonance of the prairies for Whitman and look in some detail at three of his seldom-discussed prairie poems: "The Prairie-Grass Dividing," "The Prairie States," and "A Prairie Sunset."

I

Whitman's lifelong work, the book he revised and expanded over forty years, is called *Leaves of Grass*. Readers in the twentieth century have had trouble construing this title to refer to anything but a lawn, and Whitman's key image of grass often is interpreted as though he had been imagining a flawless Chemlawned expanse of bright green cut blades, thus evoking democracy as a plot of nearly identical individuals forming a uniformly colored oneness in which all the weeds and nonconforming grasses have been eradicated. But Whitman's conception of the evolving American democracy was, of course, more rugged and variegated and interesting than a suburban lawn. His book, after all, was not "Blades of Grass"; the grasses he loved and celebrated were the tougher, sturdier ones. His eyes and his pen were more drawn to varieties like calamus and mullein and pokeweed—and to the prairie grasses that were never far from his mind's eye. Consonant with the then-familiar definitions of grass, Whitman's grass was the kind with *leaves,* usually broad leaves and firm long stems, what Whitman thought of as "manly" grasses. And on the prairies, he was intrigued with the idea that the replacement of prairie grass with wheat and corn was finally an affirmation of the transmogrifying power of prairie grass, wild grass evolving into domesticated but still vast and powerful cereal grass. One way or another, the prairies, he believed, would remain America's vast grassland: "ever the far-spreading prairies, cover'd with grass and corn" (*LG* 333).

Whitman turned to grass when he was searching for the natural trope for his characteristic of camaraderie. One of Whitman's most fervently held ideals was a political and affectional bond of man for man, which, he believed, was crucial for democracy to flourish in a capitalistic society—a new kind of intense camaraderie *among* men that would temper intense competition *between* men. His faith was that such manly love would modulate greed in an increasingly wealthy and competitive society. His poems exploring this homoerotic camaraderie were gathered in a cluster he decided to entitle "Calamus," named after what he called the "large and aromatic grass [with] spears about three feet high [that grows] all over the Northern and Middle States." He invested these "biggest & hardiest kind of spears of grass" and "their fresh, aquatic, pungent bouquet"[8] with the symbolic burden of signaling "the development, identification, and general prevalence of that fervid comradeship" (*PW* 414). Whitman's image of the phallic calamus grass has become a focus of recent critical discussions of his sexuality.

But most critics forget that he also invested two other plants with the same symbolism. Just as he turned to the calamus grass as the symbol in his own northeastern area of the nation, he sought equivalent images from the other two sections of the country: from the South, he chose the live oak with moss, and toyed with using that tree as his title image; from the West, from the emerging prairie states, he took the prairie grass. But if the northern and southern tokens of manly love suggested marginality and isolation—the calamus grass that grows by the "margins of pond waters" (*LG* 112) and the oak that stands "all alone" and is a "curious token" of "manly love" (*LG* 126–27)—the prairie grass was his near-ecstatic image of the future: tall manly grass not growing at the margins, but covering the land from horizon to horizon. "The Prairie-Grass Dividing," one of the poems in the 1860 "Calamus" cluster, explicates the image, as Whitman's poetic persona imagines himself as a kind of proleptic John Wayne man of the West, striding through the prairie, parting the waves of grass, inhaling America's future, and exhaling a string of adjectives that absorb the prairie into a new democratic speech, a new democratic way of behaving, a new democratic way of *being*:

The prairie-grass dividing, its special odor
   breathing,
I demand of it the spiritual corresponding,
Demand the most copious and close companionship
   of men,
Demand the blades to rise of words, acts, beings,
Those of the open atmosphere, coarse, sunlit, fresh,
   nutritious,
Those that go their own gait, erect, stepping with
   freedom and command, leading not following,

Those with a never-quell'd audacity, those with
   sweet and lusty flesh clear of taint,
Those that look carelessly in the faces of Presidents
   and governors, as to say *Who are you?*
Those of earth-born passion, simple, never
   constrain'd, never obedient,
Those of inland America.

                    (*LG* 129)

The poet breathes in the "special odor" of the prairie air and then sings out one of his "Prairie Airs." He would praise no art, he said, "till it has well inhaled . . . the western prairie-scent, / And fully exudes it again" (*LG* 393). As the vast representative prairie republic grew, Whitman believed, the new American character would grow like the grass. The politicians Whitman admired tended to be from the prairies, like the prairie presidents, Lincoln and Grant, who represented for him the casual and common democratic future, who were what Whitman called "vast-spread, average men," combining, like the prairies, the real and the ideal: "their foregrounds of character altogether practical and real, yet . . . with finest backgrounds of the ideal" (*PW* 208). "No wonder," he wrote, "the Prairies have given the Nation its two leading modern typical men, Lincoln and Grant" (*PW* 344). Lincoln, he said, had a "certain sort of out-door or prairie stamp" (*PW* 603) in his character. And, praising Grant on his return from his world tour in 1879, Whitman celebrated the impression Grant gave, as he "walk'd with kings," that "those prairie sovereigns of the West, Kansas, Missouri, Illinois, / Ohio's, Indiana's millions, comrades, farmers, soldiers, all to the front" were also invisibly walking with him, claiming their place of equality next to the most powerful, "justified" (*LG* 485). What Grant had was "vast-spread," as common as the prairie grass. In the 1846 edition of *Webster's Dictionary of the American Language*, which Whitman followed religiously, "prairie" is defined as "flat or rolling." So, too, are Whitman's poems and his ideal democracy: America's history, for Whitman, was a kind of accelerating flattening, a turning of high discrimination and hierarchy into a "vast-spread" equality, not erasing distinction and variety, but putting variety on a level plain.

The tallgrass prairie was, therefore, Whitman's long-sought natural analogue for American democracy. Earthbound and joined by an intricate root and seeding system, the prairie grasses, in endless close proximity, at once dug down and reached skyward: they were the perfect emblem of Whitman's odd mix of transcendentalism and descendentalism, his desire to mate the soul and the body, to experience God through the five senses. The prairies were about earth and sky—that's *all* they were about—and the grasses were the living things that most fully penetrated both: they were ruggedly rooted in the soil and slenderly waving in the air. The prairies, then, were a "strange mixture of delicacy and power," "of real and ideal" (*PW* 223). Prairies were for Whitman the landscape of democracy, flat and rolling, the very earth form of nondiscrimination. America's "Democratic spirit," he believed, would require "the strong air of prairie" (*PW* 468).

II

It is not surprising, then, that on the rare occasions when Whitman projected a "paradise"—a word that did not sit comfortably in his working democratic vocabulary, in his discourse of celebrating the fullness and joy of life in the present—it was in reference to the prairies. It was on the prairies, Whitman wrote in his notes, where "every thing is on a grander scale, with broader sweeps and contrasts—paradises—deserts" (*NUPM* 1958). You can hear as Whitman's ear picks up the tonal echoes—the alliteration and rhyme—of the two words "paradise" and "prairies," almost conflating them into a "prairiedise,"⁹ the vast democratic landscape at

the heart of America. "Democracy most of all affiliates with the open air," he said, and it "must either be fibred, vitalized, by regular contact with out-door light and air and growths, farm-scenes, animals, fields, trees, birds, sun-warmth and free skies, or it will certainly dwindle and pale." The fields and farm scenes and free skies of the prairies were to him the "health-element and beauty-element" that "really underlie the whole politics, sanity, religion and art of the New World" (*PW* 294–95).

Again and again, he would find on the prairies the "strange mixture . . . of real and ideal" (*PW* 223); thus the prairies inspired prayer, and in the prairie *soil*, Whitman found America's *soul*. "Vital to any aspiring Nationality," said Whitman, was "its autochthonic song," its "born poetic expression, coming from its own soil and soul" (*PW* 667). When he sought to join East to West, he used the imagery of the music of the Atlantic Ocean "wafted inland" to prairie soil ("Overtures sent to the solid out of the liquid, / Fusion of ocean and land"), but as the music reaches the prairies, the soil translates into soul: the music "strains for the Soul of the Prairies" (*LG* 618–19). This was how rhyme worked for Whitman—not an arbitrary convention of echoing sounds, but a metonymic conflation of words that confirmed the merging of body and spirit, of solid and liquid, of earth and heaven: soil and soul, prairie and prayer.

We come closest to Whitman's prairiedise in "The Prairie States," a brief poem that was written immediately after his trip across the prairies in 1879. The title phrase, "Prairie States," is rhymed in the fifth line by "paradise," two cretic feet (prair-ie-states / par-a-dise) echoing each other and giving Whitman his guiding trope of the prairies as the "*newer* garden":

A newer garden of creation, no primal solitude,
Dense, joyous, modern, populous millions, cities
  and farms,

With iron interlaced, composite, tied, many in one,
By all the world contributed—freedom's and law's
   and thrift's society,
The crown and teeming paradise, so far, of time's
   accumulations,
To justify the past.

(LG 402)

As in many of Whitman's poems, the syntax in "The Prairie States" is extremely slippery, leading us one way only to veer off in another. It is his prairie style—flat and rolling—where it is easy to get lost because the conventional landmarks (the syntactical pathways we are accustomed to) are absent, replaced by a waving field of adjectives. Whitman is usually quick to give us a subject but loath to give us a verb, thus leaving us to wander in a clutter of adjectives, prepositional phrases, and dead verbs—verbs frozen into infinitives or gerunds. We can feel in the very syntax of this poem the effects of culmination: the "newer garden" is never predicated; it is simply *there*, the end result of contributions and actions, but no longer the actor, now simply a static monument "to justify the past." The poem itself is a sentence fragment: jagged, jarring, itself the composite, rather than the cohesion, of many separate linguistic parts. It is inspired by what Whitman called the "Muse of the Prairies," who dismisses "the literary" (with all its hierarchies of taste and tradition) and calls instead for "free play" that will allow the poet enough freedom from restriction to "comprehend the size of the whole People" (*PW* 520).

    The first line of the poem evokes Eden, only to replace it with the present: these prairies form a "newer garden of creation," distinguished from the original by increased population. Unlike the "primal solitude" of the first paradise, this "modern" one is "teeming" and "dense," with "populous millions." This populous prairie is a stunning contrast to the first appearance of the prairies in Whitman's poetry. He had glimpsed the eastern edges of the tallgrass prai-

rie on his trip to New Orleans in 1848, and he had gained impressions then of a vast area devoid of human occupation. His impressions worked their way into "Song of Myself" in 1855, when he first published *Leaves of Grass:*

Where the sun-down shadows lengthen over the
   limitless and lonesome prairie,
Where the herds of buffalo make a crawling spread
   of the square miles far and near . . .

(LG 63)

With an alliterative flourish, Whitman turned the prairies "limitless and lonesome," even while populating them with countless buffalo carpeting the landscape. (In his early-1850s notebook, in which he wrote the originating lines of "Song of Myself," Whitman employed the image of the buffalo on the prairie as the very sign of the vast, absorptive, democratic self that he was portraying in that poem: "He drinks up quickly all terms, all languages, and meanings. To his curbless and bottomless powers, they be like ponds of rain water to the migrating herds of buffalo, who make the earth miles square look like a creeping spread—See! he has only passed this way, and they are drained dry" [*NUPM* 125].)

    But twenty-five years later, the "populous millions" that Whitman projected onto the prairies became people instead of buffalo. The animals are not even mentioned in "The Prairie States," and the multitudes are now "interlaced" with iron, not only the iron of the railroads that in the preceding twenty years had been linking prairie cities and farms into an increasingly tight web of connections (Whitman celebrated how trains had been "launch'd o'er the prairies wide" [*LG* 472]), but also the iron and steel of wire fences, especially barbed wire, the manufactured equivalent of the thorny hedges in the natural garden. Iron inventions both linked and divided the farms of the prairies and made possible civilization in the open lands of America's emerging West. Sales of barbed wire were exploding in the

51

1870s, and the enclosing of fields in this decade, turning a rancher's frontier into a farmer's domain, prompted Whitman to resurrect the word "paradise," which etymologically means "walled garden" or "enclosed park." Whitman, who often reminded himself to track every word to its origin ("get in the habit of tracing words to their root-meanings"),[10] knew that paradise on the prairies was emerging because fences were creating enclosed fertile farms, countless democratic walled gardens, and were allowing for population growth and the formation of cities. "As I cross'd Missouri State," he wrote during his 1879 trip, "I thought my eyes had never looked on scenes of greater pastoral beauty. For over two hundred miles successive rolling prairies, agriculturally perfect" (*PW* 206). He wanted his poems to urge on prairie progress: "[A]ll over the prairies," Whitman wrote, "I will make inseparable cities, with their arms about each other's necks" (*LG* 610). Paradise, etymologically and historically, was not found in pristine nature, but in the interplay between humans and the natural world, between East and West, between iron and prairie, between "law" and "freedom," a "composite" of elements, a garden to which "all the world contributed."

It is noteworthy that in his manuscript notes to "The Prairie States," Whitman emphasized that it was written "for the Irish famine" (*LG* 402n). In 1879, there had been another bad potato harvest in Ireland, raising the specter of the 1840s famine: Whitman projected his prairie-state paradise as vast enough to absorb the teeming masses of immigrants who would, like the interlaced iron, be woven into this new composite and dynamic garden. Whitman's Eden was the *result* of history, not the *cause* of it, the current culmination instead of the past inception. Instead of a linear history beginning with the expulsion from the garden and proceeding through the apocalypse, Whitman offered an alternative circular history, from one garden to a newer one, from an earthly paradise lost to an earthly paradise regained, built out of and onto the failures of the past. His new garden remained firmly planted in history; Whitman would always prefer the promise of earthly progress to that of heavenly perfection: "I shall certainly withdraw from Heaven—for the soul prefers freedom in the prairie" (*NUPM* 64).

This new paradise would be "thrift's society," marked by healthy and vigorous growth brought about by careful management, free and lawful. Whitman's unlikely phrase—"thrift's society"—has a very different resonance for us today, in the era of thrift stores, than it did in Whitman's time. "Thrift" and "thrive" are etymological twins, and "thrift" means "prosperousness." It connotes a prosperity brought about by careful oversight. Whitman's intention is to signal that this new society on the prairies would be the dividend of the careful investment "of time's accumulations": the payoff would be a justification of the past, a revelation of the horrors of history all finally culminating in this "composite" paradise—a union of individual and distinctive parts, a union "composed," not "natural." This paradise is the "crown" of history "so far"; Whitman would always hedge his evocations of paradise by allowing for further evolution. But, for now, the "crown" was a new society governed by no "crown" except the mark of honor it created for itself: regal crowns have been replaced by the sign of a "teeming" sovereignty, those millions of "prairie sovereigns" he celebrated in his poem to Grant, "What Best I See in Thee," all authority invested in the "composite" many instead of the chosen few (*LG* 485). It was the best society "so far," even as it was still "so far" to the ultimate realization of democracy.

Perfection's other name, after all, was "democracy"—a word, Whitman said, "the real gist of which still sleeps, quite unawaken'd, notwithstanding the resonance and the many angry tempests out of which its syllables have come, from pen or tongue. It is a great word, whose history, I suppose, remains unwritten, because that history has yet to be enacted" (*PW* 393). Whitman had the word "democracy," so he hardly needed paradise. And democracy's "vast-spread" crown, its flourishing, was going to happen—Whitman was convinced—on the prairies, because the tensed forces creating the true American character, the revolutionary democracy that would redefine human experience, were interacting most fertilely on the prairies: "The main social, political, spine-character of the States will probably run along the Ohio, Missouri and Mississippi rivers, and west and north of them, including Canada," he wrote in *Democratic Vistas*: "Those regions . . . will compact and settle the traits of America, with all the old retain'd, but more expanded, grafted on newer, hardier, purely native stock. A giant growth, composite from the rest, getting their contribution, absorbing it, to make it more illustrious" (*PW* 385).

III

Such beliefs lie behind another late evocation of the prairie that Whitman wrote in 1888, a poem called "A Prairie Sunset," which powerfully anticipates some of Keith Jacobshagen's prairie paintings. Whitman sensed a new art emerging from America's contact with the prairies, which, he said, "seem to me to afford new lights and shades, . . . nowhere else such perspectives, such transparent lilacs and grays." Prophesying the emergence of a new genre of prairie art, he said he could "conceive of some superior landscape painter, some fine colorist, after sketching awhile out here, discarding all his previous work

. . . as muddy, raw and artificial" (*PW* 214). "A Prairie Sunset" is a poem that grows out of Whitman's intense reactions to the sunsets he saw on his 1879 trip west, when he wrote in his notebook of "the indescribable *sentiment* of lessening light on this plains, and the far circles of the horizon" (*NUPM* 1033). There was something hugely encircling and spiritually uniting about the prairies for Whitman, and that quality seemed most apparent to him in the hovering moments between day and night. As he traveled across "*the Plains* . . . —plains—plains—plains," he noted in his journal "three beautiful sunsets—over an hour each time" (*NUPM* 1039), and his poem conflates them into one magnificent emblem:

Shot gold, maroon and violet, dazzling silver,
    emerald, fawn,
The earth's whole amplitude and Nature's multiform
    power consign'd for once to colors;
The light, the general air possess'd by them—colors
    till now unknown,
No limit, confine—not the Western sky alone—the
    high meridian—North, South, all,
Pure luminous color fighting the silent shadows to
    the last.

(*LG* 530–31)

With its initial and concluding martial imagery echoing the now-distant Civil War, this poem projects the prairie sky as the one dome large enough to unify America's old divisions, to contain enough diversity in its amplitude of color to overcome sectional confines, to overarch "North" and "South" and pull them with the West into a new "all." With their previously unknown luminous colors balancing between and mediating the blue and the gray, daylight and dusk, sun and shadow, and creating the possibility of unified "American Democracy," "in its myriad personalities," the "free skies" of the prairie are the last hope for preventing the "dwindling and paling" that Whitman feared would befall the nation like a shadow if the "Nature-element" ceased to be central to American culture. The nation had been saved once, he believed, because the prairie West had sent its brave, democratic sons to decide the conflict between North and South in favor of union: "I saw—out of the land of the prairies," he wrote in one poem, the "plenteous offspring" with "their trusty rifles on their shoulders" come "to the rescue" (*LG* 294). Whitman's composite Union soldier was a nameless "tan-faced prairie-boy" (*LG* 320)—simple, taciturn, as natural as the sun and the prairie that formed him.

When Whitman wrote "A Prairie Sunset" in Camden, New Jersey, however, nearly twenty-five years after the Civil War, his imagination still seeing the afterglow of one of the sunsets he had experienced on the prairie nearly a decade earlier, he worried about what had become of the country that so many prairie boys had given their lives to preserve. Could the prairies save the nation once again by calling it back to its nature-based democratic ideals? He continued to believe that the "Prairie States" were "*the real America*" (*Corr* 3:169), and his charged multicolored sunset was offered as a nervous symbol of hope. In the poem, the twilight moment hovers forever in an unpredicated syntactic fragment, just as in his mind that sunset symphony would hold its final note eternally. Even the seeming redundancy of Whitman's phrase "The earth's whole amplitude" subtly reveals his spiritualization of the landscape: we can hear the "s" at the end of "earth's" joining with "whole" to yield the aural pun "earth's soul." Once again, in the soil's soul, in the amplitude of the prairies, Whitman found America's culminating spirit projected into the sky's multitude of colors: "The earth's whole [earth's soul], amplitude." But it was precisely the question of the nation's amplitude that now bothered Whitman; chang-

ing conditions in the country and on the prairies made him question the direction in which America was headed.

Just how multicolored, for example, *was* the new prairiedise in Whitman's mind? Did this unifying sunset join black, red, and white, the three races in America whose destinies were at this time also being worked out on the prairies? At this stage of his life, Whitman was relatively silent about American Indians and African Americans: in his postbellum thinking, the prairies would meld North and South and the varieties of white immigrants far more efficiently than they would hybridize America across the races. But Whitman was not oblivious to the issue, and he even occasionally expressed a muted hope that the prairies might in some contingent way include all the races.

His trip west in 1879 coincided with the migration of the Exodusters, former slaves moving into the open spaces of Kansas. In his notebooks, Whitman recorded the movement, albeit in terms that equated the black settlers with the buffalo and the insects whose presence on the prairies was as inconvenient to the new white farmers as the presence of Indians. All three perceived pests had been, of course, the object of major eradication efforts in the years just before Whitman's journey. In the year Whitman headed out to the prairies, the grasshoppers that had ravaged crops in the 1870s were again under control, and the buffalo that had carpeted the prairies were virtually decimated, following a decade in which as many as 200,000 of their hides were sold at auction every day. In this context, Whitman's evocation of the black migration as a new stampede and a new swarm on the prairie suggests a kind of racist joke, the freedmen cast as the new buffalo or new grasshoppers, arriving to re-pest the plains: "The slaves are stampeding at a great rate from Western Missouri—swarm across the line in droves taking wagons, horses cattle, & one sort of truck & another. . . . In three weeks in April, 300 ran away from Lafayette county alone; they went to Kansas" (*NUPM* 1021). More than fifteen years after emancipation, Whitman was still inscribing these African Americans as runaway slaves.

Yet he could also see that this new black migration had a significance and power that transcended his own discomfort with it, and he expressed a desire that the Exodusters be included in the emerging new prairie art: "Sometimes they make a real procession (would be mighty good for an artist to paint)" (*NUPM* 1021). Whitman's genius was often his ability to rise above his own prejudices and recognize that events he found troublesome were, at some level, carrying on the democratic revolution, developing democracy in ways that even he could not conceive of: the threatening black "swarm," from another angle, became a hopeful democratic "procession."

And what about American Indians? Whitman's trip west also coincided with the end of America's bloodiest encounters with native peoples. The Battle of the Little Bighorn had been fought three years earlier, and Chief Joseph had surrendered just two years before; except for a few remnants, free and independent native cultures were gone. From the perspective of America's indigenous peoples, the prairie sunsets were now indicative of something far different from peaceful assimilation of difference, as the familiar cultural emblem of the Indian heading into the sunset suggested. But for Whitman, a kind of assimilation of Native Americans nonetheless was a reality on the prairies, where Indian place-names dominated, unlike in the East (where European and classical names had, to Whitman's dismay, overtaken the New World and smothered the native under the imported). Whitman loved native names and

lobbied for most of his life to restore them in the East, and he celebrated the increased frequency of such names as Americans headed west:

What name a State, river, sea, mountain, wood, prairie, has—is no indifferent matter.—All aboriginal names sound good. I was asking for something savage and luxuriant, and behold here are the aboriginal names. I see how they are being preserved. They are honest words—they give the true length, breadth, depth. They all fit. Mississippi!—the word winds with chutes—it rolls a stream three thousand miles long.[11]

The land of the Mississippi Valley, then, was the land of native names, and if the Indians were themselves vanishing as a presence, Whitman always insisted that at least their names could be widely absorbed into the American language, allowing the United States to embed the aboriginal in the very fabric of its nomenclature. But as Whitman traveled the prairies in 1879, native names were just about the *only* signs of Indians that he could find. Although news reports of his trip indicate that Whitman briefly saw two small bands of Indians (Eitner 44), his notebooks record but one sighting: observing a band of Potawatomis watering their horses, he wrote only: "The squad of Indians at Topeka" (*NUPM* 1039). He noted with admiration a "Wapalingua Chief [who] died 2 years ago 116 years of age a brave blind Indian never spoke English" (*NUPM* 1039); Wapalingua was one last example of the wise old natives whom white America had learned to love, Indians with nothing left to see, with no words Americans could understand, having outlived their time. So, with only remnants of Native American cultures left, Whitman put his absorptive faith in words, noting with satisfaction the names of the small towns in Kansas that he passed by: "Tongahocksa . . . Eagle Tail after a chief." And by the time he arrived in Mirage, in eastern Colorado, he could manage only a feeble joke, suggesting just how quickly what had been the native reality on these prairies was now reality no more: "Mirage see mirages" (*NUPM* 1040). The sun had already set on the Indians, and in the charged American prairie sunset of Whitman's poem, their color is nowhere to be seen.

The mirror-companion poem to "A Prairie Sunset" is another short poem that Whitman published in the same year, this one called "Yonnondio," an Iroquois term that Whitman understood to mean "lament for the aborigines" (*LG* 524). Once again, as he had done with the Exodusters, Whitman perceived the nonwhite inhabitants of the prairies to exist in "swarms":

I see swarms of stalwart chieftains, medicine-men,
  and warriors,
As flitting by like clouds of ghosts, they pass and are
  gone in the twilight.

(*LG* 524)

This is the same prairie sunset, but now, instead of suggesting the amplitude of America's future, it signals the end of the American past of native cultures. The "populous," "iron interlaced" "newer garden" of "cities and farms" in "The Prairie States," in this reminiscent twilight, all fade as the prairies go blank:

Yonnondio! Yonnondio!—unlimn'd they disappear;
To-day gives place, and fades—the cities, farms,
  factories fade;
A muffled sonorous sound, a wailing word is borne
  through the air for a moment,
Then blank and gone and still, and utterly lost.

(*LG* 524)

Once again, as with the black prairie settlers, Whitman's concern is that there is "no picture, poem, statement, passing them to the future," and so "unlimn'd they disappear," without a line in the evolving poem of America, "utterly lost." Whitman's small poem is an attempt to give the Native Americans a line, to utter their loss so

that they *won't* be "utterly lost." It is an odd and unresolved cultural moment for Whitman, a tensed "twilight," as the swarms of Indians fade at the very moment that the swarms of African Americans appear. For Whitman, finally and tragically, neither group was of clear significance for the American prairie future, yet he believed that both deserved a painting or poem that would include them in the record of the evolving national narrative.

IV

On his trip west, the people who fascinated Whitman more than the Indians or the Exodusters were the cowboys: "to me a strangely interesting class, bright-eyed as hawks, with their swarthy complexions and their broad-brimm'd hats." These swarthy men were Whitman's "tanfaced prairie-boys" grown up. He loved the way they were "always on horseback, with loose arms slightly raised and swinging as they ride" (*PW* 219). Strong and independent, yet part of a close-knit male fellowship, they were the human manifestation of the prairie grass, the living proof that Whitman's dream of democratic camaraderie on the plains was taking form. And it was the cowboys, finally, whom he remained interested in to the end of his life. He must even have been oddly comforted by one negative reviewer's parodic characterization of Whitman in an 1881 review: "American he is, of the ruder and more barbaric type, a prairie cow boy in a buffalo robe."[12]

Let's conclude, then, by turning to a cold New Jersey night in February 1889, three years before Whitman's death, when he talked, as he often did, of the West and of cowboys, greeting an emissary of sorts, a man named William Salter, who had been born in Iowa, where his father had settled forty-three years earlier. Whitman was astounded and commented on how "remarkable" it was to hear of anyone "born in Iowa forty years ago." Whitman's friend Horace Traubel commented on the poet's look as he gazed at this forty-year-old native Iowan: he "looked at Salter as if he was a curio. It amused us all."[13] Whitman was struck by the very thought that the country had come to a point where he could now be meeting a middle-aged white *adult* who had been *born* on the prairies: the nation accumulated its history quickly.

Their talk that night kept returning to the West, and Whitman proudly claimed that he was "a brevet Missourian: I reckon I'm a Westerner in spirit." As so often happened when the prairies were the subject, the conversation turned to an artist, this time Thomas Eakins, the painter and photographer who had been a frequent visitor of late to Whitman's home to paint his portrait and photograph him. What interested Whitman this night about Eakins was the source of his vitality, the experiences that generated his distinctive American art: Salter had just spoken of a German student who had gone off into the prairies and had quickly "grown from a shriveled-up sick man into an athlete." Whitman knew the truth of such tales and promptly told the version he had recently heard: "Eakins did that: he went right among the cowboys: herded: built up miraculously just in the same way." Traubel then asked Whitman, "Don't you suppose this episode helped to make Eakins the painter he is?" And Whitman answered, "Undoubtedly: it must have done much towards giving him or confirming his theory of painting: he has a sort of cowboy bronco method: he could not have got that wholly or even mainly in the studios of Paris—he needed the converting, confirming, uncompromising touch of the plains" (*WWC* 135).

This was Whitman's version of paradise on the prairies: "the converting, confirming, un-compromising touch of the plains" for him was a kind of tough rejuvenating force, and he defined American art literally and figuratively as that material produced far to the west of the "studios of Paris"—material touched by the plains, art that would have to be broken like a cowboy broke a bronco, taming the unarticulated and unformed wildness into the barely articulated and uncomfortably harnessed. The spirit of the prairies, in other words, was just what America needed to develop its own original style, to free itself from debilitating European models; Whitman despaired of the "certain snobbishness" that still infected art in America: "Instead of the storm beats, the wind blowing, the savage throat, the ecstasy and abandon of the prairie, . . . we have always a polite person amid a well-dressed assembly, in a parlor, talking about Plutarch, Astronomy, good behavior, the impropriety of laughing &c and evidently dominated by the English" (*NUPM* 1726). Whitman regarded his own unorthodox poetry as prairie work, even though it was written in the East, and he believed that his true readers would be Westerners: "I depend on being realized, long hence, where the fat prairies spread, and thence to Oregon and California inclusive. . . . I am the bard of the future" (*LG* 636).

For Whitman, then, America's hope was in the converting and confirming that were going on in the group of rough and raw but very promising prairie states, what he called "this favor'd central area . . . [which] seems fated to be the home both of what I would call America's distinctive ideas and distinctive realities" (*PW* 208). More than Yosemite or Yellowstone, more than Niagara Falls, Whitman said when recalling his one major continental trip, the prairies were "what most impress'd me, and will longest remain with me. Even their simplest statistics are sublime" (*PW* 221). And his dream was to see "these Prairies, the great Plains, and the valley of the Mississippi . . . fused in the alembic of a perfect poem . . . entirely western, fresh and limitless—altogether our own, without a trace or taste of Europe's soil, reminiscence, technical letter or spirit" (*PW* 219). This "land of ten million virgin farms" would soon, Whitman believed, boast "a hundred millions of people," and it would call forth an army of new poets, "Minstrels latent on the prairies" (*LG* 232): it already had become for him "America's Characteristic Landscape" (*PW* 220). In some of his most inflated diction, he would even confer on the prairies mythic significance, making them the very emblem of "Fecund America," casting them as a fertile democratic goddess uniting the nation and absorbing its diversity:

Thou Prairie Dame that sittest in the middle, and
  lookest out upon thy world, and lookest East, and
  lookest West,
Dispensatress, that by a word givest a thousand
  miles, a million farms, and missest nothing,
Thou all-acceptress—thou hospitable, (thou only
  art hospitable as God is hospitable.)

(LG 360)

So in 1846 when Iowa had applied for statehood, Whitman had promptly supported the move in an editorial in the Brooklyn *Daily Eagle* (June 10, 1846), applauding Iowa's unique constitution, which extended the meaning of a responsible democracy, and concluding his endorsement with an affirmation that Iowa was in fact the sign of the future, refining and perfecting American democracy and adding a distinctly American flavor as the country marched westward across the prairie: "The west is striding on ahead of us, like a giant!"[14] Out west, Whitman believed, the "friendly and flowing" (*LG* 73) new natives were busy breaking up the wilderness into fertile farms *and* breaking down the eastern conventions and pacts and constitutions into more democratic ways of governing

and behaving; out west, everything was more malleable, up for grabs, broncos that would resist breaking but could eventually be ridden by the tough and brave. Just as each newly broken bronco, though, eventually lost its fierce resistance and became tamed, so the paradise kept slipping west, leaving behind it a continually renovated East. This moving line of tense and defining encounter became for the historian Frederick Jackson Turner the site of the frontier.[15] Paradise was always somewhere, and it was somewhere *now;* in nineteenth-century America, that somewhere was an always-changing site, as the country kept moving into the "entirely unpenetrated" "vast national tracts" of the "Western Geography" (*NUPM* 1947).

If "democracy" was a word that Americans were literally growing into, they were growing into it westwardly, and it was sometimes dispiriting for Whitman to discover how quickly western experimentation gave way to eastern conventionality. He had worried in 1879 when he saw "the women of the prairie cities," "'intellectual' and fashionable, but dyspeptic-looking and generally doll-like," whose "ambition evidently is to copy their eastern sisters" (*PW* 225–26). He worried about how many small-minded Methodist ministers seemed to come back east from the prairies, carrying puritanical notions with them as though puritanism itself was what the prairies were about. For a good part of Whitman's writing life, the prairies looked as though they would last as the site of conversion and confirmation, but he also knew and feared that the East traveled west far more efficiently than the West traveled east. And that, finally, would be the battle of the prairie sunset—as the "pure luminous color" of prairie possibilities fought the "silent shadows" of conventionality and imitation always creeping in from the East (*LG* 531). Native Americans seemed to be disappearing into the shadows, just as African Americans were emerging from them. As Whitman died, he left us on the prairies at sunset, in a tense and unresolved cultural twilight.

Notes

I would like to thank the Obermann Center for Advanced Studies at the University of Iowa and its director, Jay Semel, for valuable support during the writing of this chapter. I developed some early ideas for it in a talk I gave in 1995 for the interdisciplinary public program "Utopian Visions of Work and Community," sponsored by the National Endowment for the Humanities. That talk was published in Jay Semel and Annie Tremmel Wilcox, eds., *Utopian Visions of Work and Community* (Iowa City: Obermann Center for Advanced Studies, 1996), 101–13.

1. Quoted in Walter H. Eitner, *Walt Whitman's Western Jaunt* (Lawrence: Regents Press of Kansas, 1981), 20. [Hereafter cited as *Eitner*]

2. Walt Whitman, *Prose Works, 1892*, 2 vols., ed. Floyd Stovall (New York: New York University Press, 1963, 1964), 224n. [Hereafter cited as *PW*, without volume number, as pagination is continuous]

3. Quoted in Horace Traubel, *With Walt Whitman in Camden: November 1, 1888–January 20, 1889* (New York: Mitchell Kennerley, 1912), 346. Whitman comments frequently and always favorably about Gardner in this volume and in other volumes of Traubel's *With Walt Whitman*. Gardner photographed Whitman several times during the Civil War, and the poet preferred Gardner's portraits above all others. Whitman also claimed that Gardner was a great fan of *Leaves of Grass*: "He went strong for *Leaves of Grass*—believed in it, fought for it. . . . Gardner was large, strong—a man with a big head full of ideas" (234).

4. Susan Danly, "Across the Continent," in *An Enduring Interest: The Photographs of Alexander Gardner*, ed. Brooks Johnson (Norfolk, Va.: Chrysler Museum, 1991), 84–95.

5. The most complete description of Whitman's 1879 trip can be found in Eitner, including a detailed itinerary and contemporary photographs of places that Whitman visited. While Whitman's written descriptions of his trip imply that he made the journey alone, he in fact traveled as part of a group of five (the others were journalists from Pennsylvania). The official trip lasted from September 10 to September 27, 1879, but after his traveling companions went back east, Whitman remained in St. Louis for over three months (until January 4, 1880), visiting his brother Thomas Jefferson Whitman.

6. Walt Whitman, *Notebooks and Unpublished Prose Manuscripts*, 6 vols., ed. Edward F. Grier (New York: New York University Press, 1984), 1348, 1373. [Hereafter cited as *NUPM*, without volume number, as pagination is continuous]

7. Walt Whitman, "Starting from Paumanok," in *Leaves of Grass: Comprehensive Reader's Edition*, ed. Harold W. Blodgett and Sculley Bradley (New York: New York University Press, 1965), 17. [Hereafter cited as *LG*]

8. Walt Whitman, *The Correspondence*, 6 vols., ed. Edwin Haviland Miller (New York: New York University Press, 1961–77), 1:347. [Hereafter cited as *Corr*]

9. I coin the word "prairiedise" to suggest the way that Whitman juxtaposed "prairie" and "paradise" in his writings. When he used the word "paradise," it was seldom far from "prairies," as in this line from "Enfans d'Adam, No. 11," "Time, Paradise, the Mannahatta, the prairies, finding me unchanged" (*LG* 594).

10. Walt Whitman, *Daybooks and Notebooks*, 3 vols., ed. William White (New York: New York University Press, 1977), 3:725. [Hereafter cited as *DBN*]

11. Walt Whitman, *An American Primer*, ed. Horace Traubel (1904; reprint, Duluth: Holy Cow! Press, 1987), 17–18.

12. "Walt Whitman's Poems," *Literary World*, 19 November 1881, in *Walt Whitman: The Contemporary Reviews*, ed. Kenneth M. Price (Cambridge: Cambridge University Press, 1996), 226. Early commentators on Whitman's work often evoked the prairies while criticizing him; Sidney Lanier, for example, mocked Whitman's poetics, saying that "his argument seems to be that because a prairie is wide therefore debauchery is admirable" (*DBN*, 1:101n).

13. Horace Traubel, *With Walt Whitman in Cam-

den: January 21 to April 7, 1889 (Philadelphia: University of Pennsylvania Press, 1953), 135. [Hereafter cited as *WWC*]

14. Whitman always saw the prairie men as physical giants, taking huge strides; for example, he described Union soldiers emerging from the prairie states "with large steps crossing the prairies out of Illinois and Indiana" (*LG* 282).

15. Frederick Jackson Turner, *The Significance of the Frontier in American History* (1893; reprint, New York: Ungar, 1963).

4 On Level Ground: Alexander Gardner's Photographs of the Kansas Prairies

Jane E. Simonsen

One of Alexander Gardner's best known photographs of the American prairies bears the portentous title *"Westward, the Course of Empire Takes its Way," Laying Track 600 miles west of St. Louis, Mo.* (Figure 4.1). In this image, workers crowd the newly laid rails, holding their tools and standing victorious atop the engine itself. The train is foreshortened, its engine angled toward the camera. Gardner's title seems apt. As a nineteenth-century railroad survey photographer, his job was to document the fulfillment of Manifest Destiny as the Kansas Pacific Railroad laid tracks across the prairies, plains, and mountains from St. Louis to San Francisco in the years after the Civil War. Still, the engine that represents empire in the photograph appears tiny, even toylike. Dwarfed by the enormous expanse of blank sky and deemphasized by the parade of workers who precede it, this engine is ill-placed to symbolize technology's power to forge empires out of prairie grasses. Rather than accentuating the shape and force of the machine, Gardner took his compositional cues from the prairie

landscape itself. The image is designed to emphasize levelness, distance, and a low horizon line that accents the enormity of the sky. Like prairie grasses, the workers on the railway stand shoulder to shoulder, distinguished not by their individuality but by their numbers. In his duty, subject matter, and title, Gardner promoted the conquest and transformation of the prairie environment through the technological designs of railroad transportation. In his aesthetic concerns, however, he was captivated by the artistic possibilities of the prairie landscape. Gardner's work does not represent the prairie as a landscape that would succumb to the railroad, but utilizes the railroad as a means to express the social and artistic values of prairie landscapes.

"Westward, the Course of Empire Takes its Way" is one of a set of stereograph and collodion print photographs that Gardner made of his travels in Kansas and along the thirty-fifth parallel through the American Southwest in 1867 and 1868. Gardner was hired by the Kansas Pacific Railroad to create promotional photo-

Figure 4.1. *"Westward, the Course of Empire Takes its Way," Laying Track 600 miles west of St. Louis, Mo.* (Kansas State Historical Society, Topeka)

graphs that would encourage investment in railroads and towns on the Kansas prairie, but as an accomplished portrait and Civil War photographer, Gardner was sensitive to the value of photographs as works of art. The roughly 160 photographs that compose the group entitled *Across the Continent on the Kansas-Pacific Railway, Eastern Division,* are thus an eclectic blend of carefully composed picturesque landscapes and seemingly disordered views of towns, businesses, and individuals. The series does not depict nature's cataclysms of creation; neither, however, does it isolate and dramatize such engineering feats as trains, bridges, and tracks. In a number of photographs, the prairie landscape of rivers, grasses, and hills harmonizes beauti-

fully with the curve of the railroad tracks that pass through its midst. In some images, waving grasses nearly obscure fragile new towns. In others, the technology of rail building has obviously and indelibly changed the landscape.

As these photographs plot points along the railroad line from St. Louis, Missouri, to just west of Hays City, Kansas, they also plot a story about prairie spaces. Prairies had long been considered both artistically and physically barren by Euro-American travelers and artists—the prairies were difficult to "read" using conventional understandings of the uses and artistic values of landscapes. Because of the seeming absence of prospects or viewpoints provided by mountains, forests, houses, and cultivated fields, the prairie could seem like a sea made of grasses; with no points of reference and no signs of agricultural promise, one could easily get lost. But as the nation faced west in the aftermath of the Civil War, promoters began to tell another story about the plains and prairies. The prairie's level plane became the "Great Leveler," a region where American citizens would stand on equal footing with one another, united in their purpose and struggle to create fertile farmland out of the ocean of prairie grass. Natural features reinforced this democratic vision: grand vistas of sky and grassland and gently rolling hills symbolized grand purpose. The prairie's prospect was a level one in which national democratic goals were echoed and legitimated by the very landscape on which those dreams were built.

Gardner's photographic narrative of prairie prospects celebrates the aesthetic properties of prairie landscapes that he visualized as congruent with the emerging social and economic landscape. His aestheticization of the prairie environment proposes a set of relationships between the settlers and the topography by using the railroad as an artistic construct that enhances the natural values of the terrain. The railroad would give citizens access to the landscape's resources and provide connections between points in regions previously unfamiliar to settlers. The level topography of the landscape would allow the easy construction of rail lines and the development of the prairie's potential for agriculture. Gardner's photographs of towns, natural vistas, bridges, and the railroad itself highlight the levelness of prairie topography. The series of photographs, which alternates between town scenes and open vistas, simulates the rhythm of travel on the prairie by marking signposts in spaces that could be threatening and disorienting in their vastness. The recurring image in the collection is that of the span: the river, road, bridge, or track that connotes movement across and encounter on level ground. Linking depictions of towns and vistas and serving as a visual reference throughout the sequence, the railroad itself emerges as a character in this prairie narrative. In consistently returning to the railroad in portrayals of the social and aesthetic composition of prairie life, Gardner's Kansas photographs make the prairie's natural features legible. Read in relation to the railroad, the prairie's qualities of levelness and vista could be understood and even celebrated for their beauty. Gardner, in his appreciation of the prairie's natural design, promoted not only the plans of the railroad, but also an aesthetic regard for a kind of landscape in which few artists of his era saw any design at all.

Gardner's Pastoral Landscapes

Across the Continent was not Gardner's first experiment with photographic narrative. He began his career in photography as a member of Washington artist Mathew Brady's corps of Civil War photographers and is still best known for his collection *Gardner's Photographic Sketch Book of the Civil War,* published in 1866.[1] Gardner was born in Paisley, Scotland, in 1821, and first worked as a journalist and photographer in Glasgow. The two photographers most likely met in Europe, and Brady may have asked Gardner to join his corps because of the Scot's expertise in wet-plate photography. Gardner's first trip to the United States, however, was in 1849, when he helped to settle a cooperative community on the prairie near Clydesdale, Iowa. He planned to return to Clydesdale with his family at a later date, but the community folded and its residents dispersed in the 1850s. For years afterward, Gardner continued to visit friends in MacGregor, Iowa. Biographer Josephine Cobb has proposed that these trips prompted Gardner's interest in western landscape as a subject.[2] After returning to America to join Brady, he made his home in Washington, D.C. As a member of the corps, he helped compose some of the most striking images of the Civil War. In 1862, he left the group because of Brady's practice of publishing others' work under his own name. Several photographers left with him, including well-known western photographer Timothy O'-Sullivan, and their work makes up the *Sketch Book*. While he was careful to give credit to individual photographers, Gardner ordered the images in the book and wrote the detailed captions that accompany them.

In designing the *Sketch Book*, Gardner documented the violence of war, yet foregrounded the landscapes on which battles took place. Timothy Sweet argues that the *Sketch Book* uses pastoral compositions to transcend violent death by resituating the war's casualties in an American pastoral landscape.[3] The *Sketch Book* represents battle sites as landscapes with the power to heal divisiveness, presenting death as a part of nature's cycle.[4] Instead of focusing on action (which in itself was beyond his camera's technological ability), Gardner's photographs render battle sites as views of farmhouses, churches, camps, bodies, and fields that are essentially scenic landscapes. These views hold a "restorative power," ordered through captions that present the events of the war in terms of national memory.[5] Much of both Sweet's and Alan Trachtenberg's analyses of the *Sketch Book* focuses on the extensive descriptions with which Gardner captioned each photograph. While Gardner's Civil War photos do exhibit conventional pastoral composition—such as distant horizons, eye-level views, and formal balance—it is his prose that most clearly justifies the "debris" of battle by "render[ing] it as proof of national purpose and rectitude."[6] The *Sketch Book*'s narrative is overt in its criticism of the violence and waste of

the war, its loyalty to the Union forces, and its plea for peace in a reunited America.

When he headed west after the Civil War, Gardner was an experienced landscape photographer who had demonstrated the effectiveness of artistic composition in promoting an ideological message. Yet unlike the *Sketch Book*, *Across the Continent* does not include the prose that defines the photographic narrative of Gardner's Civil War work; a simple record of place name and distance from St. Louis is all the text in the collection. Gardner did use two different ways to make his depiction of the West public. One hundred sixty prints of the Kansas portion of his journey were reproduced as stereographs for popular consumption and some of these images as 6- × 8-inch, 8- × 10-inch, and 11- × 14-inch plates. The large-print collection includes images from his entire journey across the continent, from St. Louis to San Francisco; thus there are photographs of the Sierra Nevadas, of Zuñi Pueblo inhabitants of Isletta, New Mexico, and of the plants and rock formations of the Southwest in addition to about forty photographs from the Kansas portion of the trip. Stereographs were a much cheaper and more accessible way to view these prairie portraits; it would have been prohibitively expensive for most people to purchase the entire collection of prints. The stereographs, furthermore, in showing only the prairie portion of the journey, present a narrative and an aesthetic appreciation of plains and prairie landscapes that can contribute to our understanding of the print collection that does span "across the continent." The series of prairie stereographs does not depict a divisive and violent confrontation between nature and technology, but a nonhierarchical and mutually beneficial relationship between the West and its new population. By emphasizing the unique visual characteristics of the prairie and stressing parallels between the natural and built environments, Gardner represented the social and physical transformation of the prairie as in harmony with its aesthetic qualities.

Railroad Promotion and the Aesthetic of Levelness

The desire of railroad companies to depict the way west as a level one in order to emphasize the ease of travel was one of the reasons Gardner was hired to photograph the existing railroad in Kansas and to travel with General William Jackson Palmer as he surveyed the land along the thirty-fifth parallel in the fall of 1867. Gardner photographed the construction of a branch line of the railroad as it crept west to join the Union Pacific's main line; he stayed with Palmer's group of surveyors as they continued southwest toward San Francisco. Palmer included twenty of Gardner's photographs in his official report to illustrate his argument that the route he had surveyed was the most plausible way west.[7] The photographs exhibit the absence of obstacles to rail construction and record the grades, timber availability, and natural resources of the landscape for potential investors. Because of this "documentary" approach, many of Gardner's photographs have been labeled as merely topographic.[8] Moreover, part of the series is devoted to depicting social concerns: blacks and whites working in prairie communities, Native American reservations, and schools, churches, and businesses that represent new growth on the prairie landscape. Gardner's seeming inability to find a consistent aesthetic angle for the blank spaces of prairies and the clutter of new towns along the railroad has made it difficult for critics to find compositional themes in his work. Gardner's photographs do not have the cataclysmic qualities that are found in the more famous tradition of western photography—for example,

the work of his colleague Timothy O'Sullivan. O'Sullivan's rakish angles, sweeping prospects, and ominous close-ups of canyons, geysers, and precipitous mountain ranges have become the standard example of nineteenth-century landscape photographs of the West.

To dismiss photographs of less sublime landscapes as topographic or social records without artistic merit, however, is to dismiss the prairie aesthetic of levelness, which Gardner located in both natural and social landscapes. The tradition of the threatening or awe-inspiring in nature does not necessarily appreciate the qualities of the prairie landscape. Many of the views in Gardner's prairie collection do not follow the conventions of landscape painting, which many photographers used to order their representations. There is little of the classic composition that rendered a landscape overtly sublime, beautiful, or picturesque. Some of Gardner's photographs focus on a central object, animal, or person; others are characterized by their disorderliness. Yet others attempt a humorous or an ominous depiction of sites on the prairie. Some lack balance, and some contain photographic flaws that Gardner chose to include. What binds the photographs together is not their consistent composition, but their attention to diverse but repeated features and the relation of these features to the social and aesthetic construct of the railroad.

Railroad surveys of the prairie were meant to address all the things that Gardner illustrated, including the landscape's beauty, potential, population (both animal and vegetable), and topography. Throughout his report of the survey, Palmer stressed the southerly route as the most feasible way for the railroad to cross the continent: "Its cost will be due rather to the remoteness and wildness of the country, the absence of supplies, high cost of labor and risk from Indians, than to any serious engineering obstacles."[9]

The way west was smooth, he argued, and the building of the railroad would solve the other problems in time. Palmer believed that a railroad in the interior would subdue the Native American inhabitants, would transport the necessary supplies and labor, and could even contract the distance that made the country "wild" and "remote." The railroad would physically level uneven terrain as bridges were built and land was graded to accommodate the tracks. For surveyors like Palmer and for his investors, the railroad also figuratively leveled the landscape by promoting exchange and communication between sites along its route. If one area along the line lacked certain resources, another area could provide them, and these resources could move as easily along the rails as water along a riverbed—but faster and more economically. By promoting levelness and the easy distribution of goods as a feature of the railroad's proposed path, Palmer ensured its economic viability as well as its democratic purposes.

Some of Gardner's photos were reproduced as wood engravings and included in *New Tracks in North America*, an account of the survey written by Dr. William A. Bell. Bell, who accompanied Palmer on his expedition, was an affluent Englishman whose primary interest in the West was as an investor.[10] After the completion of the survey, Bell and Palmer formed a partnership to establish a new railroad company, the Denver and Rio Grande Railway. *New Tracks,* which includes information about the geography, population, politics, and history of the West, was written to promote tourism and to encourage investment in the new business. Bell's appreciation of the beauty of western landscapes was influenced by his promotional designs, and he emphasized the prairie's flatness as a boon to cross-continental travel: "surveys and explorations, undertaken by private companies and others . . . [have] disclosed a certain regularity of

design throughout the entire 'Summit Plateau' system, which greatly simplifies its topography."[11] The towns and inhabitants of the "vast flat" of Kansas particularly interested him. Bell lauded not only the promise of booming commercial success for towns on the railroad network, but also the "social system" of the state, in which women took an active role in politics and education, and the progressive mind-set of the population.[12]

In his own narrative of the survey, Palmer continually argued for the suitability of certain terrain for the construction of a railroad. Accordingly, Gardner's photographs depict the prairie's gentle grades and levelness as well as its expanse. The region is, of course, characterized by this topography; however, Gardner's decisions about how to emphasize these physical traits were shaped by his professional awareness. The railroad and the prairies themselves had, by the late 1860s, become allegories in artistic and literary representations of national expansion: the prairies were the continent to be crossed, and the railroad was the means of crossing it.[13] Thus Gardner's project was to unite the artistic and the economic terms through which the prairie could be appreciated, to develop a prairie aesthetic that promoted development of rather than disregard for its resources.

Kansas topography is notoriously lacking in the visual forms—mountain peaks, valleys, wind-warped trees, and rushing cascades—that so thrilled many early photographers of the West.[14] Photographer Charles R. Savage complained to the *Philadelphia Photographer* in 1867 that on the prairies and plains, "rarely were the circumstances favorable for producing fine views":

From Fort Kearney on to the crossing of the South Platte . . . a more uninteresting road can hardly be found. Very few trees to be seen, and what with the swarms of green flies and mosquitoes, and the strong wind that blows regularly every day, your photographic enthusiasm gets cooled down so much that you see nothing worth taking under the circumstances of such a trip.[15]

The prairie topography was repetitive, the distance was long, and settlements were few and far between. Yet Gardner seemed fascinated by the very distance and repetition that so discouraged Savage. While the relative lack of forms or drama and the emphasis on space and distance suggest an early aesthetic of abstraction, his photographs are not without narrative.[16] The photographs continually refer the viewer back to their primary subject: the railroad. The forms of the prairie, both natural and human-created, are united in the photographs through their mutual relation to the railroad as a social and aesthetic sign.

Grounding the View: The Railroad as Reference

Gardner's photographs document a reordering of prairie space, for the advantage of a position along the railroad determined the evolution of towns, the development of travel routes, and the uses of natural resources. The first image of the series is the depot at the Mississippi River in St. Louis. At each developed location along the route, Gardner photographed the depot. Sequences begin with the railroad itself: *Railroad Shops, Wyandotte, Kansas; Depot, Lawrence, Kansas; Depot, Leavenworth, Kansas; Depot Tonganoxie on Branch Road Between Lawrence and Leavenworth*, and so on. The depot tends to fill the space of the photograph to the exclusion of the surrounding openness, clearly marking the landscape as a developed and commercial one. The building is not dwarfed by the space of the sky or the breadth of the prairie, and signs are

visible on or around it, naming its location and function. It is in these depot pictures that the train and the business of building the railroad are most prominent, for the business of the railroad gives structure to the landscape and makes threatening, empty space recognizable. Following the views of the depot are sequences of photographs of the towns: streets, businesses, schools, and churches. Photographs such as *Massachusetts Street, Lawrence, Kansas* (Figure 4.2); *Indian Farm in Delaware Reservation, Kansas; Catholic Cathedral, Leavenworth, Kansas;* and *Packing House, Junction City, Kansas,* show the profusion of built structures that follows when a point on the prairie is favored by the railroad as a stopping place. In the series of photographs of Leavenworth, for example, the crowd of people and buildings in the first image is followed by views of the town that increasingly emphasize abstract form and distance. Some of the towns appear only at a distance, with a wide strip of ground between the camera and the stark, square buildings of the treeless communities (Figure 4.3). These photographs make the expanse of the prairie palpable by establishing depots and surrounding towns as points of reference.

Town scenes are followed by series of vistas or "views" of spaces between communities. Blank spaces, blurred horizons, and tonal gradations predominate over sharply defined shapes. A number of these vistas are characterized by low horizon lines that stress the limitless sky and the flatness and distance of the prairie, which often goes beyond the scope of the camera's ability to define it. In two photographs, Gardner felt compelled to try to quantify this distance in his caption: *View Embracing 12 Miles of Prairie from Moore's Summit, on Branch Road Between Lawrence and Leavenworth* (Figure 4.4), and *Section Men at Salina, Kansas (The extreme distance is five miles off)*. In others, however, the horizon

Figure 4.2. *Massachusetts Street, Lawrence, Kansas (Cattle in foreground)*. (Kansas State Historical Society, Topeka)

Figure 4.3. *Junction City, Kansas.* (Kansas State Historical Society, Topeka)

is high, and swaths of barren ground or prairie grasses rise up to balance the forms of town buildings or human figures. In *View on the Plains, Six Miles West of Fort Hays, Kansas,* the figures appear to the left while the "vista" stretches out before them (Figure 4.5). The stereograph viewer is encouraged to look with them, to survey what they survey, and thus looks from left to right, from the near figures to the distant, blurred horizon. The next stereograph in the series is *View on the Plains, Kansas,* which projects the viewer right into the observed space (Figure 4.6).

Gardner's town scenes do not disrupt the prairie aesthetic of his landscapes; in fact, social disunity is deemphasized by a stress on natural rather than political or economic design. Expanses of sky as well as prairie grasses foreground and provide a backdrop for the buildings and people who appear in the photographs. Towns rise as naturally from the prairies as stands of trees. The figures and facades in *Massachusetts Street, Lawrence, Kansas,* divide like prairie grasses, opening into a view into the indeterminate distance (see Figure 4.2). His depictions of Kansas towns that were in actuality riddled with political strife and conflicts among settlers, railroad companies, and Indian

Figure 4.4. *View Embracing 12 Miles of Prairie from Moore's Summit, on Branch Road Between Lawrence and Leavenworth.* (Kansas State Historical Society, Topeka)

Figure 4.5. *View on the Plains, Six Miles West of Fort Hays, Kansas.* (Kansas State Historical Society, Topeka)

commissioners instead stress the same compositional themes that characterize his landscape
photographs: distance, perspective, repetition,
and the juxtaposition of open space with solid
forms. Gardner's fondness for photographing
towns at a distance portrays the business of
town building as itself a kind of vista or prairie
prospect. In the view entitled *Lecompton, Kansas,* the white houses that dot the prairie do not
disrupt the emphasis on flatness and perspective
(Figure 4.7). The new town blends with the expanse of sky, maintaining the compositional
balance between dark and light, earth and sky,
which distinguishes his natural vistas as well.

The vistas, buildings, and natural features of
the landscape gain meaning through Gardner's
insertion of the railroad as a reference point
throughout the series of photographs. The sequence negotiates the formal differences between the blank spaces of vistas and the solid
forms of the built environment by proposing the
railroad as the mediator between the space of
the prairie and the forms of human activity, between emptiness and profusion. Palmer and his
fellow surveyors and backers saw the railroad
the same way. As Palmer wrote in his report,

There are vast stretches of unwooded prairie, and
there are mountains at intervals covered with dense
forest of timber; there are rich mines in rocky ranges,
and elsewhere extensive fertile valleys and numerous
rich but scattered basins and cañadas; . . . extended
rolling plains covered with the most nutritious
grasses . . . ; and cañons whose water-power is able to
reduce the ores to metal and convert the wool into

Figure 4.6. *View on the Plains, Kansas.* (Kansas State Historical Society, Topeka)

clothing. . . . Now these are precisely the conditions that are most favorable to the business of transportation. A railroad thrives in the proportion that one portion of its line lacks that which another has a great facility for supplying.[17]

The lack of one part of the route could be balanced by the wealth of another: the railroad, like the prairie itself, was the Great Leveler. With a system of transportation that could connect one end of the continent to the other, there would be no reason for one part of the country to revel in natural resources while another part languished in aridity and mineral deficiency. Moreover, Palmer asserted, inequalities in resources are a boon to railroads. Thus Gardner's project was not to hide differences in the distribution of timber, water, and grass, but to work those differences into a sequence organized by connections to the railroad line. The prairie was no longer a vast, unmarked expanse, but a series of points ordered through a single visual and ideological line of reference.

Figure 4.7. *Lecompton, Kansas.* (Kansas State Historical Society, Topeka)

The Democratic Aesthetic

The railroad could take resources, average them, and redistribute them along the route until each location had an equal amount—until a balanced distribution of gifts had been achieved. This leveling provided economic balance and thus promised commercial success that promoted social "leveling." In *New Tracks,* Bell hinted that the rapid development of western lands would destroy all previous conceptions of hierarchy: "when, in fact, we commence to be aristocratic, and ask, Who is who? we find, to our astonishment, that the rich old gentleman we have learned to look up to was once the happy owner of no more than an acre of waste land along Main Street."[18]

Gardner leveled the landscape he confronted by composing photographs that stress balance and harmony in both their aesthetic and their social implications. In a number of them, the railroad provides compositional balance for the features of the prairie landscape. Some of Gardner's best-known prairie photographs are composed less in terms of their components than in terms of the relationships between these parts, usually visualized as equal in value. Two of these images are *Railroad Bridge Across Grasshopper Creek* and *View on Kansas River at Fort Riley, Kansas* (Figure 4.8), in which a rail bridge, in the former, and tracks, in the latter, are fully integrated into the landscape, providing balance and structure for the photographs. The verticality of trees is balanced by the horizontal stretch of bridge, and the graceful curve of the river is reinforced by the curve of the rails. The railroad does not intrude on the serenity of the landscape, but is one of its essential features.

The violent changes effected on the prairies as a result of Manifest Destiny are tempered by the distribution of these photographs among others that depict a prairie pastoral or the social conditions of towns. Because the stereographs illustrate the railroad's impact on just several hundred miles of the continent to be crossed, they explore different ways that the railroad was transforming the prairies, rather than stressing only the forward motion and invasive power of the locomotive. Gardner made images of towns both on and off the main rail line; a number of photographs were taken on the branch line between Lawrence and Leavenworth.[19] An article that appeared in the *Lawrence Daily Tribune* indicates that the citizens of Kansas regarded Gardner's arrival as an opportunity in several ways:

Mr. Gardner, a photographic artist from Washington City is in Lawrence, having come to Kansas for the purpose of taking photographic views of remarkable and noted places in our state. He comes here, we believe, under the auspices of the Union Pacific Railway to make draughts of points on the road. He will take a view of Massachusetts Street this forenoon. These views will be a fine advertisement for our state and we hope that the artist may have all the assistance and courtesy which our citizens can render him.[20]

The residents of Lawrence placed Gardner's work into several categories, indicating the multiple contexts in which prairie towns and landscapes might be viewed. The writer was equivocal about the purpose of Gardner's work. Were towns like Lawrence and Leavenworth "remarkable and noted places" or merely "points on the road?" Was Gardner an advertiser or an "artist?" Was prairie topography primarily natural or social? The image that resulted from the photo session on Massachusetts Street is a picture of a bustling town, the dirt road crisscrossed with tracks and crowded with people, cattle, horses, and carts. The street is lined with buildings that stretch into the distance, a perspective that makes the commercial "vista" as boundless as the natural vista. This was the prairie environment envisioned by such proponents of settlement as William Gilpin, governor of Colorado Territory, and poet Walt Whitman, who saw the prairies as the limitless interior that would one day teem with industry, trade, and agriculture. This was the Lawrence that would be home to the state university and the location of the Catholic cathedral, under construction when Gardner made images of them.

But this was also the state that was attempting to put a violent past behind it through economic and social development. The pre–Civil War years of "Bleeding Kansas," in which the state had become the center of a bitter battle between pro- and antislavery forces and between speculators and settlers, were only a decade in the past. As a free-state stronghold, Lawrence had been raided in 1856. John Brown's Pottawatomie Massacre and the Waukerusa War had turned Kansas into a battleground years before Antietam became a subject for Gardner's camera. Gardner photographed former free-state cities Manhattan, Topeka, and Lawrence as well as proslavery towns Leavenworth and Lecompton, even though he had to go off the railroad's main line to do so. The "remarkable and noted" places in the state were not photographed in the context of their violent past, but their expansive

Figure 4.8. *View on Kansas River at Fort Riley, Kansas.* (Kansas State Historical Society, Topeka)

Figure 4.9. *Waukerusa Valley (Blue Mount in Distance) from Fort. Lawrence, Kansas.* (Kansas State Historical Society, Topeka)

future. This limitless future, the photographs suggest, could be read in the natural design of the prairie landscape. Gardner took a number of views of Waukerusa Valley from Mount Oread in Lawrence and from Fort Union. They depict a peaceful valley dotted with farmhouses, barns, and white rail fences. In one image of the valley, a high horizon calls attention to the deep color of the fields and the contrast of white buildings and fences against the landscape (Figure 4.9).

The photograph, he noted in the title, was taken "from [the] Fort," but he directed the viewer to the distant horizon, by pointing out parenthetically "(Blue Mount in Distance)"—a hazy, rolling prospect on the far horizon. Thus he averaged past with future, social with natural, in this photograph in which Fort and Mount are on the same plane, with the wide, fertile—and regenerative—valley stretching between them.

The series's design of levelness and emphasis

Figure 4.10. *U.S. Express Overland Stage Starting for Denver from Hays City, Kansas.* (Kansas State Historical Society, Topeka)

on unity rather than disruption depict the prairie as a place where ruptures in the social fabric might be mended. Like the rest of the United States, Kansas's prairies were now "free soil," where the reconstructed nation would begin to construct the interior using the labor of free men and women. The railroad was one place where blacks and whites worked together. The multitude of gandy dancers preceding the engine in *"Westward, the Course of Empire Takes its Way"* appears to include some blacks among its number (see Figure 4.1). In another photograph, a group of African American soldiers appears atop a stagecoach bound across the plains for Denver (Figure 4.10). Neatly attired, facing front, and weapons at the ready, the soldiers are portrayed as playing an important part in the

national project of traversing the prairies. Some ten years after Gardner made these stereographs, the Union Pacific Railroad Company was to offer hundreds of thousands of acres for homestead sale in the "Golden Belt of Kansas," an offer that blacks from the post–Reconstruction South were to take up eagerly.[21] *U.S. Express Overland Stage Starting for Denver from Hays City, Kansas,* depicts an important social aspect of prairie settlement: the interior was not a place to escape society, but a place where individuals of different descent confronted one another.[22] The enemy against whom these soldiers were prepared to defend the coach was, of course, Native American.

Gardner did not neglect this prairie population as problem or prospect. His contact with

Native Americans, both before and after his trip to Kansas, no doubt gave him insight into the complex problem of the "Indian question" in the nineteenth century. He photographed Indian delegations in Washington, D.C., and in 1868 joined one of the last peace commissions to treat with Native American tribes as independent nations. He traveled to Laramie, Wyoming, to record the signing of a treaty with Red Cloud.[23] In *Across the Continent*, Gardner's several photographs of native peoples and their lands stress both racial difference and the prospect of assimilation. *Indian Farm at Delaware Reservation, Kansas*, and *View on Kansas River in Delaware Reservation, Kansas*, make clear that the landscape being photographed belongs to Indians confined to reservations. Yet in both images, reservation lands are depicted as fully incorporated into the vision of the prairies as farmland connected to the rest of the country by rail lines. *View on Kansas River in Delaware Reservation, Kansas*, is a near mirror image of *View on Kansas River at Fort Riley, Kansas* (see Figure 4.8). Its classic picturesque composition shows the river and railroad tracks curving together through the reservation landscape. Gardner also made several images of St. Mary's Mission and the Potawatomi who attended school there. *Pottawatomie Indians at St. Mary's Mission* calls attention to the Native American faces in the gallery of individuals arrayed in front of the building; all are in western dress, and the faces of white children appear scattered among those of the Potawatomi (Figure 4.11).

The reservation lands that Gardner photographed for the railroad were, however, under contested ownership. The picturesque composition of this landscape suggests railroad companies' designs on Potawatomi lands. The arrival of the railroad and settlers on this territory legally and physically reordered the terrain on which the native population lived, marking it

out into lots and sections to allow for allotment, trading, and sales. The Union Pacific Railroad pressed for this redesigning of prairie spaces in a grid plan in order to gain control of plots along the proposed routes. The Potawatomi and other Native American owners of the land were given allotments by the federal government and were expected to farm their designated acreage—or to sell it to speculators and settlers. The land not given away as allotments fell, more often than not, to railroad companies that wrangled over the right to purchase lucrative reservation lands. Gardner's images depict the assimilation of both native people and their lands into the carefully designed enterprise of settlement and development.

Bridging the Distance

Rail routes were the focus for these changes in the prospects of the prairies, both social and physical. The value of land and the success of certain towns were determined by their connection to railroad lines as well as their proximity to bridges that reorganized travel across the prairie. Railroads and bridges, by making a level road out of the disruption caused by rivers, eventually replaced rivers as transportation routes. The construction of bridges was an essential component in the leveling of the West, and Gardner recognized this in his photography by emphasizing bridges as aesthetic components of his photographs. He explored the bridge as a feature of town life, in its power as a span and in its aesthetic possibilities as both a part of the landscape and a location from which to view it. While a bridge is highlighted as an architectural feat in one image, in another it might become a device for framing a group of townspeople or a means of providing perspective for the prairie landscape it crosses.

Figure 4.11. *Pottawatomie Indians at St. Mary's Mission.* (Kansas State Historical Society, Topeka)

One of Gardner's most frequently reproduced prairie pictures is *Trestle Bridge near Fort Harker, Kansas,* in which a bridge spans the entire length of the image (Figure 4.12). The level line of the bridge and the flatcars atop it bisects the photograph, leaving a swath of sky above and a wide stretch of stubbly ground below. Several figures, both on the ground and etched against the sky as they ride the cars, lend perspective to the photograph. Art historian Susan Danly Walther has written of this image, "It is only in the ordered structure of the railroad bridge and train that man can equal the expansiveness of na-ture. . . . [T]he train, from its engine to its passenger car, fills the horizon. The trestle upon which the train sits defines the topography of the land, giving shape to the endless panorama of the prairie."[24] It is significant that the shape that the bridge gives to the prairie is an absolutely level one. The trestle bridge takes the prairie's natural topography and enhances it, straightening the gently rolling land. Gardner literally redesigns the prairie horizon, as the line where sky meets earth is rendered indistinct by distance and the imposition of the line of the bridge. The span is a recurring element in Gard-

Figure 4.12. *Trestle Bridge near Fort Harker, Kansas.* (Kansas State Historical Society, Topeka)

Figure 4.13. *Leavenworth, Lawrence, and Galveston R.R. Bridge across Kansas River, Lawrence, Kansas.* (Kansas State Historical Society, Topeka)

ner's series, as various types of spans add visual interest to an image, influence composition by providing directional contrast to the lines of the landscape, and cut across space, raising the level of the prairie.

Leavenworth, Lawrence, and Galveston R.R. Bridge across Kansas River, Lawrence, Kansas, is a carefully composed photograph of river and railroad bridge (Figure 4.13). In this view, the train is small but prominent, suggesting that nature has been changed by the presence of the locomotive. The change, however, is not represented so much as a technological advance as an aesthetic design. Without losing the sense of vista and distance that is characteristic of his photographs, Gardner stressed the visual interest that the curve of the bridge adds to the land-

scape. While the sweep of the bridge dominates the image, the perspective of the photograph emphasizes the flatness of the bridge rather than the height of the locomotive. The bridge winds across the river in the same way that a river might wind across the prairie itself. From this perspective, the bridge takes on the compositional function that rivers themselves traditionally serve in images of landscapes. The photograph renders visually the design of railroad promoters: railroads could redesign the prairie by replacing rivers as transportation routes.

Gardner's photographs manipulate perspective to emphasize the railroad's ability to negotiate the landscape and to make it level; this is particularly noticeable in the images that depict the locomotive in motion. In one of his rare "action shots," the motion of train and figure adds an energy and dynamism to the photograph that is missing from others. *Trestle Bridge near Abilene, Kansas,* foregrounds a man who, back to the camera, waves his hat in the air, his body bent as though to spring into motion (Figure 4.14). He stands at the edge of the trestle bridge, which spans a gulch in the center of the photograph. On the horizon, an engine steams directly toward the man—one can almost see the smoke and hear the whistle as the train rushes toward the bridge. The perspective emphasizes both the flat landscape and the span's part in keeping the ground level; it also places the man—and the viewer—on a level with the engine itself. In the gulch below the tracks, a wagon, that outmoded means of transportation, accentuates the ease of railroad travel. Gardner composed this photograph along both horizontal and vertical lines, combining an extensive vista with the verticality of the man, made taller by his waving hat, and of the lines of bridge and track. The train and track accentuate distance and vista, raising the level of the prairie in contrast to that of the natural gully, which could only impede travel. The result is the parity of the common person, the faceless, nameless man, with the locomotive, the bridge, and the prairie itself. This "action shot" anticipates an exuberant and dramatic moment of encounter that celebrates the expansiveness of the prairie as well as the locomotive's ability to move across it.

Visual Transformations

This kind of engagement with the composition is crucial to the stereoscopic experience. Because all these images are stereographic, viewers would have been forced to situate visually the train, the bridge, and the man, heightening the simulation of confrontation. Nega-

tives that were suitable for stereographs had to be fairly strongly foregrounded, so that the makers of the stereocards would have a central object on which to center the two views to produce a three-dimensional effect. The stereoscope was based on an understanding of the way the eye works: each eye sees from a slightly different perspective from and views independently of the other. These images are fused in the viewer's mind, causing distance, space, and form to appear in three-dimensional images.[25] Robert J. Taft, in his description of Gardner's Kansas stereoviews, praised the technology of viewing that "produces a sense of perspective and reality that the flat prints do not possess."[26] Indeed, the depth of these images does come close to a "realistic" encounter, yet it is important to remember that the views that Gardner took for the stereograph had to be constructed in a specific way in order for the viewer to "see" them with the stereoscope. One object or area, such as a building, a bridge, a figure, or a foreground sweep of land, has to be emphasized in order to structure the photograph. The stereoscope functions on the interplay between objects near and far, between detail and distance, between clutter and space. In his selection of subject matter and in his compositions, Gardner created more than a topographic record—he revealed his understanding of the values of prairie environments and conveyed it to history.

The stereoviews, in their multiple perspectives, emphasis on flatness and form, and juxtaposition of space and clutter, offer a visual equivalent to a social apprehension of the prairies. The prairies had to be visually anchored; the railroad offered a way of establishing a logical sequence and proposing a set of connections, commercial and cultural, between sites. Using buildings and bridges as foci and combining them with vistas that demanded a far-reaching apprehension of space, Gardner dramatized the

Figure 4.14. *Trestle Bridge near Abilene, Kansas.* (Kansas State Historical Society, Topeka)

difference that development could make in the way the prairies were viewed. Close views of waving grasses are less common than long views that accent a single line, such as a horizon or train track. Conflicts with the topography—riverbeds, gulches, and barren stretches—are arranged into beneficial visual searches for level ground. The railroad does not disrupt, but enhances the physical properties of the natural environment that Gardner's photographs celebrate. At the same time, conflicts between prairie populations are naturalized as Gardner represents social change as part of the process of leveling.

Gardner's photographs do not provide the "instant gratification" of a sublime or cataclysmic mountain range. His attention to the expansiveness as well as the details of the social fabric in new communities distinguishes his work from that of his contemporaries who refused to grapple with the prairie aesthetic. Rather than downplaying the facets of prairie topography that were considered monotonous, Gardner's photographs highlight flatness, sweep, and repetition as useful and artistic elements of landscapes. Refusing the vision of the prairie as uneventful expanse, Gardner instead insisted on the interplay between components of its composition, both natural and constructed. Gardner, however, did not fail to recognize that the ideology and aesthetics of levelness were more often socially and physically constructed than naturally endowed. His position as railroad photographer and landscape artist gave him a dual responsibility in his accountability to the geographic facts of the environment and to artistic fictions. Even as it celebrates the prairie's distinctive aesthetic qualities, Gardner's work naturalizes a tale of the prairie's levelness as a sign of its inevitable development by rail traffic. His series of Kansas prairie photographs publicized the level beauty of the prairie by establishing the railroad as the simple and easily legible key to ordering—and to understanding—prairie places. The series stands as a rare example of an early aesthetic appreciation of flat lands, yet it is also a reminder that our ability to "see" the prairies and plains has always been mediated by the stories we tell ourselves about those landscapes.

Notes

1. This book was republished as Alexander Gardner, *Gardner's Photographic Sketch Book of the Civil War* (New York: Dover, 1959).

2. The fate of this community is in dispute. Josephine Cobb's account has the entire community wiped out by consumption in 1856 and proposes that Gardner's visits to MacGregor were to see the orphaned daughter of his friend Robertson Sinclair. She also reports that during the Civil War, Gardner sent his family to live in MacGregor. Donald McCoo, however, has the community breaking up in 1852 as a result of financial difficulties and reports that Robertson Sinclair moved to MacGregor's Landing along with his wife and daughter. For biographical information on Gardner, see Cobb, "Alexander Gardner," *Image,* June 1958, 124–36; McCoo, "Gardner and His Contemporaries: The Years in Scotland," in *An Enduring Interest: The Photographs of Alexander Gardner,* ed. Brooks Johnson (Norfolk, Va.: Chryster Museum, 1991), 11–15; and D. Mark Katz, *Witness to an Era: The Life and Photographs of Alexander Gardner* (New York: Viking Penguin, 1991).

3. Timothy Sweet, *Traces of War: Poetry, Photography, and the Crisis of the Union* (Baltimore: Johns Hopkins University Press, 1990), 77.

4. Alan Trachtenberg, *Reading American Photography: Images as History, Mathew Brady to Walker Evans* (New York: Hill & Wang, 1982), 99.

5. Sweet, *Traces of War,* 122.

6. Trachtenberg, *Reading American Photography,* 93.

7. Two of the Kansas photographs were also published in William E. Webb, *Buffalo Land: An Authentic*

Account of the Discoveries, Adventures, and Mishaps of a Scientific and Sporting Party in the Wild West, with Graphic Descriptions of the Country; of the Red Man, Savage and Civilized; Hunting the Buffalo, Antelope, Elk, and Wild Turkey; etc., etc., Replete with Information, Wit, and Humor (Philadelphia: Hubbard, 1872). As evidenced by its title, Webb's book was a picaresque account of prairie life. It featured the foibles of Professor Paleozoic, Tammany Sachem, and Dr. Pythagorum and characterized the West as wild, violent, weird, and romantic.

8. Robert Sobieszek, "Conquest by Camera: Alexander Gardner's 'Across the Continent on the Kansas Pacific Railroad,'" *Art in America,* March–April 1972, 83.

9. William Jackson, Palmer, *A Report of Surveys Across the Continent, in 1867–68, on the 35th and 32nd Parallels, for a Route Extending the Kansas Pacific Railway to the Pacific Ocean at San Francisco and San Diego* (Philadelphia: Selheimer, 1869), 76.

10. For information on Bell, Palmer, and the use of imagery to promote investment in the West, see Joni L. Kinsey, *Thomas Moran and the Surveying of the American West* (Washington, D.C.: Smithsonian Institution Press, 1992), 153–60.

11. William A. Bell, *New Tracks in North America,* 2nd ed. (New York: Scribner, Welford, 1870). While he also learned photography, the Englishman Dr. William A. Bell is not to be confused with William A. Bell, the American photographer with the Wheeler survey.

12. Ibid., 15.

13. Susan Danly Walther, "The Railroad in the Western Landscape, 1865–1900," in *The Railroad in the American Landscape, 1850–1950* (Wellesley, Mass.: Wellesley College Museum, 1981), 37–51.

14. For a discussion of artists' renderings of "prospects" on the prairie landscapes, see, especially, Joni L. Kinsey, *Plain Pictures: Images of the American Prairie* (Washington, D.C.: Smithsonian Institution Press, 1996).

15. Charles R. Savage, "A Photographic Tour of Nearly 9000 Miles," *Philadelphia Photographer* 4 (1867): 314–15.

16. Susan Danly Walther, "The Landscape Photographs of Alexander Gardner and Andrew Joseph Russell" (Ph.D. diss., Brown University, 1983), 46.

17. Palmer, *Report of Surveys Across the Continent,* 167–68.

18. Bell, *New Tracks,* 13.

19. Robert J. Taft, "A Photographic History of Early Kansas," *Kansas Historical Quarterly* 3 (1934): 12; Robert W. Richmond, "Kansas Through a Camera in 1867: Stereographs from Alexander Gardner's Photographic Art Gallery," *American West* 2 (1965): 53.

20. Quoted in Walther, "Landscape Photographs," 35.

21. Nell I. Painter, *Exodusters: Black Migration to Kansas After Reconstruction* (New York: Norton, 1992).

22. Patricia Nelson Limerick, *The Legacy of Conquest: The Unbroken Past of the American West* (New York: Norton, 1987).

23. Gardner published these photographs, entitled *Scenes in Indian Country,* as a select number of bound portfolios. For a detailed description of this trip as well as a selection of photos, see Raymond DeMallie, "'Scenes in the Indian Country': A Portfolio of Alexander Gardner's Stereographic Views of the 1868 Fort Laramie Treaty Council," *Montana, the Magazine of Western History* 31 (1981): 42–59.

24. Walther, *Railroad in the American Landscape,* 97.

25. Weston J. Naef and James N. Wood, *Era of Exploration: The Rise of Landscape Photography in the American West, 1860–1885* (Boston: New York Graphic Society, 1975), 19.

26. Taft, "Photographic History of Early Kansas," 7.

5 Cosmopolitan Vistas: Willa Cather, Hamlin Garland, and the Literary Value of Regionalism

Tom Lutz

Locations and Locutions

Willa Cather is perhaps the most often quoted prairie writer. It sometimes seems that a piece cannot be written about Nebraska that does not somewhere manage to quote, approvingly or not, the observation of the narrator of *My Ántonia:* "the only thing very noticeable about Nebraska was that it was still, all day long, Nebraska."[1] But more common than this is the borrowing of landscape descriptions by authors like Cather, most often as paeans to the beauty and power of the land and the dignity and virtue of its inhabitants. Many people devoted to the prairies find in the distinguished literary history of the Middle West a celebration of a landscape, an aesthetic, and a culture that they hold dear and that they feel to be now, as it was then, embattled—threatened by what is called progress, its eco-disasters, and its homogenizing culture. As "all day long, Nebraska" shows, however, there is something else at work in Cather's work and in that of literary regionalists in general,

something in addition to their more lyrical passages of pastoral beauty and their critique of progress. Language is an unwieldy tool that can turn swords into plowshares and back again without warning. In Richard Ford's novel *Independence Day,* a verbally subversive or perhaps verbally gifted real-estate agent tells a new salesman that the three laws governing real-estate sales are "locution, locution, locution."[2] As writers like Cather show, literary language can be even slipperier than that of realtors, as when she describes the prairies, sometimes within the same paragraph, as both barren and fecund, bitter and sweet, wilderness and paradise.

In this chapter, I argue that Cather and the other regionalist authors of her period were at best ambivalent about their regions, and ask what that means for our understanding of regionalism. In his first trip back to Iowa, four years after having published the full version of his regionalist classic *Main-Travelled Roads*

(1899), Hamlin Garland complained about the "uncouth" people he met, claiming that "all this commonplaceness . . . cuts me off from the past—or rather it separates me from these people and scenes. . . . My old-time world, the world that appealed to my imagination, is gone."[3] It is an old game in literary studies, of course, to hack away at the old hacks and show that they really were not saying what they were meaning or meaning what they were saying, and that is not my intention. The regionalist authors continue to have something to offer, including something to offer today's regionalists. I am going to argue, though, that that something is tied not to a regionalist ethic, but to a cosmopolitan one. Garland and Cather and the other literary regionalists were linked to a worldwide web of literary production, and their representations of Iowa and Nebraska were always shaped by and directed not to the people of the plains states primarily, but to those who thought of themselves as part of a cosmopolitan literary community. The values of this community, as clearly displayed in regional fiction, were very similar to those of today's prairie regionalists, whether or not authors or readers shared modern-day regionalists' love of the region itself.

Cather and Garland maintained a double or even triple set of attitudes toward the prairie, and similar multiplicities can be seen in the representational strategies used by most regionalist artists. Literary regionalists from the heyday of local-color fiction in the late nineteenth century until the present have balanced their positive representations of their regions with negative ones, and they have done the same thing with the metropolitan interlopers who appear in their fictions. They do not simply represent a noble peasantry and a corrupt metropolis; their works are full of characters who represent the "idiocy of rural life" and the genius of metropolitan modernity as well. They do so, I will argue,

as part of an advertisement for the cosmopolitan perspective, which has been the core value for American literary culture over the past century and a half. Their texts are over and over again allegories of the value of cosmopolitanism, and thereby allegories of the value of literature itself. In this project, writers' regions are often sacrificed to their ideas of art.

Of course, many literary regionalists would object to this characterization, claiming that what is important about regionalism is its embattled region, which they are helping to preserve, as in the works of Kathleen Norris and Wendell Berry, for instance, and before them the Southern Agrarians.[4] The "critical regionalists" in architecture would go even further, suggesting that regionalism can be a form of active resistance to global capitalism, the behemoth both abstract and real that is, after all, the very threat to local culture.[5] (The Agrarians wanted this to be true, but admitted that it probably wasn't.) In literary studies recently, a similar attempt has been made to find resistance in regionalism. David Jordan, for instance, speaks of regionalist art and literature in terms of marginalization, with the assumption that regionalism "necessarily proceeds from a decentered worldview" and that it is, therefore, good and "resistant."[6] Josephine Donovan links local-color literature, or at least a reading of such literature, with the recuperation of Foucauldian "subjugated knowledges," which Michel Foucault also described as "local, regional" knowledges.[7] The feminist recovery of local-color literature starting in the 1970s included a good dose of similar talk, if less theoretically bulwarked.[8] And in American literary history, the two iconic moments in the prehistory of this "resistance to hegemony" strain of regionalist discourse are Hamlin Garland's *Crumbling Idols* (1894), with its condemnation of the literary imperialism of New York and Boston, and the Southern Agrarian manifesto, *I'll Take My Stand* (1930), with its cultural secessionist pronouncements and anti-modern rhetoric.[9]

At least since the 1920s, though, literary regionalists have been accused of exploiting their regions, selling a false, mythic vision of rural and marginal cultures to jaded city folk interested in buying images of the quaint or degraded. Each generation of regionalist writers has tended to make this charge against the writers who came before it: Garland took great pains to explain that he was not espousing "picturesque" renderings of country folk, as had the local-color writers before him, and the regionalists in the 1920s and 1930s dismissed the writers of Garland's generation as quantifiers and carpetbaggers. The latest proponents of this line in literary studies, such as Richard Brodhead and Amy Kaplan, believe that all local-color writing is urban mythmaking.[10] In a way neither and in a way both of these opposing views are correct. Literary regionalists have always been much more interested in art and its values than in the debate about the relative merits of provincial and metropolitan life, and the conventions and narrative forms associated with regionalism betray their particular aesthetic, which privileges a broad, somewhat distanced overview. The authors may have fond memories of their regions and may present loving portraits of some local characters, but they tend to subsume the cultural values of specific regions, and those espoused in urban centers, to a third, overarching set of values—those of the cosmopolitan literary community.

When it comes to literary regionalism, the region in some ways does not seem to matter. The stories that were told in literary forums, from the end of our regional conflict in the 1860s until our engulfment in the global conflicts of the 1910s, and again in the 1920s and 1930s, were largely the same, whether they were set in Iowa, Georgia, Maine, California, or, as in Cather's case, Nebraska. In each of these fictions, the moral of the story was remarkably similar: the literary sensibility, literary culture, was better than either the local cultures in which these dramatizations of literary value were staged or the urban cultures across the country in which the texts were produced and found the larger part of their audience.

I say "larger" because literary culture was clearly not simply the combined activities of an urban clique, as Brodhead and Kaplan have argued. In a special issue of *Life* edited by Algonquin round-table wits and consummate metropolitans Robert Sherwood and Robert Benchley, a list of literary commandments included the following complaint: "Omnipotent shall be the presence of half a million women subscribers in the small town in the Middle West." The double-damning involved in their charge of female provincialism is, in part, the familiar complaint of literary writers about the lack of taste among their potential readers. But Sherwood and Benchley were also noting that the movement westward of the literary market prophesied by Garland had come about, and that Midwesterners were now important players in literary production and consumption. When Herbert Ross said that the *New Yorker* was *not* published for the "little old lady in Dubuque," he did not mean that he didn't want to sell magazines in Dubuque; the *New Yorker* had 149 subscribers in Iowa in 1929, and sold another 35 copies at newsstands and bookstores each month, or almost as many copies as Iowa's regionalist magazine, the *Midland* (which itself topped 1,000 copies an issue only after having gone bimonthly, moved to Chicago, changed its subtitle to *A National Literary Magazine,* and received plugs from H. L. Mencken and other eastern editors in the early 1930s). However much New York still functioned as a mecca, literary production and consumption were dispersed, and those who avoided a cosmopolitan openness doomed themselves to a niche market.

Local-color writers of the hundred years after the Civil War thus tended to represent both the city and the provinces from a cosmopolitan point of view that few of their rural characters *and* few of the urban interlopers in the texts possess. While this cosmopolitan aesthetic may not have had much directive force in the culture as a whole in the latter part of the nineteenth century (at least not as much as its proponents wished or suggested it had), it clearly was adopted, in its most general form, by the majority of those who considered themselves literary writers and readers, and as such was central to the formation of the literary culture of the middle class then coming into dominance. This literary ideology has a particular cast in regional writing, one that takes as its specific charge the keeping of cultural memory, as we will see in the case of Cather's *O Pioneers!*

Regionalism has once again become an important topic in American (and other) literary studies, energized in part by the decidedly economic cast of some recent theorists. Joni Kinsey, in *Plain Pictures: Images of the American Prairie,* uses the word "prospects" to signal the confluence in prairie paintings of the aesthetic (the prospect that is the organizing point of view in landscape aesthetics) and the economic (the actual social and economic promise of the place represented).[11] Such an inextricable relation between aesthetic and economic concerns, especially in relation to the land, is a theme of many regionalist writers. Cather, for instance, praises those farmers who make works of art out of their farms, like Alexandra Bergson in *O Pioneers!,* while those who simply squeeze a living out of the land without adding to its beauty are damned. Like Kinsey's use of the term "prospects," "cosmopolitanism" is a word that tends

to collapse the distinctions among the economic, ideological, and artistic realms, and thereby helps to demonstrate their interconnectedness. The "prospect" of literature of the prairie and other regions, its purview, has always been cosmopolitan, and rightly so, for therein lies its value.

Cosmopolitan Vistas

"Cosmopolitanism" is a word with fairly extreme semiotic vagrancy and increasingly prevalent usage after a couple of lean decades. Its first meaning in most dictionaries is related to the basic universalizing ethic of the Enlightenment, in which the *philosophes* declared themselves citizens of the world, rather than subjects of a sovereign or state.[12] It is this meaning that Julia Kristeva invokes in *Nations without Nationalism* (1993), for instance, when she claims that she "is a representative of what is today a rare species, perhaps even on the verge of extinction in a time of renewed nationalism: I am a cosmopolitan."[13] But rather than going extinct, the word is clearly being revived. The geographer Yi-Fu Tuan's memoir is subtitled *A Cosmopolite's Viewpoint* (1996).[14] Arnold Krupat, in *Ethnocriticism* (1992), uses "cosmopolitanism" to describe an ethnocritical perspective that "is consistent with a recognition and legitimation of heterogeneity," and Homi Bhabha, less clearly, says something quite similar in *The Location of Culture* (1994).[15]

Krupat and Bhabha are reversing the stance of the postcolonial critics, who rejected the culture-vulture aspects of the cosmopolitan ethos. These earlier critics adopted the use of "cosmopolitan" as an insult that had first been advanced at midcentury by the international socialists, who used the word to denote a form of blinkered relativism subscribed to by uncommitted intellectuals, as in the work of Antonio Gramsci. What the socialists and postcolonial critics objected to most was the notion of cosmopolitanism as a kind of up-to-date connoisseurship, as in "cosmopolitan tastes," a false sophistication that replaces the political with the aesthetic, with taste, and thereby with irresponsible consumption, going shopping for fiddles while Peoria burns. According to Gramsci and, more recently, Tim Brennan, cosmopolitanism is the enemy of a "national culture" that might resist imperialism: the Roman Empire is Gramsci's example of a society in which cosmopolitan culture served the ruling class and fostered imperial power over that of more local cultures.[16] In another register altogether, Robert Reich, a former Secretary of Labor, also writes about the "darker side of cosmopolitanism." The true cosmopolitans of our day, according to Reich, are the multinational corporate operators who are beholden to no nation, no local group: "Citizen[s] of the world," such corporate types "feel no particular bond with any society."[17] As Christopher Lasch pointed out, "the cosmopolitanism of the favored few, because it is uninformed by the practice of citizenship, turns out to be a higher form of parochialism."[18]

As these quick takes suggest, the word "cosmopolitanism," after a fairly quiet few decades, is very much in circulation again. Many use it as a bridge beyond multiculturalism, as David Hollinger does in arguing for his vision of a "postethnic" society.[19] There are two strands in the history of American thinking about multiculturalism, according to Hollinger: a cosmopolitan strand, which is wary of traditional labels and boundaries and emphasizes voluntary association, and a pluralist strand, which respects traditional labels and boundaries and emphasizes fixed identities. He traces the cosmopolitan strand back to Randolph Bourne, the favorite intellectual of American intellectual his-

torians when they are arguing about cultural politics, and the pluralist strand back to Horace Kallen, and sees the two at odds and often confused with each other. The postethnic society that Hollinger envisions is very close to Bourne's cosmopolitanism, his notion of a "transnational America." Similar recapitulations of Bourne's position have also been made by Mitchell Cohen and Bruce Ackerman, each of whom has called his theory "rooted cosmopolitanism," and they add into their mix the elaborations to Bourne's ideas made by John Dewey, Lewis Mumford, and Scott Nearing in the 1920s as well as aspects of the debate since. It is cosmopolitanism with a progressive face.[20]

Something very much like the apolitical cosmopolitanism chastised by the socialists and Reich was important to certain literary circles in the late nineteenth century, including, for instance, the decadent writers—Edgar Saltus, Percival Pollard, Gelett Burgess, and the like—and the remnants of a truly genteel literary world. But the more engaged form of cosmopolitanism, the one Hollinger credits to Bourne, is at the center of regionalism (and realism more broadly) as a cultural force and literary tradition. The regionalists, from the early local-color writers through the regionalists of the 1920s and 1930s, are cosmopolitans in the senses that Amanda Anderson has analyzed in her survey of the term in current critical discourses: they "cultivated detachment from restrictive forms of identity," "manifest[ed] a complex tension between elitism and egalitarianism" at a time "when the world . . . suddenly seemed to expand in unassimilable ways," and, unlike universalists, required "at least limited self-reflexivity" within "cultural multiplicity."[21] Bruce Robbins's use of "cosmopolitanism" to mean "trans-local connecting" and James Clifford's notion of "discrepant cosmopolitanisms" are attempts to correct both the universalizing elitism of the Enlightenment and "ethnic enclave" thinking, while they explicitly acknowledge the elite position that makes their cosmopolitan thinking an option.[22] The local-color writers and regionalists, I want to argue, were writing in precisely this vein.

What Robbins calls his "willfully provocative" use of the word is particularly germane, since he is writing about the way in which many academics in the humanities—because of their social position and relation to knowledge production, their professional need for self-legitimation, and the current imperatives to cross-disciplinary, cross-cultural, and multicultural study—are perfect examples of a certain kind of cosmopolitanism. Many essays on such topics as global culture, local knowledge, postcolonialism, and the like, says Robbins, are "allegories of vocation": "while doing whatever other interpretive tasks they set themselves, [such essays] also perform a second, most often implicit function; they invent and arrange their concepts and characters so as to narrativize and argue for the general value and significance of the intellectual vocation they exemplify."[23] Thus, in the most obvious case, attacks on privileged, or totalizing Western, hegemonic writers are often also allegories of the critic's vocation, which he or she would like to align with the "people" whom these terms exclude. It is my contention that *O Pioneers!* and many other regionalist texts are allegories of the writer's vocation as well, allegories of art, in which the cosmopolitan perspective is both means and fulfillment.

Wendell Berry, who as a farmer, English professor, poet, essayist, and novelist knows something of vocations, has for many years written stories based in fictional Port William, Kentucky. Best known for *The Unsettling of America: Culture and Agriculture* (1977), Berry is a committed localist, but, at the same time, he is an avowed cosmopolitan. "My work has been moti-vated," Berry says, giving credit to both sides of the regionalist equation, "by a desire to make myself responsibly at home in this world and in my native and chosen place."[24] He long ago made a distinction among various kinds of regionalism, including one that "behaves like nationalism" and one that "behaves like an exploitative industry." Both of these are the result of a narrowing of perspective—in the one case narrowed by pride and in the other by condescension—and both mean that "a man is unable to bring to bear on the life of his place all that he is able to know." This narrowed regionalism is the opposite of literary regionalism. "If they had written under its standard," Berry writes, "Faulkner would have to disavow that part of his mind that knew the 'Ode to a Grecian Urn,' Thoreau's knowledge of the Orient would have been a mere flourish, not useful, William Carlos Williams would have had to shrug off the influence of Villon and Chaucer and Fabre."[25]

Pride and Condescension

Notions of pride and condescension similar to those Berry refers to have been at the center of current literary debates on regionalism. Critics on what I called the "resistance to hegemony" side of the debate do not have a problem with regional pride. In their introduction to the *Norton Anthology of American Women Regionalists*, Judith Fetterly and Marjorie Pryse maintain a distinction between "regionalists" and "local colorists," and not the one that has long been made, which is strictly historical—the local-color writers wrote before World War I and the regionalists after. For them, the difference is attitude. The regionalists, they claim, avoid holding up "regional characters to potential ridicule by eastern urban readers," but instead "present regional experience from within."[26] Local colorists, on the contrary, are condescenders. The rap that local-color fiction demeaned its subjects was initiated in the 1920s and 1930s by the new regionalists, the Southern Agrarians and the academic folklorists, and Fetterly and Pryse try to rescue their favorite local colorists from the charge. This leads them to odd conclusions: Hamlin Garland, George Washington Cable, and Mark Twain are local colorists, while Charles Egbert Craddock (the pen name of Mary Noilles Murfree), Sarah Orne Jewett, and the early Harriet Beecher Stowe are regionalists. Such categorizations are debatable, of course, but, more important, they are ahistorical. The distinction between a representation from within and a representation from without would have seemed strange to nineteenth-century writers or readers of local-color fiction. The idea that Mary Wilkins Freeman was more or less sympathetic to her provincial characters than was Hamlin Garland, or that one was more or less than the other exploiting a local culture for the pleasure of genteel readers, never entered contemporary commentary on the genre, in part because the minimal qualification for good regionalist writing was the author's ability to do both.

On the other side of the debate from the view of Fetterly and Pryse is the idea that all regionalism is necessarily a representation from without. As Robert Dorman puts the historical consensus in his excellent history of regionalist thought from 1920 to 1945, regionalism is "the signal of a critical juncture in the centuries-long transformation of this country from a rural, frontier, decentralized, producerist, farm and village society—the older America—into the modern, commercialized, consumerist, and mechanized mass society of the metropolis," along with, we might add, the accompanying great waves of immigration and internal migration.[27] Larzer Ziff argued some time ago and Richard Brodhead

more recently that in the context of these changes, local-color stories produced for readers, in Brodhead's words, a "real-sounding yet deeply fictitious America . . . whose diversities were ranged under one group's normative sway," and that group was the urban moneyed classes.[28] Amy Kaplan suggests that the imperatives of post–Civil War nation building and overseas empire building, fears of immigration, and the march of commercial culture all contributed to the making of regionalist narratives, which she refers to as "allegories of desire generated by urban centers."[29] For writers like Brodhead, Kaplan, and Ziff, Fetterly and Pryse's defense of local color is hopelessly naive, as though they had been duped by the ideological formation they should have been analyzing.

These two approaches need each other. Local-color stories—both those dismissed by Fetterly and Pryse as patronizing and those valued for their empathetic respect—did, in fact, tend to represent local cultures from the inside, with at least a partial approbation of the values of those cultures. But they also, simultaneously or in alternating textual moments, represented them from the outside, thereby offering a large dose of reaffirmation (again, only partial) of the values of the business, professional, and leisure classes across the country that provided the bulk of readers for the genre. Cheryl Herr has argued, through reference to theoretical notions of a "third space" and Deleuzian "in-betweenness," that the complex perspective of regional texts is the result of an "oscillation" between a subjective view and a cold objectivity, or, finally, between individual desires and social facts.[30] But regionalist texts also offer an oscillation between competing sets of social or cultural facts. Local-color fiction both celebrated and criticized the provinces and both celebrated and criticized the urban centers, and it did the same for farmers and bankers, immigrants and natives, and the rest of the active cultural dichotomies. This doubleness was exactly what performed these texts' ideological, or (as we like to say now) cultural, work.

We can see this doubleness in the standard form of these fictions, especially those that use the framing device of a visitor. Sarah Orne Jewett's *The Country of the Pointed Firs,* for instance, represents the people of Maine through the eyes of a summer visitor from Boston who has come to Maine to write.[31] Frank Norris's eastern protagonist Presley refracts the "story of California" in *The Octopus.*[32] When Edith Wharton wrote her genre piece, *Ethan Frome,* she used a narrator who is an engineer from the city.[33] The prairie writers often used the same technique. Hamlin Garland's "Up the Coolly" is a story told from the perspective of an actor who is returning to the home of his youth in Wisconsin, but who has fully assimilated the values of New York City, now his home.[34] Willa Cather's city-living Jim Burden tells us the story of Ántonia. Again and again, the very form of local-color stories suggests a rural perspective framed by an urban one.

And even when the frame does not signal the cosmopolitan perspective, the narrator, protagonist, or plot does. In Garland's "A Branch Road," for instance, the protagonist, Will, is introduced to us as a young man who, unlike the truly local men around him, has a primarily aesthetic relation to the land and is sneered at as one of the "seminary chaps."[35] In the opening pages, he feels rapture at the dawn and is moved by the "interest, picturesqueness of it all," despite how "accustomed to it" he is (15). He and his love interest, Agnes, have an aesthetic response to his labor, enjoying the fact that "he made a fine figure to look at" and that while he is working "the scene . . . had a charm quite aside from human companionship" (16). The other workers "vulgarize" his experience, and

so he takes "no part in the race of the dust-blackened, half-famished men" (18). Will "assumed a reserved and almost haughty air toward his fellow workmen" (19), and "he wanted them to understand that he could do as much pitching as any of them and read Caesar's Commentaries besides" (25). He is our literary-cosmopolitan "visitor" right from the start. He then goes away and comes back as the classic returning cosmopolitan, awash in the pastoral beauty of the land after the bleak Southwest, meditating on Darwin and "the eternal procession of types" (33). He experiences literary-cosmopolitan nostalgia in his "bittersweet reveries" and "strange and powerful feeling of the passage of time," a "feeling hardly to be expressed in words" (34). His disgust at the way Agnes is living when he returns is couched in aesthetic terms rather than economic ones: weeds have choked the flowers out of her garden because of her husband's belief in nothing but "petty utility" (40).

And many of the authors themselves, including Cather, were not native informants but emigrants who may have loved but also famously hated their former lands. Cather, Freeman, Garland, Jewett, Mary Austin, Sherwood Anderson, Theodore Dreiser, among others, all left small towns and wrote novels about the way small towns attempt to squash the art out of people. These writers could no more have spoken with some pure, authentic voice of provinciality than their audience could have heard or wanted to hear such a voice. Although Fetterly and Pryse and some of today's lovers of regional fiction continue to insist that it is the time spent in a region that qualifies someone to represent that region, the time spent elsewhere is obviously much more important. As Kathleen Norris has written, regionalist writers have always had to spend some time in a cosmopolitan literary center before they could write their narratives. Their fear of provincialism leads them to New

York, she says, and a touch of cosmopolitanism allows them to reapproach the provinces with new perspectives, new prospects, and a sense that (here she paraphrases Czeslaw Milosz) "language is the only homeland."[36] Neil Jackson, reviewing the proceedings of the Pomona Critical Regionalism seminars, notes that the best-known proponents of critical regionalism in architecture are also "itinerants" of the global village.[37]

Regionalist writers have long been well aware that their texts were available for many different readings, and some wrote directly to the issue. Irvin Cobb, a largely forgotten writer of Kentucky local-color stories, published one in 1914 that was clearly a fable about the question of regionalism and authenticity.[38] "Local Color" is about a writer who has written well-respected prison stories but wants to write more authentically. He manages to have himself arrested and sent to jail. While all the other prisoners are miserable, he is ecstatic: he is living the life he wishes to depict, he is taking surreptitious notes, he looks forward to each new day and each new prison experience. This lasts for a year, after which he loses interest in his notes and becomes more and more like the other prisoners. When he is released after three years, he walks the streets for a day, and then mugs a man and is sent back to prison, fully hopeless. The point, fairly obviously, is that if the writer lives the life he is writing about authentically enough, he ceases to be a writer. It is the writer's distance from his subject that allows him to write it.

But neither are regionalist stories, therefore, as Kaplan and others argue, simply "urban" folk tales or, as Brodhead suggests, the literary equivalent of the middle-class vacation in the country. In Garland's "Up the Coolly," the eastern actor does not come off too well; he has let his family sink into poverty while he buys diamond stickpins and goes yachting, and he is surprised that they are angry. Jim Burden is not the hero

of *My Ántonia*. Carl Lindstrum and Emil Bergson, the two characters in *O Pioneers!* who leave and return, do so without being very much improved. The representations of urban folk and values follow the same pattern as that of local folk; we see from within, and then we see from without. In Garland's story, we see through the eastern actor's eyes and feel his euphoria at the beautiful scene and the bracing air; and we see his moody, depressive brother through his eyes; then we see the actor through the poor farmer's eyes, and see a selfish, small-minded fop.

The prospect in this story keeps changing, from the actor's prospects to his brother's lack of prospects (he literally keeps his eyes to the ground through most of the story). And only we, and the implied author, see the full picture; neither the actor nor his brother ever does. That full picture is not just one of the available prospects, but a cosmopolitan overview of all the prospects represented in the text. In *Country of the Pointed Firs,* this need for an overview gets literalized. When the narrator-author is living in Mrs. Todd's house, she cannot write; she has to remove herself to a small schoolhouse, set on a hill with a commanding vista of the town, in order to write her observations of it. Brodhead is wrong to summarily dismiss the writing labor of Jewett's narrator. She has not come to Maine, as he argues, for resort and vacation, but in order to do her work, the work that is the novel itself. The narrator's "cross-cultural cosmopolitanism" is not meant to mark the vacationing "leisure class as a class apart," as though her sole project were claiming Veblenian distinction, or to "facilitate the urban reappropriation of the New England shore as a vacation site," as though she were a real-estate sales adjunct.[39] Instead, like today's new cosmopolitans, Jewett adopted cosmopolitan detachment as a way to assert the ethical claims of literary cosmopolitanism within a world of discrepant cosmopolitanisms. She marked her awareness of these other cosmopolitan possibilities by giving voice to the retired whaling ship captains, who had sailed all over the globe, and by celebrating the wily perspective of Mrs. Todd, who comprehends more than we expect her to at first, more than the narrator does at various points, but less than the implied author and reader eventually do. And Jewett's readers understood all of this. Charles Miner Thompson wrote in 1904 that the audience Jewett "seeks, quite naturally and unconsciously, is made up of people of her own social and intellectual class. . . . The attitude is always felt to be that of an observer *de haut en bas*." [40]

Culture and Competition

William Dean Howells, the "Dean of American Literature," as he was known late in his life, and arguably the most important literary writer of the nineteenth century, was born and raised in the Middle West and was very influential in the production of local-color literature. As editor of the *Atlantic Monthly* and later of *Harper's*, he regularly held forth on literary topics and gave many of the most popular local-color writers their start. For Howells, local-color writing was one of the central facts of "our literary decentralization," and he claimed that Americans could construct a true nation, at the cultural level, only through the kind of representation that the local colorists were providing. [41] Like the House of Representatives, hundreds of authors, each with his or her own regional sensibilities and interests, would collectively write the bills of an American literature. (And Howells included not just the local-colorists, but writers like Abraham Cahan, Charles Chesnutt, and Paul Laurence Dunbar, who represented ethnic subregions.) Regional literature was as American, Howells claimed, as our political system. And the hallmark of both was a dual attention to local and national interests. In the 1930s, and again recently, regionalism has been held up as

an alternative to the political violence of nation-states; but as Wendell Berry and Roberto Dainotto point out, regionalism is often the same thing as nationalism, only on a smaller scale— Serbian regionalism became Serbian nationalism, just as northern Italian regionalism quickly became a nationalist movement, and so on. [42] Howells, despite his political imagery, espoused a cosmopolitanism that was neither regional nor national, neither urban nor rural, but encompassed both; it was not really political, but philosophical and literary. It was not a choice between political allegiances, but an attempt to transcend them.

Howells's cosmopolitanism was a nineteenth-century version of Enlightenment cosmopolitanism. If the eighteenth-century *philosophes* had made little distinction among literature, science, and politics, the nineteenth-century writers did. Both Howells's career and the heyday of local-color fiction were made possible by the newly expanded magazine market, which was not just an eastern metropolitan phenomenon, but a national one. What made for the expanded magazine world was industrialism and, therefore, the rise of a middle class with some discretionary cultural spending power. Pierre Bourdieu has outlined a similar set of changes in France in the nineteenth century, although the full opposition to the bourgeois world he takes to have been central to the structure of the literary field in France was not as important in the United States, anymore than Howells was as antibourgeois as Flaubert. [43] This was, in part, because of the nature of the struggle for cultural authority in America, which was not between classes but within the middle class.

In this scramble for cultural authority, the ministers, physicians, businessmen, politicians, scientists, journalists, and social scientists were all making their pitches. In that melee, the literary writers, along with their editors and reviewers, staked out a specific place in the cultural landscape by making specific claims.[44] They could not very well, in the face of science, claim to have final say about objective reality (although some tried); they did not do a very good job battling doctors and ministers for primacy in the cure of bodies and souls (although, again, some tried); and so on. What they did do quite successfully is claim, in a world of increasing specialization and fragmentation, that they maintained the broadest possible perspective.

In fiction, which after the Civil War was the dominant literary genre in America, this claim to cultural authority was a central structuring principle, especially in such emerging genres as realism, regionalism, and naturalism. In these fictions, the businessmen were as parochial as the Brahmins (think, for instance, of Howells's depiction of the local culture of Boston in *The Rise of Silas Lapham*), and the scientists were as parochial as the divines; only literary writers, they claimed, could see it all. In "The Man of Letters as a Man of Business" (1893), Howells described literary writers as workers, but of a sort that is not recognized by the masses, while the "classes," or the elite, are different from authors because they do not work. Estranged by their special perspective from both the masses and the classes, literary writers nonetheless are the only true egalitarians, helping to bring about "the accomplishment of human equality of which the instinct has been divinely planted in the human soul."[45] Their cosmopolitanism was announced as both their stock in trade and central to the service they were providing society; their broad perspective was both their process and their product.

The local-color writers' first commitment was to this new ethic of the evolving literary market. In *Crumbling Idols,* Garland—never as subtle a writer as Howells—took turns attacking the older literary establishment and the popular-fiction writers, who owned the lion's share of the

market for fiction. He also sometimes cast the sciences as competitors, at which points he argued that literature does much more than relay sociological facts; it can "touch, and lift, and exalt men."[46] At other times, the competitors are the effete aesthetes of the schools, and then he was willing to claim that "literary power" of the sort he was championing "is at bottom sociologic" (140). These obvious contradictions would be simply ludicrous if they were not part of a fairly widely agreed on catholicity of literary perceptions. Literary culture is locked in a battle with competitors, and the only things holding back the new flowering of localist literature are "first, lack of a market; and, second, lack of perception" (16): that lack of perception, Garland suggested, can be corrected by the cosmopolitan perspective, which contains both aesthetics and its scientific antipode, sociology, and which surveys and transcends both the classic and the popular.

The academics make two basic errors, according to Garland. One is thinking that the market should be closed: "We have books and paintings enough in the market," he has them say. "When we want a book, we buy a classic, and know what we are getting" (132). The other is having too provincial an outlook: "From your library, or car-window, you look upon our life, that is the extent of your knowledge of our conditions" (133). Garland claimed that there were potential readers—readers equipped with a more true cosmopolitan appreciation than the aristocrats and academics—everywhere: "All over America, in towns and cities, there are groups of readers who . . . have not only all the substantial acquirements . . . but possess . . . a more intimate knowledge of American life than the aristocrat who prides himself on never having been farther west than Buffalo" (129).

Garland also argued that the new literature is made possible by the "splendid light" of Darwin and Spencer, and just as these scientists have shown the path of physical development, so will literary writers provide our social development with a "search light" (38–39). The past is feudalistic, the future democratic, he wrote, and if the past ignored women and children, the future will include them, "and fiction will embody these facts" (39). The academics are stuck in the past, but the new literary sensibility sees both past and future. The biologists see only the physical, but literature comprehends the physical and the spiritual. The sociologists understand types, but the "veritists" understand both types and individuals. The academics are absolutists, while Garland and his gang are the avenging "relativists in art" (64).

The professional reviewers of local-color fiction consistently praised such inclusive relativity. A review of *Where the Battle Was Fought* by Charles Egbert Craddock (Mary Noailles Murfree) claimed that a close reading of the text will show "how rich and varied a material can be found in a dull, deserted country neighborhood by an imagination keen in detecting the poetic value" there.[47] Almost thirty years later, the *New York Times* reviewed *Raid of the Guerrilla:* "In her latest work, she gives some admirable stories of these mountains and their picturesque people, all presented with the true artistic idealization, which is truer than the realism of actuality."[48] William Baskerville claimed that Craddock's "real power . . . rests upon a sympathetic understanding of human life." She realizes that "untutored souls are perplexed with the same questions and shaken by the same doubts that baffle the learned . . . in any environment."[49] And Harry Toulmin compared her to a social psychologist who had "served an apprenticeship in a stupendous human laboratory," so that she had made a "genuine contribution to the science of social organization as well as to the creation of an artistic and literary success."[50]

Similar reviews were given to all the local colorists. They were praised first for their literary accomplishments in strictly aesthetic terms—style, interest, clarity, balance, harmony—and then for their achievement in relation to the other professions, as in Garland's and Craddock's contributions to sociology, Bret Harte's to ethical philosophy, Jewett's to political science, and so on. "American life," Howells wrote, "is getting represented with unexampled fullness. It is true that no one writer, no one book, represents it, for this is not possible; our social and political decentralization forbids this, and may forever forbid it." But, he continued, the literary text that transcends pure entertainment is characterized by a broader view than that available to other arts and sciences: "The world was once very little, and it is now very large. Formerly, all science could be grasped by a single mind; but now the man who hopes to become great or useful in science must devote himself to a single department." The individual novelist may not comprehend it all either, but "the whole field of human experience was never so nearly covered by imaginative literature in any age as in this."[51]

No one believed, of course, that literary writers were making actual contributions to other sciences—such talk was simply critical hyperbole helping to assert literary value. But local colorists did develop a set of generic conventions for addressing the sociological, political, and philosophical issues of their day, which had the effect of displaying both sides of pressing cultural debates without promoting either side. Whether the lines of cultural division are urban/rural, farmer/townsman, eastern/western, capital/labor, agricultural/industrial, Anglo/Other, poverty/wealth, progress/tradition, or marriage/spinsterhood, what these narratives offer again and again is a third term, a vantage point from which the distinctions represented are erased in favor of a cosmopolitan ethic, which usually respects and disrespects both poles. These texts promote a superior cultural position that transcends all difference and dismisses difference as atavistic. Thus every text becomes, whatever else it is, also a parable of the value of the cosmopolitan literary sensibility. This ethic of cosmopolitanism has remained the central tenet of the literary class, from the 1870s to the present, and membership in the supposedly exclusive club of the broad-minded and artistic is what these texts offered their readers.

Willa Cather's *O Pioneers!*, published in 1913, is a case in point. Today's regionalists tend to find the novel to be quite elegant and effective in its rhapsodic passages about the plains and prairies, but it opens with a somewhat darker image, which has become a classic image of the plains: "One January day, thirty years ago, the little town of Hanover, anchored on a windy Nebraska tableland, was trying not to be blown away."[52] Wind-blown opening scenes of cobbled-together buildings like this work to suggest that everything human is endangered. Cather says that none of the buildings in the town "had any appearance of permanence" (3) and that the rest of the land was even less marked by human habitation:

The houses on the divide were small and tucked away in low places; you did not see them until you came directly upon them. Most of them were built of the sod itself, and were only the unescapable ground in another form. . . . The record of the plow was insignificant, like the feeble scratches on stone left by prehistoric races, so indeterminate that they may, after all, be only the markings of glaciers, and not a record of human strivings. (15)

The prospect of the prairie here is to always be what it is, inhospitable, with ant-like humans washed out with every rain and their efforts indistinguishable from natural signs.

The only thing that changes the prairie, in Cather's estimation, is imagination. The differ-

ence between Alexandra Bergson and the other farmers is her vision; when we first meet her, we are told that "her blue eyes were fixed intently on the distance" (5), and it is a distance that few of the other characters can see. "A pioneer should have imagination" (37), Cather tells us, in explaining the unfitness of Alexandra's dull-witted brothers Lou and Oscar for the life. A pioneer "should be able to enjoy the idea of things more than the things themselves" (37). The result is that Alexandra manages to wring her vision from the land and make a farm that is "a brighter pattern [of] life" (59) than what came before. "There was something individual about the great farm" that Alexandra built over the next fifteen years, "a most unusual trimness and care for detail," and "it is in the soil that she expresses herself best" (63). Alexandra is, in other words, not just a farmer, but an artist. In her flower garden, "you feel again the order and fine arrangement manifest all over the great farm; in the fencing and hedging, in the windbreaks and sheds, in the symmetrical pasture ponds" (63), and so on.

Cather represents art, and its absence, in other ways as well. Alexandra's childhood friend Carl Lindstrum starts out as an artist, but then leaves for the city and gets work as an engraver. He doesn't paint anymore, he says at one point, but just engraves for newspapers and magazines; and he doesn't do wood engraving any more, but steel engraving, which he suggests is even less artistic. One of the enemies of art, in other words, is mass culture, and we get a series of other images of the paucity of representation and truth in newspapers and other mass formats. Alexandra is as close to an artist as we see represented.

The novel is, in fact, a kind of a fable about art, a parable of authorship, but not simply because Alexandra is an artist. Alexandra's imagination fails her at times as well. Her brother Emil has been in love with her married friend

Marie for some time, and "if Alexandra had had much imagination she might have guessed what was going on in Marie's mind, and she would have seen long before what was going on in Emil's. But that, as Emil himself had more than once reflected, was Alexandra's blind side" (151). Farther along in the same paragraph, Cather writes: "Her personal life, her own realization of herself, was almost a subconscious existence" (151). For example, Alexandra has a recurring dream and daydream of being picked up and carried across the fields by a big, strong, muscular man. Whenever she has the dream, Alexandra takes a cold bath, feels disgusted with herself, and refuses to think about it. This is one of the many places in the text where the implied author of the text, who I'll call Cather, forges a bond with her readers, which says that Emil knows something of Alexandra's lack of imagination, but that she, Cather, and now her readers, know even more. This theme of "understanding" is central: early in the story, as the young Carl is leaving, Alexandra says to him "It's by understanding me, and the boys, and mother, that you've helped me. I expect that is the only way one person ever really can help another" (39). This is a very odd statement from a character who would have to know, as a pioneering farm woman, that people not only can but necessarily do help one another in much more fundamental and material ways. But it is in terms of such understanding that readers meet the implied author in a silent agreement outside the discursive movement of the text and agree with her about what really matters.

At one point, for instance, Alexandra has a quarrel with her brothers Lou and Oscar about whether she should marry Carl. She then turns to her younger brother and favorite, Emil. As one reviewer pointed out in 1913, Alexandra sends Emil to college in order to "procure for him the advantages of education which shall give him a larger horizon, more flexible inter-

ests, than her own."[53] But it doesn't quite work. At first, he is too self-involved to listen; then, finding the idea far-fetched, he tells Alexandra to do what she wants, but assumes that she will do nothing. "I had hoped you might understand, a little," she says, "but I suppose that's too much to expect" (132). Again we see Alexandra alone with her problem and realize the limitations of her culture, especially compared with the culture we share with Cather. The only ones who have the breadth of understanding necessary to the situation are ourselves and the author, and we bond over this mutual understanding by seeing its lack represented. We never make the same imaginative bond with Alexandra, in part because the author keeps giving us cues not to, pointing out Alexandra's lack of "imagination," her unconsciousness of her own unconscious.

And we bond, finally, in the realm of art, an art that is tied to both understanding and memory. Carl and Emil are almost artists, and they almost understand what they have to; Alexandra is a better artist, but she still does not understand enough. We do, however, because, unlike Alexandra, we are modern, cosmopolitan people, as was Cather, the real artist. And we know that this is "thirty years ago" and that in imbibing this story we are accepting the pastness of the past and imaginatively remembering rather than understanding the region's present.

The book is pro-modern in other ways as well. The dullard brothers are stuck in tradition and conformity; they "hated experiments" (34) for the smallest of reasons: "Even Lou, who was more elastic than his older brother, disliked to do anything different from their neighbors. He felt that it made them conspicuous and gave people a chance to talk about them" (34). Alexandra, of course, wants to experiment (because she is almost a modern artist) and goes to the university to talk to people about new crops and new methods. Her reliance on modern science makes her success.

Anti-modern in its rejection of mass culture, pro-modern in its respect for agricultural science and psychology; anti-modern in its respect for old Ivar (the crazy holy man from the old country who can talk to the animals), pro-modern in its rejection of social convention, *O Pioneers!* asks us to agree not with either the anti-modern or the pro-modern position, but with a very specific way of integrating them—in effect, annihilating the differences between them. It is such negotiations of difference that were central to the cosmopolitan ethic of literary culture as it was developing in the late nineteenth century.

Of course this openness to difference could take various forms, as it was variously motivated. When we and Cather "understand" old Ivar, we do so not as a representative of biblical authority, which he cites regularly, and not as a representative of pre-Christian Nordic animism and therefore immigrant culture, which he is also associated with, and not as a representative of the new spiritualists and psychic researchers, although we get hints of that as well. The novel provides an almost divine, ecumenical view of the religious possibilities alive in the culture, a reading of the varieties of religious experience that refuse to privilege one over another. Readers are offered and assumed to comprehend a cosmopolitan multiplicity of perspectives and are absolved of specifically endorsing any one; we are allowed, in effect, to have our faith and deny it too.

At the beginning of *O Pioneers!* we see Emil as a young boy, in from the farm: "He was a little country boy, and this village was to him a very strange and perplexing place, where people wore fine clothes and had hard hearts" (5). He sees this tiny, wind-blown village, in other words, as villagers stereotypically see the city,

and we are encouraged to notice this, to smile at the boy's lack of perspective. And the rest of the text works to build up our perspective, visiting the "foreign" cultures of the French settlements, taking us down crazy Ivar's religious path, and even, in the end, forcing us to understand the murderer, Marie's jealous husband. Alexandra gives us a parable of the value of such perspective: the sister of one of her hired men had grown despondent and tried to commit suicide. She went to visit relatives in Iowa and was amazed at what she saw, the new modern bridges spanning the Platte and the Missouri Rivers, and so she returns content "to live and work in a world that's so big and interesting" (93). Alexandra then provides the moral she took from this story: "it's what goes on in the world that reconciles me" (93).

And so Cather can write of the "frank and joyous and young . . . open face of the country" (58) because she has a similar and more inclusive cosmopolitan perspective. Enough of one, indeed, to say that "like the plains of Lombardy, it seems to rise a little to meet the sun." Nebraska is both wind-blown barrenness and a place where "the air and the earth are curiously mated and intermingled, as if one were the breath of the other. You feel in the atmosphere the same tonic, puissant quality that is in the tilth, the same strength and resoluteness" (58). But you feel the latter in such lyrical abundance because you feel the former in its full dreadfulness. The celebration of Nebraska is possible because you know something of the plains of Lombardy.

Discrepant Cosmopolitanisms

The particular form that cosmopolitanism takes in local-color fiction is not the same as that which it takes in other literary genres. It is not, as with the "decadent" writers of the 1890s, for instance, the kind of cosmopolitanism that adopts values promiscuously wherever they are found, exercising the connoisseurship of cultural value that completely obliterates and consumes the local; it is not primarily a cosmopolitanism based in taste. Nor is it the cosmopolitanism of the genteel writers who are open to only that which passes the test of Christian propriety. Nor is it the cosmopolitanism of the literary realists like Rebecca Harding Davis, Frances Harper and Upton Sinclair, for instance, with their reform motives and their insistence on the inevitability of progress. In contrast to these writers, one of the special claims that regionalists make, as I suggested earlier, is to be the repositories of cultural memory: they promise to keep the old places from being blown away. Alexandra Bergson may apply the newest agricultural methods in order to create a garden-like work of art out of the desert of the uncultivated prairie, but Cather, even more of an artist, makes art out of both garden and desert, and keeps the past alive for readers in ways that it is not quite alive for most of the characters in the book and is not truly alive in the culture. And the other local-color writers did the same thing, in varying shades of nostalgia, for their regions, always in transition, always newly challenged by the demands of modernity, and always depicted as in need of the representation that will save them from obliteration.

This is the real tie with ethnic fiction, which began, as Brodhead has argued (and as Howells argued before him), as a subgenre of local-color writing. A paradigmatic figure for the ethnic capture of the past appears at the end of Anzia Yezierska's *The Bread Givers*, in which the assimilated protagonist and her husband listen to her Old World, rabbinical, tyrannical father intoning his prayers from down the hall, appreciating as music what she detests as religion and ideol-

ogy. Her husband is going to take Hebrew lessons from the old man, not for the purposes of worship, but because he feels it is important to remember one's heritage. On their first date, they talk about having come from the same area of Poland as young children, and they bond in remembrance, after which the heroine says an odd thing: "And the whole story of my life poured itself out to him. . . . And as I talked my whole dark past dropped away from me." He encourages this process: "Next time we are together . . . try to remember more about Poland." The past drops away in being recounted, even as it is remembered. She continues to feel her father's tyranny until she comes to realize the "pathos of this lonely old man": "In a world where all is changed, he alone remained unchanged—as tragically isolate as the rocks." In the final image of the book, the father begins to chant the biblical phrases she associates with tyranny, but which her husband has encouraged her to reconceive as tradition. As they walk down the hall away from him, they can no longer hear the insulting words of his scripture: "Still we lingered for the mere music of the fading chant."[54] The aesthetic act of adopting cultural memories as aesthetic objects in the process of forgetting one's own life is exactly the kind of ground prepared by local-color fiction for the staging of ethnic identity.

Cather's complex act of remembering and forgetting in her Nebraska novels is clearly one of the models for Yezierska's story. As today's cosmopolitan theorists suggest, this may be the only viable ethics of difference we have. Sarah Orne Jewett, the regionalist author who was Cather's mentor, wrote: "There is a saying of Plato's that the best thing one can do for the people of a State is to make them acquainted with each other, and it is with some instinctive feeling of this sort which led me to wish that the town and country people were less suspicious of one another." Jewett wrote to Cather, before she had written *O Pioneers!*, that in order to write the book she needed the opposite of a more authentic identification with the Nebraska folk; she needed more distance from her material: "You don't see them [Nebraskans] yet quite enough from the outside,—you stand right in the middle of each of them when you write, without having the standpoint of the looker-on who takes them each in their relations to letters, to the world."[55] Among other things, Jewett is here anticipating Yi-Fu Tuan's notion that the difference between space and place is a quality of contemplative distance that transforms the local into the regional.[56]

Cather obviously did have a great love for aspects of the Nebraska experience she described, just as she did for the New York of those same years she described in *My Mortal Enemy* (1926). But she did not offer a regionalist agenda as such, and she certainly did not find in regionalist literature, as John Crowe Ransom and Wendell Berry and many others have, a balm for the wounds inflicted by modernity. Such a view has done long service in literary studies; for instance, Harold P. Simonson wrote that "a sense of place is what heals the separations—self and society, mind and body, individual and community, soul and soil, symbol and fact, writer and region, words and feeling—that are the fate of modern beings."[57] Cather's belief, I am arguing, is that it is literature that accomplishes this healing, not an attachment to Nebraska, where she had not lived for years before writing *O Pioneers!*, and where she never wanted to live again. She loved Nebraska—and hated it—just as she loved and hated New York.

In "Cosmopolitanism and Schizophrenia," Claude Lévi-Strauss argued that the Chinook, because they were "traders and intermediaries between near and distant tribes," were cosmopolitan. One effect of this is that their mythology "seems less like an original corpus than an ensemble of secondary elaborations," in which they "reconcile, by transforming them, miscellaneous mythic materials."[58] As economic and social life became more and more a product of trade between near and distant tribes in the United States in the period after the Civil War, as the isolated communities across the country were connected by commerce, a cosmopolitan transformation of the "miscellaneous mythic materials" of various groups was effected in the literary world, and nowhere so explicitly or vigorously than in regional fiction.

As regionalism was reinvented in the 1920s and 1930s, people like John Crowe Ransom contrasted it to cosmopolitanism. But Ransom, like the earlier regionalists, found that the "important benefit" of the regional way of life is that it "feels right, it has aesthetic quality."[59] In his very cosmopolitan pose in "The Aesthetic of Regionalism," as the "philosophic regionalist," Ransom pushed the transformation more forcefully into the arena of myth, arguing that the object is not to argue for regionalism, but "to try, to feel" it. Truly regional people like the southwestern Indians "do not have to formulate the philosophy of regionalism," Ransom claimed, but we do. Regionalism is more reasonable than any other philosophy because it is "more natural." What Ransom's contemporaries Mumford, Dewey, and Nearing argued for in the 1920s and 1930s was not the mythical regionalism that Ransom described so much as the rooted cosmopolitanism that is now in the process of being reinvented. Regionalist writers in the same period— Ellen Glasgow, O. E. Rölvaag, Sherwood Anderson, William Faulkner, Ruth Suckow—often evoked a generalized nostalgia, whereas localcolor writers had insisted on specific memories, but in other ways they continued local colorists' multifaceted critique of local ways of life; they did not revolt just from the village, that is, but from the city as well. As John T. Frederick, editor of the *Midland*, wrote, "regionalism is an incident and a condition, not a purpose or motive. . . . [T]he regionalist's work has literary importance only in so far as it meets the standard of good writing at all times and in all places."[60] Allen Tate wrote, in "The New Provincialism," that the genuine regionalist uses local details, "but otherwise offer[s] as an imaginative subject the plight of human beings as it has been and will continue to be, here and in other parts of the world."[61] The regionalist writers in the 1920s and 1930s were interested primarily, after all, in art and its uses, just as the local-color writers had been. And so they continued the project of transforming the "miscellaneous mythic materials" of the various American tribes into a literary lingua franca, not by holding them up to ridicule, of course, and not by arguing for their continued viability, but by equal parts forgetting and remembering, employing an overview that was a kind of overlooking. We will, they suggested, add colors to the palate of a national literature until we have achieved pure white. This last prediction comes from William Carlos Williams's image of the effect of local color in literature, a mark of the common ground between the cosmopolitan regionalists and the cosmopolitan modernists in the 1910s to 1930s.[62]

This was not always the ethic of literary production, of course. In Samuel Johnson's dictionary, the "Cosmopolite" is "at home in every place," and the regionalists clearly had this eighteenth-century definition in mind. But in the mid-nineteenth century, Noah Webster's first definition was a person "with no fixed residence." Herman Melville's appraisal, like Webster's, was that the cosmopolitan is a close relative of the confidence man, similar to Robert Reich's view of multinational corporate executives.[63] According to Lévi-Strauss, the cosmopolitan is a close relative not just of the schizophrenic, but of the businessman. More ethnographers than moralists, more businesspeople than schizophrenics, the regionalists side more

with the anthropologist than with the novelist. These regions, these local colors, these multiple perspectives are not lost in their integration into national and international commerce, the regionalists claim, because their uniqueness is guaranteed by representing their historical specificity and ultimate universality. And it is done so in the *New Yorker* and the *Midland* and the *Overland Monthly* and the *Nation*. Local cultures will not be obliterated by the stampede of modernization, the literary regionalists reassure their audience, because they are being preserved and are available on newsstands and in bookstores, written with a sensibility that advertises itself as being as wide as the prairie sky.

Cosmopolitanism is also at work in today's nonliterary regionalisms, which are, especially when they are tied to ecological politics, almost entirely the products of cosmopolitan university training; fueled by national and international publications, institutes, and meetings; and legitimated with globally gathered and disseminated data and theories. For example, Wendell Berry's "Rules for a Local Economy" is reprinted on the Global Ideas Bank home page, sponsored by the Institute for Social Inventions, an institute for developing "non-technological ideas" in London, England, with a sister institute in Australia. This globalism should be embraced rather than disguised. Whatever regional commitments we have are the result, as they were for the literary regionalists, of thinking globally. It is not the prairie that reconciles us; it is, as Alexandra Bergson says, the world.

Notes

1. Willa Cather, *My Ántonia,* in *Willa Cather: Early Novels and Stories,* ed. Sharon O'Brien (New York: Library of America, 1987), 716.

2. Richard Ford, *Independence Day* (New York: Knopf, 1995), 113.

3. Diary entry, 1–5 June 1903, in *Hamlin Garland's*

Diaries, ed. Donald Pizer (San Marino, Calif.: Huntington Library, 1968).

4. Kathleen Norris, *Dakota: A Spiritual Geography* (Boston: Ticknor and Fields, 1993); Wendell Berry, *The Unsettling of America: Culture and Agriculture,* 3rd ed. (San Francisco: Sierra Club Books, 1996); Twelve Southerners, *I'll Take My Stand: The South and the Agrarian Tradition* (1930; reprint, Baton Rouge: Louisiana State University Press, 1977).

5. Kenneth Frampton, "Towards a Critical Regionalism: Six Points For an Architecture of Resistance," in *The Anti-Aesthetic: Essays on Postmodern Culture,* ed. Hal Foster (Port Townsend, Wash.: Bay Press, 1983); Jean-Louis Cohen, "The Search for a Critical Practice," *Casabella* 60 (1996): 21–27; Spyros Amourgis, ed., *Critical Regionalism: The Pomona Meetings Proceedings* (Pomona: California Polytechnic State University, 1991); Botond Bognar, "On the Critical Aspects of Regionalism," *A + U,* March 1990, 11–18; Alexander Tzonis and Laine Lefaivre, "Why Critical Regionalism Today?" *A + U,* May 1990, 23–33.

6. David M. Jordan, *New World Regionalism: Literature in the Americas* (Toronto: University of Toronto Press, 1994), 8.

7. Josephine Donovan, "Breaking the Sentence: Local-Color Literature and Subjugated Knowledges," in *The (Other) American Traditions: Nineteenth-Century Women Writers,* ed. Joyce W. Warren (New Brunswick, N.J.: Rutgers University Press, 1993), 227; Michel Foucault, *Power/Knowledge: Selected Interviews and Other Writings, 1972–1977* (New York: Pantheon, 1980), 82.

8. Josephine Donovan, *New England Local Color Literature: A Women's Tradition* (New York: Ungar, 1983); Josephine Donovan, "Sarah Orne Jewett's Critical Theory: Notes Toward a Feminine Literary Mode," in *Critical Essays on Sarah Orne Jewett,* ed. Gwen L. Nagel (Boston: Hall, 1984), 212–25; Emily Toth, ed., *Regionalism and the Female Imagination* (New York: Human Sciences, 1985). For a more recent discussion of these issues, see June Howard, "Unraveling Regions, Unsettling Periods: Sarah Orne Jewett and American Literary History," *American Literature* 68 (1996): 365–84.

9. Hamlin Garland, *Crumbling Idols: Twelve Essays on Art Dealing Chiefly with Literature, Painting and the Drama* (1894; reprint, Cambridge, Mass.: Harvard University Press, 1960); in *I'll Take My Stand* see especially the essays by Ransom, Lytle, Young, and Davidson.

10. Richard Brodhead, *Cultures of Letters: Scenes of Reading and Writing in Nineteenth-Century America* (Chicago: University of Chicago Press, 1993); Amy Kaplan, "Nation, Region, Empire," in *Columbia History of the American Novel,* ed. Emory Elliott (New York: Columbia University Press, 1991).

11. Joni L. Kinsey, *Plain Pictures: Images of the American Prairie* (Washington, D.C.: Smithsonian Institution Press, 1996).

12. Thomas J. Schlereth, *The Cosmopolitan Ideal in Enlightenment Thought: Its Form and Function in the Ideas of Franklin, Hume, and Voltaire, 1694–1790* (Notre Dame, Ind.: University of Notre Dame Press, 1977); Amanda Anderson, "Cosmopolitanism, Universalism, and the Divided Legacies of Modernity," in *Cosmopolitics,* ed. Pheng Cheah and Bruce Robbins (Minneapolis: University of Minnesota Press, 1998).

13. Julia Kristeva, *Nations without Nationalism,* trans. Leon S. Roudiez (New York: Columbia University Press, 1993), 15.

14. Yi-Fu Tuan, *Cosmos and Hearth: A Cosmopolite's Viewpoint* (Minneapolis: University of Minnesota Press, 1996).

15. Arnold Krupat, *Ethnocriticism: Ethnography, History, Literature* (Berkeley: University of California Press, 1992), 3; Homi Bhabha, *The Location of Culture* (New York: Routledge, 1994).

16. Antonio Gramsci, *Selections from the Prison Notebooks,* ed. Quintin Hoare and Geoffrey Nowell Smith (New York: International Publishers, 1971), 17; Timothy Brennan, "Cosmopolitans and Celebrities," *Race & Class* 31 (1989): 1–19; Timothy Brennan, *At Home in the World: Cosmopolitanism Now* (Cambridge, Mass.: Harvard University Press, 1997).

17. Robert Reich, *The Work of Nations: Preparing Ourselves for 21st-Century Capitalism* (New York: Knopf, 1991), 310.

18. Christopher Lasch, *The Revolt of the Elites and the Betrayal of Democracy* (New York: Norton, 1995), 47.

19. David A. Hollinger, *Postethnic America: Beyond Multiculturalism* (New York: Basic Books, 1995).

20. Mitchell Cohen, "Rooted Cosmopolitanism: Thoughts on the Left, Nationalism, and Multiculturalism," *Dissent,* Fall 1992, 478–83; Bruce Ackerman, "Rooted Cosmopolitanism," *Ethics* 104 (1994): 516–35; John Dewey, "Americanism and Localism," in *Characters and Events: Popular Essays in Social and Political Philosophy* (New York: Holt, 1929), 2: 259–79; Lewis Mumford, special issue of *Survey Graphic,* April 1925, and "Roots in the Region," in *Faith for Living* (New York: Harcourt, Brace, 1940); Scott Nearing, *Where Is Civilization Going?* (New York: Vanguard, 1927).

21. Anderson, "Cosmopolitanism," 3, 7, 14.

22. Bruce Robbins, "Comparative Cosmopolitanism," *Social Text* 10 (1993): 169–86. See also Bruce Robbins, *Secular Vocations: Intellectuals, Professionalism, Culture* (London: Verso, 1993); Cheah and Robbins, eds., *Cosmopolitics;* and James Clifford, *Routes: Travel and Translation in the Late Twentieth Century* (Cambridge, Mass.: Harvard University Press, 1997).

23. Robbins, "Comparative Cosmopolitanism," 170, 178.

24. Wendell Berry, "Rules for a Local Economy," in "Conserving Communities," *Resurgence,* May 1995, available at http://www.newciv.org/GIB/BI/BI-123. HTML or http://www.geocities.com/RainForest/5780/bi-123.htm.

25. Wendell Berry, "The Regional Motive," *Southern Review* 6 (1970): 972, 975.

26. Judith Fetterly and Marjorie Pryse, eds., *American Women Regionalists, 1850–1910* (New York: Norton, 1992), xii.

27. Robert L. Dorman, *Revolt of the Provinces: The Regionalist Movement in America, 1920–1945* (Chapel Hill: University of North Carolina Press, 1993), xii.

28. Larzer Ziff, *The American 1890s: Life and Times of a Lost Generation* (Lincoln: University of Nebraska Press, 1979); Brodhead, *Cultures of Letters,* 126.

29. Kaplan, "Nation," 252.

30. Cheryl Herr, *Critical Regionalism and Cultural Studies: From Ireland to the American Midwest* (Gainesville: University Press of Florida, 1996), 8–11.

31. Sarah Orne Jewett, *The Country of the Pointed Firs* (1896; reprint, New York: Norton, 1994).

32. Frank Norris, *The Octopus: A Story of California,* in *Frank Norris: Novels and Essays,* ed. Donald Pizer (New York: Library of America, 1986).

33. Edith Wharton, *Ethan Frome,* in *Edith Wharton: Novellas and Other Writings,* ed. Cynthia Griffin Wolff (New York: Library of America, 1990).

34. Hamlin Garland, "Up the Coolly," in *Main-Travelled Roads* (1891; reprint, New York: Penguin, 1962).

35. Hamlin Garland, "A Branch Road," in *Main-Travelled Roads,* 16. [Hereafter cited in the text]

36. Kathleen Norris, *Leaving New York: Writers Look Back* (New York: Hungry Mind, 1995), 35.

37. Neil Jackson, "Critical Regionalism," *Architectural Review,* March 1993, 11–13.

38. Irvin S. Cobb, "Local Color," in *Local Color* (New York: Doran, 1916).

39. Brodhead, *Cultures of Letters,* 149, 151.

40. Charles Miner Thompson, "The Art of Miss Jewett," in *Appreciation of Sarah Orne Jewett: 29 Interpretive Essays,* ed. Richard Cary (Waterville, Me.: Colby College Press, 1973), 43–44.

41. William Dean Howells, "Criticism and Fiction," in *Criticism and Fiction and Other Essays,* ed. Clare Marburg Kirk and Rudolf Kirk (New York: New York University Press, 1959), 64.

42. Berry, "Regional Motive," 972; Roberto Maria Dainotto, "'All the Regions Do Smilingly Revolt': The Literature of Place and Region," *Critical Inquiry* 22 (1996): 486–505.

43. Pierre Bourdieu, *Rules of Art: Genesis and Structure of the Literary Field,* trans. Susan Emanuel (Stanford: Stanford University Press, 1996).

44. David Shumway, *Creating American Civilization: A Genealogy of American Literature as an Academic Discipline* (Minneapolis: University of Minnesota Press, 1994); Thomas Haskell, *The Emergence of Professional Social Science: The American Social Science Association and the Nineteenth-Century Crisis of Authority* (Urbana: University of Illinois Press, 1977); Bruce Kuklick, *The Rise of American Philosophy: Cambridge, Massachusetts, 1860–1930* (New Haven, Conn.: Yale University Press, 1977); T. J. Jackson Lears, *No Place of Grace: Antimodernism and the Transformation of American Culture, 1880–1920* (New York: Pantheon, 1981); Carol Klimick Cyganowski, *Magazine*

Editors and Professional Authors in Nineteenth-Century America: The Genteel Tradition and the American Dream (New York: Garland, 1988); Burton J. Bledstein, *The Culture of Professionalism: The Middle Class and the Development of Higher Education in America* (New York: Norton, 1976).

45. Howells, "The Man of Letters as a Man of Business," in *Criticism and Fiction,* 309.

46. Garland, *Crumbling Idols,* 133. [Hereafter cited in the text]

47. Review of *Where the Battle Was Fought,* by Charles Egbert Craddock, *Nation,* 4 November 1884, 314.

48. Review of *Raid of the Guerrilla,* by Charles Egbert Craddock, *New York Times Book Review,* 9 June 1912, 358.

49. William Malone Baskerville, "Charles Egbert Craddock," in *Southern Writers: Biographical and Critical Studies* (1897; reprint, New York: Gordian Press, 1970), 1:357–404.

50. Harry Aubrey Toulmin, "Charles Egbert Craddock," in *Social Historians* (Boston: Gorham Press, 1911), 59–97.

51. Howells, "Criticism and Fiction," 68.

52. Willa Cather, *O Pioneers!* (1913; reprint, New York: Penguin, 1989), 3. [Hereafter cited in the text]

53. Review of *O Pioneers!* by Willa Cather, *Nation,* 4 September 1913, 210–11.

54. Anzia Yezierska, *The Bread Givers* (1925; reprint, New York: Persea, 1975), 278, 296, 297.

55. Sarah Orne Jewett, *Letters,* ed. Richard Cary (Waterville, Me.: Colby College Press, 1967), 83–84, 248.

56. Yi-Fu Tuan, *Space and Place: The Perspective of Experience* (Minneapolis: University of Minnesota Press, 1981).

57. Harold P. Simonson, *Beyond the Frontier: Writers, Western Regionalism, and a Sense of Place* (Fort Worth: Texas Christian University Press, 1989), 23.

58. Claude Lévi-Strauss, "Cosmopolitanism and Schizophrenia," in *The View from Afar,* trans. Joachim Neugroschel and Phoebe Hoss (New York: Basic Books, 1984), 171–79.

59. John Crowe Ransom, "The Aesthetic of Regionalism," in *Selected Essays of John Crowe Ransom* (Baton Rouge: Louisiana State University Press, 1984), 46.

60. John T. Frederick, Introduction to *Out of the Midwest,* ed. John T. Frederick (New York: McGraw-Hill, 1944), xv.

61. Allen Tate, "The New Provincialism" in *Essays of Four Decades* (Chicago: Swallow, 1968), 545.

62. William Carlos Williams, *Imaginations* (New York: New Directions, 1971), 311.

63. John Bryant, "'Nowhere a Stranger': Melville and Cosmopolitanism." *Nineteenth-Century Fiction* 39 (1984): 275–91; Karen Halttunen, *Confidence Men and Painted Women: A Study of Middle-Class Culture in America, 1830–1870* (New Haven, Conn.: Yale University Press, 1982), 198.

6   Prairie Politics and the Landscape of Reform

Shelton Stromquist

What defines a region as a historically and culturally distinctive place? How does landscape shape patterns of living, a sense of place, and the imagined space that invests a region with meaning and identity? In what ways does a region's cultural and physical landscape shape its political environment?

Such questions invite us to cross conventional boundaries of historical investigation and scholarly discourse. They ask us to consider the influence of the environment—in this case, the prairie—on society and politics. This chapter is a preliminary attempt to cross those boundaries by examining the imprint of the prairie or, more generally, "the West" on different strands of American reform politics in the late nineteenth and early twentieth centuries. John A. Johnson, the reform governor of Minnesota, defined the regional character of that movement for reform in 1905, when he envisioned a new political alignment:

The great center of political power should be in the Mississippi valley, instead of on the Atlantic Coast. The best brain and the surest brawn of the nation is found here, and it should be organized into one mighty moral, material, and patriotic force to over-

throw the new paternalism and plunder, and regenerate politics and the Republic. To the resources, the energies and genius of the West, the nation looks, not only to build up its commercial and industrial greatness, but its moral and political strength.[1]

Nearly all sources see the roots of that midwestern reform movement in the agrarian protests of the late nineteenth century that grew with the settlement of the region beyond the Mississippi, but also influenced the politics of other parts of what came to be known as the Midwest.[2] Woodrow Wilson in 1911 referred to the Midwest as "a region of political protest," or what historian Russel Nye once called "a culture area of discontent," which he argued was "compounded out of its geography, its culture, its economic and social history." That lineage of protest ran from the Grangers through the Farmers' Alliance and Populists to the particular brand of midwestern progressivism represented by reform governors of Wisconsin, Iowa, and Minnesota: Robert M. La Follette, Albert Cummins, and John A. Johnson. This culture of discontent was grounded in a strong sense of western democratic virtue, cultivated in the soil of prairie settlements and hostile to the corruption and paternalism of eastern interests, most notably the railroads and other monopolies. In characteristic fashion, a Minnesota farmer in the late nineteenth century reputedly expressed a preference for "the old buccaneers"—the gamblers, land speculators, and flamboyant individual entrepreneurs of the early settlement era—over the "cold, shrewd men of business"—the railroad tycoons and eastern robber barons, like J. P. Morgan and E. H. Harriman—because "the old ones 'left a little for seed.'"[3]

A useful entry point for a consideration of prairie reform politics is poetry. The prairies have nurtured a brand of poetry animated by a political vision of reform and layered with imagery of the landscape. That poetic/political vision took varied, even conflicting forms. No single poem captures the voice of regional reform and its contradictions better than Vachel Lindsay's "Bryan, Bryan, Bryan, Bryan." Before turning to the political landscape of the prairie and its varied manifestations, it pays to listen for the cadence and meaning of that vision in the verse of one "prairie poet" and his lament for the "boy orator" of the Platte:[4]

These creatures were defending things Mark Hanna
   never dreamed;
The moods of airy childhood that in desert dews
   gleamed,
The gossamers and whimsies,
The monkeyshines and didoes
Rank and strange
Of the canyons and the range,
The ultimate fantastics
Of the far western slope,
And of prairie schooner children
Born beneath the stars,
Beneath falling snows,
Of the babies born at midnight
In the sod huts of lost hope,
With no physician there,
Except a Kansas prayer,
With the Indian raid a howling through the air.

And all these in their helpless days
By the dour East oppressed,
Mean paternalism
Making their mistakes for them,
Crucifying half the West,
Till the whole Atlantic coast
Seemed a giant spiders' nest.
      · · ·
Election night at midnight:
Boy Bryan's defeat.
Defeat of western silver.
Defeat of the wheat.
Victory of letterfiles
And plutocrats in miles
With dollar signs upon their coats,
Diamond watchchains on their vests
And spats on their feet.
Victory of custodians,
Plymouth Rock,
And all that inbred landlord stock.
Victory of the neat.
Defeat of the aspen groves of Colorado valleys,
The blue bells of the Rockies,
And blue bonnets of old Texas,
By the Pittsburg alleys.
Defeat of alfalfa and the Mariposa lily.
Defeat of the Pacific and the long Mississippi.
Defeat of the young by the old and silly.
Defeat of tornadoes by the poison vats supreme.
Defeat of my boyhood, defeat of my dreams.

Lindsay imagined a West unified by common rugged, earthy values set in diverse western landscapes, counterposed to a "dour," "mean paternalism" of eastern "plutocrats" and "inbred landlord stock." His fellow prairie poet Edgar Lee Masters saw even more directly a vision of the land as the wellspring of the people's capacity to revolt:

But let the vision of this land appear;
Let duty to the heritage that is ours
Come to the minds of leaders: then the people,
Waiting like winter fields for April time,
Will rise and shake their banners like the corn.[5]

Whether it was a prairie painter or poet, midwestern journalist or politician, plain-spoken reformer or standpatter, a sense of place profoundly colored their vision and the texture of their identity.

Beginning in the years immediately following the Civil War, a politics of democratic reform, rooted in the Midwest's distinctive landscape, economy, and social structure, grew and flourished. The burst of postwar settlement redefined the axis of political tension from north–south to east–west. While the colonization of new lands and the contrasts between settled society and frontier were by that time well-established themes in the history of the new nation, the sense of a distinctive and coherent region (Frederick Jackson Turner would call it a "section") bounded by the western edge of the Great Lakes and extending westward was new. Vachel Lindsay, Edgar Lee Masters, and Carl Sandburg would capture its democratizing spirit in their poetry. William Jennings Bryan sought to mobilize it in his political campaign of 1896. His famous "cross of gold" speech to the Democratic Convention in July 1896 conjured up that region and its values as a source of political virtue and material prosperity:

You come to us and tell us that the great cities are in favor of the gold standard; we reply that the great cities rest upon our broad and fertile prairies. Burn down your cities and leave our farms, and your cities will spring up again as if by magic; but destroy our farms and the grass will grow in the streets of every city in the country.[6]

But this "prairie politics" of reform, as I would call it, contained a profound tension, even contradiction. One strand celebrated the social and cultural solidarity in western communities that transcended differences of class. Late-nineteenth-century reformers, who contested the encroachment of railroads and banks and the new aggregations of corporate power that threatened the independence of western communities, conjured up a sense of place created through face-to-face relations, tied to the soil and its products, and resistant to the wealth and power accumulating in distant, usually eastern, cities and corporations. They sought to revitalize democratic institutions locally and nationally and to carry out antimonopoly reforms that would restore competition and vigor to smaller places and their interests.[7] Bryan (and Lindsay) embodied this politics of reform emanating from the prairie. They sentimentalized the virtue of the West and demonized the corrupting influences of the East. They also discounted differences of class and interest among Westerners, as in Bryan's proclamation:

We have come to speak of this broader class of businessmen. The man who is employed for wages is as much a business man as his employer; . . . the farmer who goes forth in the morning and toils all day, who begins in spring and toils all summer, and who by the application of brain and muscle to the natural resources of the country creates wealth, is as much a business man as the man who goes upon the Board of Trade and bets upon the price of grain.[8]

Historians Robert Wiebe and Samuel Hays have argued that these western reform impulses grew naturally out of "island communities," resistant to the tides of modernization that swept out of the urbanized East. In Wiebe's and Hays's view, "progressive reform" heralded the awakening of a new middle class committed to organization and efficiency and prepared to use state power to curtail wasteful competition, corruption, and corporate inefficiency, which bred poverty and injustice.

One interpretation that suggests an alternative perspective points to the influence of those middle-class reformers who embraced Bryan's project of restoring democracy through reforms that bridged class differences. Like Bryan, Robert La Follette, Jane Addams, and a host of midwestern progressives translated their sense of community and their grievances against the corrupting influence of corporate power into a program of reform that transcended the regional interests from which it sprang.[9]

A second strand of reform politics, more radically oppositional and utopian, also drew vitality from the Middle West. Beginning in the post–Civil War era, adherents of this position were less sanguine about the process of colonization and settlement. Farmers found that they did not have to look east to find the engines of accumulation and inequality. They found those interests present in the activities of *local* banks, grain elevators, land speculators, and railroad agents. They infested the employment practices of manufacturing establishments and mining operations that were *locally* capitalized.[10] Proponents of this oppositional politics crafted solidarity around "producerist" values, which sharply demarcated their interests as a class from those of nonproducers. The democratic renewal *they* promised required attacking the sources of class power and unjust accumulation, whether eastern or not, and organizing to uproot a social system based on class privilege. Producerists articulated these values through the Knights of Labor and its political expression, the United Labor Party; in the Farmers' Alliance and the Populist Party; and as "grassroots socialists," whether in Terre Haute or Milwaukee, rural North Dakota or Oklahoma. Mary Elizabeth Lease, the so-called Kansas Pythoness, spoke from within this tradition of reform, colored as it sometimes was by racism, for a radical redistribution of property. For her readers in 1895, she solved the "Riddle of the Sphinx":

[I]n our own time they who have "eyes to see" and "ears to hear," may yet discern the Sphinx—not dim and fabled, but grim and real—sitting by the high-

way of human progress,—the tear-stained, prayer-worn path leading up the march of centuries,—propounding as of old her riddle to the children of men:—

"Here, O, Passers-by, in the bosom of mother earth are richest gifts and blessings, enough for all. How shall we convert this fertile bounty of Nature into wealth, and how shall we so divide this wealth that none may want, and each shall have according to what each has produced."

These reformers professed faith in their ability to constitute a cooperative commonwealth as an alternative to the social order based on wage slavery that they saw taking shape around them.[11] They drew inspiration for their social vision from the rugged egalitarianism of the West and from the real social power they mobilized in newly settled areas to use state government as a means to control corporate power. The most dramatic instance of this was the capture of state power in North Dakota by the Nonpartisan League in 1916, what one historian has termed the "daybreak on the prairie."[12]

The two traditions of reform—what I will call sentimental and oppositional—mingled in the political culture of the prairie, at times opposing each other, at times in seeming harmony. By sentimental reform, I mean a program that sought to reinstitute in a modern setting the class harmony and democratic culture that many midwestern reformers associated with the era of settlement and community formation on the prairies. By oppositional reform, I mean a culture whose searching critique of American capitalism and the inequality it produced implied the need for a fundamental redistribution of property and power. Each has influenced in different ways the politics of the region down to the present—represented by figures as different as Henry Wallace and Milo Reno, Robert La Follette and Julius Wayland, Walter Mondale and Paul Wellstone.

Nineteenth-century Americans prided themselves on their distinctiveness as a people. This originality acquired mythic stature in the accounts of European travelers, who saw it reflected in Americans' dress, language, democratic sensibilities, and voluntary associations.[13] The unfolding epic of the exploration and colonization of the North American continent reinforced that sense of difference as Americans encountered, settled, and, in Alan Trachtenberg's felicitous phrase, "incorporated" an extraordinary range of landscapes.[14] By at least midcentury, a "middle-western" region, distinct in character, if inexact in boundaries, took shape in the imagination of Americans. Russel Nye noted the difficulties in defining such a region. Lord Bryce considered it to be "that which was not East." Virtually all observers agree "that there is a Midwest, but the region is too fluid, too subdivided and disunified, to be defined as more than a state of mind, a regional self-consciousness that knows no clear demarcation lines."[15] Its prairies proved to be unusually well adapted for agricultural pursuits; its rivers, navigable for access to long-distance markets; its "great lakes," oceanlike in their vastness and in the connections they offered to the world's commerce. The Middle West, encompassing some measure of prairie and plain, invited the formation of smallholding communities of farmers, serviced by a hierarchy of towns and cities that distributed goods, processed agricultural products, maintained transportation facilities, and organized government activity.[16] These communities, democratic in principle, if not always in fact, seemed to replicate older Jeffersonian values. As the East grew more like Europe—industrial, congested, overrun by migrating poor—middle Americans came to see their region as the distinctive repository of republican values that were jeopardized in the slave-holding South and the industrial East alike. By the end of the

Civil War, that sense of regional exceptionalism profoundly stamped the culture of the prairies and their politics. Even opposition to the Civil War was colored by that consciousness. Copperhead leaders in Dubuque, Iowa, mobilized anti-eastern sentiment as the touchstone of their "western" opposition to the war. In the late 1850s, newspaperman Joseph Dorr denounced the "railroad cormorants and Wall Street vultures" who "fatten upon the toils of the laboring and agricultural classes." His colleague Dennis Mahony accused local investors of having delivered a Dubuque-owned railroad to "the animals who control the Stock Board in Wall Street."[17] While community boosters celebrated the period of prairie settlement, which had stamped the region's development forever, other observers and writers noted the changes marking the countryside and its cities.[18] Even before the Civil War, communities like Sugar Creek in Sangamon County, Illinois, according to John Mack Faragher, had seen a "'common' landscape give way to a landscape of class," as substantial farmers distanced themselves from tenants and poor laboring households. Edgar Lee Master lamented in the twentieth century, "But ah the landscape changes! Not merely the disappearance of a barn or a house or a corncrib here and there, but by the vanishment of orchards and strips of forest. . . . I had been over this neighborhood a thousand times. . . . I looked about me and did not know where I was."[19] Frank Norris and other novelists writing at the turn of the century captured the enormity of Chicago's impact on the region. But the growth of "nature's metropolis," as William Cronon defined it, reinforced the region's exceptional place in America. As Norris described Chicago,

It was Empire, the resistless subjugation of all this central world of the lakes and the prairies. Here, midmost in the land, beat the Heart of the Nation, whence inveitably must come its immeasurable power, its infinite, infinite, inexhaustible vitality. Here, of all her cities, throbbed the true life—the true power and spirit of America.[20]

The roots of prairie reform politics lay in the peculiar configuration of economic activity and land settlement that stamped the region. Despite the promise of abundant land and the Homestead Act of 1862, the activities of speculators and the disposition of railroad land grants significantly influenced the process of land acquisition in large areas west of the Mississippi. In the years immediately following the Civil War, farmers settling the prairies found the costs of settlement rising, their access to the best lands restricted, and farm prices beginning what would be a long deflation that threatened their ability to survive on the land.[21]

Small wonder that in the early 1870s farmers across the prairies organized in Granges to combat inequitable railroad charges, rising interest rates, and excessive fees at grain elevators. Small merchants and retailers in towns and villages who shared, directly and indirectly, these grievances joined efforts with the farmers.[22] A new reform politics grounded in the cross-class solidarity of farming communities enjoyed considerable influence in the prairie states as Grange-dominated legislatures passed measures to regulate the freight rates charged by railroads headquartered in Chicago and eastern metropolises. Although the Grangers experienced only short-lived success, "Greenbackers," who advocated an antimonopoly politics based on currency reform, took up the cudgel. Operating in the interstices of the two-party system, the Greenbackers rarely marshaled the numbers of voters required to win office in their own name, but they disrupted the stability of the "party system" and won important accommodations to their demands from one or another of the major par-

ties. Outcroppings of an insurgent, reform politics appeared in various forms and places. In Iowa, an "antimonopoly" fusion of Democrats and Greenbackers in the mid-1880s threatened the political hegemony of the Republicans in the state and the stability of the two-party system. Workers in Dubuque and Waterloo, Iowa, organized the Union Labor Party in 1887 and won control of city government, leaving local Democrats and Republicans briefly in disarray. The Knights of Labor, which by the mid-1880s was growing rapidly in the West, spread such disruption of local politics to all parts of the country.[23]

The antimonopoly culture of reform that gained strength in rural communities and market towns of the prairie states could also be a hospitable medium for the cultivation of grievances of wage workers against their employers. At times, these contests were waged against local employers; at other times, they were fought against distant corporations.[24] In Creston, Iowa, we see both operating. A local paper, the *Creston Daily Advertiser,* found itself in 1885 the object of a strike by its own printers, who enlisted support from local members of the Knights of Labor, railroad brotherhoods, union cigar makers, and locals of the Farmers' Alliance in the surrounding townships. Publisher S. A. Brewster argued that this strike pitted "labor against labor" and that "all the people of this city with but very few exceptions are working people."[25] Despite this position, he found himself alienated from large segments of the community that supported a new, rival newspaper, the *Workingmen's Advocate,* started by his striking printers. But three years later, he emphasized the countervailing community interest. In the midst of a bitter strike of railroad workers against the Chicago, Burlington and Quincy, the *Advertiser* again voiced the antimonopoly perspective, which, in its view, separated the interests of all members of the Creston community from outside corporations like the "arrogant" C. B. & Q.:

Aside from the principle involved, we deem it of vast interest to us and to every citizen of Creston and every town along the Q. line and every businessman, especially, that the boys win the present struggle. They are part of us; they are our best citizens. . . . Some have their all invested in a home, others have homes part paid for, and others have obligations contracted which if the strikers lose and were compelled to look elsewhere for employment, would be such a blow to the financial condition of our city that she would not recover for years to come.[26]

On such occasions, antimonopoly reform could fuse the interests of town promoters and members of the producing classes in opposition to the machinations of outside, eastern corporations. It encouraged a sentimental attachment to community that transcended differences in class and that celebrated an environment and sense of place in which sturdy values took root. A correspondent to the *Burlington Weekly Hawkeye* decried the way the corporate officers of the Chicago, Burlington and Quincy Railroad made "it a practice (warrior-like) of demanding tribute money every time they visit us, and threaten us, if we do not comply with their request, with total annihilation."[27] When strikes erupted in western towns, railroad company officials bemoaned the support that the strikers enjoyed from the "pastoral" governments and people in such states as Iowa and Nebraska. A lumber dealer from rural Afton, Iowa, reported to Charles Perkins, the C. B. & Q. president during the 1877 strikes, that "the railroad enemies here are confined to the 'granger element' with a few exceptions."[28] A few years later, a railroad official from Galesburg, Illinois, saw a regional pattern in the rapid growth of the Knights of Labor: "the farther west we go, the stronger the rolls of these 'Communist' societies seem to be."[29] Faced with polarized interests between outside, eastern

corporations and aggrieved community members, *Advertiser* publisher S. A. Brewster asserted that "leading citizens" had come to "feel that the proper thing is for us to stand up like men and ask for our rights" and to support "our *resident, property-owning, taxpaying, striking* brotherhood men."[30] Such alliances proved unstable, however, in the rapidly changing economies of western towns and their hinterlands.

In contrast to such sentimental reform built on cross-class alliances in local communities, a different kind of reform politics developed across the prairie and plains states in the late nineteenth century, reaching its fullest flower in the Populist movement of the 1890s and the Nonpartisan League of the World War I era. While the character of oppositional reform varied a good deal from region to region, and even state to state, the Populists carried antimonopoly sentiments to new heights and in some states elevated political reform to an alternative social and cultural vision of a cooperative commonwealth.[31] The Populists offered a program of practical reforms and a "democratic promise" of broader change. They looked toward government ownership of railroads, telegraphs, and mines; to a national currency and publicly financed cooperative marketing; to the eight-hour day and the enhancement of government power, even as they promised a revival of local democratic institutions.[32] Animating the Populists' vision, according to historian Lawrence Goodwyn, was a cooperative "movement culture" constructed by the Farmers' Alliance in the late 1880s. While the texture of the Populists' reform culture varied, as did its political practice, the Populists in the West functioned outside the two-party system, until a schism in their ranks led to fusion with the Bryan wing of the Democratic Party. Populist culture could be antiurban, as was Bryan, and racist, as it became with Georgia's Populist leader Tom Watson; its rhetoric of conspiracy could, with some leaders, take on an antisemitic, anti-immigrant cast.[33] But, even after fusion, Populists constituted a political movement that was at times covert and at other times volatile, fusing not with Democrats but with local socialists and urban workers, and occasionally manifesting near-insurrectionary impulses, as in the Oklahoma Green Corn Rebellion of 1917. Populism reconstituted itself on the northern plains in the World War I era as the Nonpartisan League and became a powerful, independent political force on the prairies of North Dakota and Minnesota. On the Canadian prairie, a political movement, paralleling that of the Populists and the Nonpartisan League, took shape and had lasting influence on Canadian reform politics in the twentieth century.[34]

Out of a shared legacy of nineteenth-century, midwestern antimonopolism, then, two different reform traditions crystallized by the 1890s and became powerful forces in American public life. The first, what I have called sentimental reform, celebrated western virtue and community solidarity. The second, oppositional reform, mobilized producers as a class to attack the sources of accumulation locally and nationally and to expand the power of government to build the economic foundations of an alternative, cooperative social order.

Sentimental reformers promised to restore health to American democracy through cross-class alliances and to cleanse society of the corrupting influence of corporate (usually eastern) power. If they did not seek the restoration of some pristine frontier condition of agrarian democracy, they rhetorically applauded the virtues of such a society. Sentimental reform provided one powerful influence in constituting what we have come to label "the progressive movement."[35] Russel Nye, whose perspective is perhaps closest to that of the sentimental reformers themselves, argued that for "the progressive

movement in the Middle West . . . the agricultural class, its roots deep in nineteenth-century agrarian radicalism, provided the impetus, while insurgent Republicanism provided the means of expression." It was "a distinctly regional movement, growing logically out of the recent past and consciously local in application."[36]

Progressivism drew from many sources in American political culture at the turn of the century. Campaigns against boss rule in American cities, led by mugwump reformers of middle-class and elite backgrounds, provided one source of inspiration. In the name of a finer and purer democracy, they sought to restrict the franchise, neutralize the influence of political parties, and narrow the scope of local government.[37] But progressives also drew inspiration from reform factions within both major parties that exercised great influence in key prairie states, primarily Iowa, Minnesota, and Wisconsin. Standpatters in the Republican Party, tied to the corporate colonization of the prairie states, found their control challenged by party insurgents who sought, in "the laboratory of the states," to use government to regulate corporate excesses and protect vulnerable populations. A third influence on progressivism lay in what some historians have referred to as the "domestication of American politics." Growing out of their experience on the home front during the Civil War, a new generation of female activists entered American reform politics in specific spheres—notably temperance, suffrage, and social settlement work. Each of these campaigns enjoyed strength in the prairie states and the West, where battles over temperance reshaped party loyalties, early suffrage victories were won, and the first settlement houses appeared. Through successful organization building and ideological innovation, women enlarged those outposts of reform in ways that made claims for their voices in public life.[38] By the turn of the century, women were playing central parts in a developing reform movement that attacked political corruption, corporate greed, and the social inefficiency bred by industrialization. Having grown accustomed to organizing on a gendered, cross-class basis, female reformers carried their experience into the wider progressive movement. They looked to the state and their own voluntary efforts to curtail the poverty, disease, and urban congestion spawned by industrialization.[39]

Progressive reformers sought to bridge the class chasm and renew democracy.[40] Influenced by the antimonopoly political culture they inherited, progressives hoped to rebuild democratic institutions by awakening a new civic responsibility that transcended class divisions. This progressive political culture continued to be nourished in direct and powerful ways by midwestern sources. Two vignettes illustrate those sources with particular clarity.

No state political figure looms larger in the midwestern reform movement of the late nineteenth century than Robert M. La Follette.[41] As a young, talented, and ambitious politician, La Follette had risen rapidly in the ranks of the Republican Party of Wisconsin. Unwilling to bide his time in loyal service to party bosses Philetus Sawyer and Henry Payne, La Follette ran successfully in the 1880s against his own party's incumbent for Dane County district attorney and for Congress. He developed a direct style of campaigning in rural parts of his district. He recalled driving through the country at harvest time, climbing fences, and talking to farmers and their hired help in the fields. These "hardheaded old pioneers . . . who thought as they plowed, went far toward roughing out the doctrine in regard to railroad control which the country has since adopted." He "never fully lost the effect" of that "movement of Grangers swirling about" him as he was growing up on a farm

in rural Dane County, Wisconsin.[42] Defeated in the Democratic landslide of 1890, he returned to the party fold and his law practice.

The turning point in La Follette's development as a "progressive" came in 1891. In his own carefully constructed autobiographical account, written years later, La Follette portrayed his career as a constant battle with "the special interests." He claimed to have been offered a bribe by Philetus Sawyer to use his influence in thwarting an investigation into Republican Party financial abuses.[43] (Sawyer asserted that he was only seeking to retain the best defense lawyer he could find for the pending court case.) Although read out of the Republican Party after he publicized the incident, La Follette campaigned throughout the state for young, insurgent Republicans. Their gratitude and La Follette's own ambition led to the formation of a reform faction based in rural, Scandinavian areas of the state that had always felt neglected by the machine. A new politics of reform crystallized by 1900 within the Republican Party and catapulted La Follette into the governorship. Only gradually did his full program of progressive reforms take shape, defined as much by the changing times in the Midwest as by his own vision of democratic renewal.[44] The progressive program in Wisconsin, like that in Iowa, Minnesota, and other midwestern states, focused on three areas of long-standing interest to reformers and their constituents: direct democracy (direct primaries, initiative and referendum, restrictions on lobbying), corporate regulation (of railroads, grain elevators, banks, and insurance companies), and health and safety of the people (factory and mine safety, pure food and drugs, workmen's compensation, protective legislation for women and children). This reform program, rooted in the politics of the prairies, made its way into the national reform agenda of progressives.

In Jane Addams, the progressive movement acquired its saint. Addams, too, shaped her identity autobiographically by representing the influences that had nurtured her reform sensibilities and the tough-minded reform politics she shared with an influential group of women of her generation.[45] Her values were cradled in the culture of a prairie village in northern Illinois. In Cedarville, destitution was hardly known and social harmony seemed a by-product of the soil itself. When she was just a few years into the Hull House experiment in a poor immigrant neighborhood of Chicago, Addams encountered bitter class conflict during the Pullman strike of 1894. Her response to the strike drew on the political culture of her Illinois roots, embodied in a mythical Abraham Lincoln, whom she had learned as a child to revere.

Coming on the heels of two decades of bitter class conflict, the massive Pullman strike seemed to portend the utter breakdown of society into warring classes. For Jane Addams, whose Hull House had opened its doors to the poor in 1889, the strike brought enormous distress. She depended on the goodwill and financial support of Chicago's elite, but settlement workers confronted directly the tribulations of the strikers and their families. Addams recalled that because "the settlement maintained avenues of intercourse with both sides," it had "the opportunity for nothing but a realization of the bitterness and division along class lines." She recalled having encountered an acquaintance, as she left a "futile" meeting of the arbitration committee on which she served, who declaimed that "'the strikers should all be shot.'" But she also remembered the broken, blacklisted English workingman of "a superior type" who, she said, "seemed to me an epitome of the wretched human waste such a strike implies." The strike and its poignant human consequences revealed her own "constant dread of spreading ill will."[46]

Addams most clearly revealed her determination to bridge the divisions between classes and restore social harmony in the pilgrimage she undertook at the height of the strike to the newly erected statue of Abraham Lincoln near Chicago's lakefront. She gave the episode a prominent place in her autobiography:

I walked the wearisome way from Hull-House to Lincoln Park—for no cars were running regularly at that moment of sympathetic strikes—in order to look at and gain magnanimous counsel, if I might, from the marvelous St. Gaudens statue. . . . Some of Lincoln's immortal words were cut into the stone at his feet, and never did a distracted town more sorely need the healing of "with charity towards all" than did Chicago at that moment, and the tolerance of the man who had won charity for those on both sides of "an irrepressible conflict."[47]

For many midwestern progressives like Addams, the Lincoln of their imaginations functioned as a political touchstone. Both Ida Tarbell and Albert Beveridge periodically took up Lincoln as a consuming passion.[48] And none provided a more popular (even if more flawed) rendering of Lincoln as the embodiment of prairie political virtue than Carl Sandburg in his multivolume celebration of the formative influence of Lincoln's "prairie years." His Lincoln was, as one historian has noted, "a profoundly indigenous character, one who grew from the common folk and the great national experience of pioneering." Sandburg's words evoke the prairie environment that nurtured Lincoln's democratic values:

He lived with trees, with the bush wet with shining raindrops, with the burning bush of autumn, with the lone wild duck riding a north wind and crying down on a line north to south, the faces of open sky and weather, the ax which is an individual one-man instrument, these he had for companions, books, friends, talkers, chums of his endless changing soliloquies. . . . He grew as hickory grows, the torso lengthening and toughening. The sap mounted, the branches spread, leaves came with wind clamor in them.[49]

In his representation of Lincoln, and even more in his construction of himself as what Ben Hecht has termed the "peepul's poet" of his Chicago years, Sandburg celebrated his own humble prairie roots. He dedicated his Lincoln biography to his parents, August and Clara Sandburg, as "Workers on the Illinois Prairie." His Lincoln was, as he wrote, "the biography of the son of an illiterate mother written by the son of an illiterate father." But Sandburg also shaped his identity as a prairie poet of the common people through his explicit emulation of Walt Whitman. In *Chicago Poems,* Sandburg defined for himself a poetic and political identity that explicitly echoed Whitman's "Song of Myself." As Blair Whitney notes, Sandburg connected the people's strength to the land in his poem "I Am the People, the Mob":

I am the people—the mob—the crowd—the mass.
Do you know that all the great work of the world is
    done through me?
I am the workingman, the inventor, the maker of the
    world's food and clothes.
I am the audience that witnesses history. The
    Napoleons come from me and the Lincolns. They
    die. And then I send forth more Napoleans and
    Lincolns.
I am the seed ground. I am a prairie that will stand
    for much plowing. Terrible storms pass over me.
    I forget. Everything but Death comes to me and
    makes me work and give up what I have. And I
    forget.
When I, the People, learn to remember, when I, the
    People, use the lessons of yesterday and no longer
    forget who robbed me last year, who played me
    for a fool—then there will be no speaker in all the
    world say the name: "The People," with any fleck
    of a sneer in his voice or any far-off smile of
    derision.
The mob—the crowd—the mass—will arrive then.[50]

Sandburg's poetry, like his political identity, tacked through the prairie's varied political cultures of reform. As the son of a railroad shopman, hungry for education and aware of his precarious social position, he cultivated a persona that merged the talents of an aspiring lecturer, a dogged poet, and an encyclopedia salesman. But as a young organizer for Eugene Debs's Socialist Party, he marshaled his own immigrant, working-class background to attack the class structure of American society, seeking to empower its workers and himself. In his Chicago poems, he conceived a proletarian city of "big shoulders"—restless, powerful, but driven only to immediate gratification. In his poems collected in *Cornhuskers,* his portrait of Lincoln, his folkloric renderings of America, and his Depression-era poetry, *The People, Yes,* he conjured up a classless America and a diffuse midwestern progressivism that celebrated a common democratic culture, community solidarity, and social harmony.

Two traditions of reform politics were nurtured in the social and economic changes that swept across the prairie states in the late nineteenth century. One, represented in the poetry of Carl Sandburg (and Vachel Lindsay) and in the political vision of midwestern progressives like Robert La Follette and Jane Addams, cultivated a social and cultural solidarity that embodied democratic virtue and transcended class divisions. It called forth a sentimental appreciation of past communities and the common people, but it also served as a reservoir of antimonopoly sentiment critical of political corruption that threatened the region's democratic social order.

The second tradition was more explicitly oppositional and utopian. It stressed exploitation and inequity in the past, not some idealized community; it attacked the hegemony of capitalist power and the need for solidarity of plain people, regardless of race. In its most expansive form, this vision explicitly encompassed women, Native Americans, blacks, and the latest immigrants. It is expressed in the "one hoss philosophy" of Julius Wayland, the editor of the socialist weekly *Appeal to Reason,* published in Girard, Kansas; in Jack Conroy's Depression-era literary/political journal, the *Anvil,* published in Missouri; and among "grassroots socialists" from North Dakota to Oklahoma. By the 1930s, Jack Conroy, Meridel Le Sueur, Nelson Algren, and other midwestern radical writers hoped to forge an independent, revolutionary culture in the Midwest as part of a broader cultural and social revolution. Rejecting what she termed the "idealistic duality of New England culture," Le Sueur spoke for the group at the American Writers' Congress in 1935: "Now we know where to put down our roots, that have never been put down, that have been waiting through a bad season. . . . We, of the petty bourgeois and the working class, have been dissenters, individual madmen, anarchists against the machine; but now the Middle Western mind is finding its place."[51] This search for a more revolutionary prairie political culture has been at various times subterranean, always unofficial, and usually subversive of more established traditions of political progressivism.

The prairie roots of the oppositional culture of reform are nowhere captured better than in Le Sueur's poetry. Her connections to that tradition were lineal, direct, and powerful. From the harsh beauty of the prairie landscape and the struggles of the people who inhabited it, she drew personal and political nourishment. Her poem "The Ancient People and the Newly Come" both echoes a tradition of prairie radicalism and illustrates its endurance:

Born out of the caul of winter in the north, in the swing and circle of the horizon, I am rocked in the ancient land. As a child I first read the scriptures written on the scroll of frozen moisture by wolf and rabbit, by the ancient people and the newly come. In the beginning of the century the Indian smoke still mingled with ours. The frontier of the whites was violent, already injured by vast seizures and massacres. The winter nightmares of fear poisoned the plains nights with psychic airs of theft and utopia. The stolen wheat in the cathedrallike granaries cried out for vengeance.

Most of all one was born into space, into the great resonance of space, a magnetic midwestern valley through which the winds clashed in lassoes of thunder and lightning at the apex of the sky, the very wrath of God. . . .

I had been conceived in the riotous summer and fattened on light and stars that fell on my underground roots, and every herb, corn plant, cricket, beaver, red fox leaped in me in the old Indian dark. I saw everything was moving and entering. The rocking of mother and prairie breast curved around me within the square. The field crows flew in my flesh and cawed in my dream.

Crouching together on Indian land in the long winters, we grew in sight and understanding, heard the rumbling of glacial moraines, clung to the edge of holocaust forest fires, below-zero weather, grasshopper plagues, sin, wars, crop failures, drouth, and the mortgage. The severity of the seasons and the strangeness of a new land, with those whose land had been seized looking in our windows, created a tension of guilt and a tightening of sin. We were often snowed in, the villages invisible and inaccessible in cliffs of snow. People froze following the rope to their barns to feed the cattle. But the cyclic renewal and strength of the old prairie earth, held sacred by thousands of years of Indian ritual, the guerrilla soil of the Americas, taught and nourished us.[52]

Le Sueur conveys not a tranquil, sentimental, and harmonious landscape of some arcadian midwestern past, but a violent and severe "ancient land" whose "cyclic renewal" and strength as a "guerrilla soil" nourished her oppositional sensibilities, as it had a long tradition of reform in which she situated herself.

Notes

1. John A. Johnson, quoted in Russel B. Nye, *Midwestern Progressive Politics: A Historical Study of Its Origins and Development, 1870–1958* (Lansing: Michigan State University Press, 1959), 223–24.

2. On the meaning of the Midwest as a region, see James R. Shortridge, *The Middle West: Its Meaning in American Culture* (Lawrence: University Press of Kansas, 1989).

3. Russel B. Nye, "Has the Midwest Ceased to Protest?" in *The Midwest: Myth or Reality?* ed. Thomas T. McAvoy et al. (South Bend, Ind.: University of Notre Dame Press, 1961), 1; Nye, *Midwestern Progressive Politics,* 13, 4, 21–22.

4. Vachel Lindsay, "Bryan, Bryan, Bryan, Bryan," in *Collected Poems* (New York: Macmillan, 1923), 98–99, 103–4.

5. Edgar Lee Masters, "Give Us Back Our Country," quoted in *The Vision of This Land: Studies of Vachel Lindsay, Edgar Lee Masters, and Carl Sandburg,* ed. John E. Hallwas and Dennis J. Reader (Macomb: Western Illinois University Press, 1976), 8.

6. William Jennings Bryan, "A Cross of Gold," in *Myth and Reality in the Populist Revolt,* ed. Edwin Rozwenc and John C. Matlon (Boston: Heath, 1967), 28.

7. The literature on late-nineteenth-century antimonopoly reform is enormous. On the cross-class character of these movements, see, for instance, George Miller, *The Railroads and the Granger Laws* (Madison: University of Wisconsin Press, 1971); Herbert Gutman, "Workers' Search for Power: Labor in the Gilded Age," in *The Gilded Age: A Reappraisal,* ed. H. Wayne Morgan (Syracuse, N.Y.: Syracuse University Press, 1963), 31–53; and Robert Wiebe, *Self-Rule: A Cultural History of American Democracy* (Chicago: University of Chicago Press, 1995). On the reformist disposition of the Farmers' Alliance and the political dynamics of reform in a two-party system, see Jeffrey Ostler, *Prairie Populism: The Fate of Agrarian Radicalism in Kansas, Nebraska, and Iowa, 1880–1892* (Lawrence: University Press of Kansas, 1993). Robert Wiebe stresses the reform impulses that emanated from the efforts of midwestern "island communities" to restore an order of small producers in *The Search for Order, 1877–1920* (New York: Hill and Wang, 1967).

8. Bryan, "Cross of Gold," 25.

9. Wiebe, *Search for Order;* Samuel P. Hays, *The Response to Industrialism* (Chicago: University of Chicago Press, 1957). I would not want to make too exclusive a claim for the regional origins of progressive reform. Clearly, other influences were also at work, sometimes with different agendas. However, it is undeniable that midwestern progressivism, especially at the state and municipal levels of politics, had a particular vitality and did exert a powerful influence nationally. For an account of the progressive movement that stresses its cross-class reform agenda, see Shelton Stromquist, *Reinventing a "People": The Progressive Movement and the Class Question* (forthcoming).

10. The more radical, utopian strand of reform is also found within the producerist movements of the nineteenth century. For a discussion of those tendencies in the Knights of Labor, see, for instance, Leon Fink, "The New Labor History and the Powers of Historical Pessimism: Consensus, Hegemony, and the Case of the Knights of Labor," *Journal of American History* 75 (1988): 115–61; and Robert Weir, *Beyond Labor's Veil: The Culture of the Knights of Labor* (State College: Pennsylvania State University Press, 1996). Lawrence Goodwyn explores the distinctive "movement culture" of the Farmers' Alliance and the early Populist Party in *Democratic Promise: The Populist Moment in America* (New York: Oxford University Press, 1976). On the utopian strains of political thought, see John L. Thomas, *Alternative America: Henry George, Edward Bellamy, Henry Demarest Lloyd, and the Adversary Tradition* (Cambridge, Mass.: Belknap Press, 1983). For a discussion of the structure of class relations in new areas of settlement, see Alan Trachtenberg, *The Incorporation of America: Culture and Society in the Gilded Age* (New York: Hill and Wang, 1982), 11–37, and Shelton Stromquist, *A Generation of Boomers: The Pattern of Railroad Labor Conflict in Nineteenth-Century America* (Urbana: University of Illinois Press, 1987), 164–87.

11. The life of Eugene V. Debs embodies in many ways the course of nineteenth-century producerism, which transformed a strand of republican ideology into a socialist vision that retained its commitment to democratic principles and a cooperative economy. See, especially, Nick Salvatore, *Eugene V. Debs: Citizen and Socialist* (Urbana: University of Illinois Press, 1982). On the capacity of producerist movements to overcome racist and nativist visions of community, see Lawrence Goodwyn, "Populist Dreams and Negro Rights: East Texas as a Case Study," *American Historical Review* 76 (1971): 1435–57; Peter Rachleff, *Black Labor in Richmond, 1865–1890* (Urbana: University of Illinois Press, 1989); and Walter Nugent, *The Tolerant Populists: Kansas Populism and Nativism* (Chicago: University of Chicago Press, 1963). But, alternatively, several works stress the racial construction of working-class and reformers' identities in the nineteenth century, notably David Roediger, *The Wages of Whiteness: Race and the Making of the American Working Class* (London: Verso, 1991); Alexander Saxton, *The Rise and Fall of the White Republic: Class Politics and Mass Culture in Nineteenth-Century America* (London: Verso, 1990); and Michael Kazin, *The Barons of Labor: The San Francisco Building Trades and Union Power in the Progressive Era* (Urbana: University of Illinois Press, 1987). On the debate over conspiracy thinking in the populist movement, see Jeffrey Ostler, "The Rhetoric of Conspiracy and the Formation of Kansas Populism," *Agricultural History* 69 (1995): 1–27.

12. Still the most useful general study of the Nonpartisan League is Robert Morlan, *Political Prairie Fire: The Nonpartisan League, 1915–1922* (Minneapolis: University of Minnesota Press, 1955).

13. American exceptionalism is deeply intertwined with nineteenth-century political thought and popular politics. A range of foreign travelers helped to construct that sense of national identity, especially Alexis de Tocqueville, *Democracy in America* (Cambridge, Mass.: Sever and Francis, 1862). See also J. Hector St. John de Crevecoeur, *Letters from an American Farmer; and Sketches of Eighteenth-Century America* (1782; reprint, New York: Penguin, 1981), and, on the construction of a distinctive American

language, Kenneth Cmiel, *Democratic Eloquence: The Fight over Popular Speech in Nineteenth-Century America* (New York: Morrow, 1990). Exceptionalist rhetoric came to pervade political rhetoric as well as early academic thought. See Dorothy Ross, *The Origins of American Social Science* (New York: Cambridge University Press, 1991). Contesting that exceptionalist paradigm, which continues to infect historical scholarship on nineteenth-century reform, see Sean Wilentz, "Against Exceptionalism," *International Labor and Working-Class History* 26 (1984): 1–24, and Kim Voss, *The Making of American Exceptionalism: The Knights of Labor and Class Formation in the Nineteenth Century* (Ithaca, N.Y.: Cornell University Press, 1993). For discussion of the racial formation of white Americans' identity with respect to African Americans and Indians, see George Fredrickson, *The Black Image in the White Mind: The Debate on Afro-American Character and Destiny, 1817–1914* (New York: Harper & Row, 1971), and Robert F. Berkhofer, Jr., *The White Man's Indian: Images of the American Indian from Columbus to the Present* (New York: Random House, 1978).

14. Trachtenberg, *Incorporation of America*, 11–37. On the ways in which western railway travel reshaped Americans' perceptions of the landscape and themselves, see Wolfgang Schivelbusch, *The Railway Journey: The Industrialization of Time and Space in the 19th Century* (Berkeley: University of California Press, 1986).

15. Nye, *Midwestern Progressive Politics*, 4.

16. For the imprint of a distinctive geography on the social and economic development of the Midwest, especially the Mississippi Valley, see Timothy R. Mahoney, *River Towns in the Great West: The Structure of Provincial Urbanization in the American Midwest, 1820–1870* (New York: Cambridge University Press, 1990). The influence of transportation and urban growth are discussed in Michael Conzen, "A Transport Interpretation of the Growth of Urban Regions: An American Example," *Journal of Historical Geography* 1 (1975): 361–85, and William Cronon, *Nature's Metropolis: Chicago and the Great West* (New York: Norton, 1991). Case studies that emphasize regionally distinctive patterns of social development are Don

Harrison Doyle, *The Social Order of a Frontier Community: Jacksonville, Illinois, 1825–70* (Urbana: University of Illinois Press, 1983), and Nellie Kremenak, "Urban Workers in the Agricultural Middle West, 1856–1893: With a Case Study of Fort Dodge and Webster County, Iowa" (Ph.D. diss., University of Iowa, 1995).

17. On the anti-eastern rhetoric of Copperhead opposition to the Civil War, see Russell Johnson, "An Army for Industrialization: The Civil War and the Formation of Urban-Industrial Society in a Northern City" (Ph.D. diss., University of Iowa, 1996), 142–45.

18. Doyle discusses the "inversion of boosterism" that colored representations of the past in communities bypassed by substantial urban and manufacturing development in the later nineteenth century in *Social Order of a Frontier Community,* 255–59.

19. John Mack Faragher, *Sugar Creek: Life on the Illinois Prairie* (New Haven, Conn.: Yale University Press, 1986), 190; Edgar Lee Masters, *The Sangamon,* quoted in Faragher, *Sugar Creek,* 234–35.

20. Frank Norris, *The Pit,* quoted in Cronon, *Nature's Metropolis,* 3.

21. Fred Shannon, *American Farmers' Movements* (Princeton, N.J.: Princeton University Press, 1957); Ray Allen Billington, *Westward Expansion: A History of the American Frontier* (New York: Macmillan, 1982); Ostler, *Prairie Populism,* 14. Allan Bogue describes the changing conditions in the late-nineteenth-century Midwest that led prairie farmers to relocate westward as farm prices rose in *From Prairie to Cornbelt: Farming on the Illinois and Iowa Prairies in the Nineteenth Century* (Chicago: University of Chicago Press, 1963), 266, 283–87.

22. Solon Buck, *The Granger Movement: A Study of the Agricultural Organization and Its Political, Economic, and Social Manifestations, 1870–1880* (Lincoln: University of Nebraska Press, 1963); Miller, *Railroads and the Granger Laws;* Thomas A. Woods, *Knights of the Plow: Oliver H. Kelley and the Origins of the Grange in Republican Ideology* (Ames: Iowa State University Press, 1991); Margaret Dorsey Phelps, "Farmer Deprivation and Organization in 1872: Anti-Railroad Sentiment Before the Granger Law" (master's thesis, University of Iowa, 1985).

23. The turmoil in midwestern politics engendered by popular insurgencies of one variety or another are discussed in Frederick Emory Haynes, *Third Party Movements Since the Civil War, with Special Reference to Iowa: A Study in Politics* (Iowa City: State Historical Society of Iowa, 1916); Ostler, *Prairie Populism;* Dorothy Schwieder, *Iowa: The Middle Land* (Ames: Iowa State University Press, 1996); Kremenak, "Urban Workers in the Agricultural Middle West"; Leon Fink, *Workingmen's Democracy: The Knights of Labor and American Politics* (Urbana: University of Illinois Press, 1983); and Ralph Scharnau, "Workers and Politics: The Knights of Labor in Dubuque, Iowa, 1885–1890," *Annals of Iowa* 48 (1987): 353–77.

24. For differences in antimonopoly sentiment among cities and towns in the Midwest, see Stromquist, *Generation of Boomers,* 158–74.

25. *Creston Daily Advertiser,* 30 March, 28 April 1885.

26. *Creston Daily Advertiser,* 4 March 1888.

27. *Burlington Weekly Hawkeye,* 11 May 1858.

28. C. E. Perkins to Mr. Walker, 22 July 1877; G. W. Beymer to C. E. Perkins, 25 July 1877, Strike Papers, 1887, Burlington Archives, Newberry Library, Chicago.

29. R. W. Colville to G. W. Rhodes, 25 August 1885, "Engineers Grievance Committee Papers, 1885–86," Burlington Archives, Newberry Library.

30. *Creston Daily Advertiser,* 12 August 1885, 4 April 1888.

31. In *Democratic Promise,* Goodwyn has offered the most compelling portrait of the alternative political vision the populists articulated. See also Peter Argersinger, *The Limits of Agrarian Radicalism: Western Populism and American Politics* (Lawrence: University Press of Kansas, 1995).

32. "The Omaha Platform," in *The Populist Mind,* ed. Norman Pollack (Indianapolis: Bobbs-Merrill, 1967), 96–100.

33. On the populists and fusion, see Argersinger, *Limits of Agrarian Radicalism,* and Robert C. McMath, *American Populism: A Social History, 1877–1898* (New York: Hill and Wang, 1993). Also useful is Chester M. Destler, *American Radicalism, 1865–1901: Essays and Documents* (New York: Octagon Books,

1965). The debate over the populists' racism and anti-Semitism has generated considerable heat in the historical literature, including Richard M. Hofstadter, *The Age of Reform* (New York: Knopf, 1955); Norman Pollack, *The Populist Response to Industrial America: Midwestern Populist Thought* (Cambridge, Mass.: Harvard University Press, 1962); Nugent, *Tolerant Populists;* and Ostler, "Rhetoric of Conspiracy." The most dramatic shift in populist appeals toward racism was represented in the career of Georgia's Tom Watson, as recounted in C. Vann Woodward, *Tom Watson: Agrarian Rebel* (New York: Macmillan, 1938).

34. James Green, *Grassroots Socialism: Radical Movements in the Southwest, 1895–1943* (Baton Rouge: Louisiana State University Press, 1978), 360–66; Elliot Shore, *Talkin' Socialism: J. A. Wayland and the Role of the Press in American Radicalism, 1890–1912* (Lawrence: University Press of Kansas, 1988); Robert L. Morlan, *Political Prairie Fire: The Nonpartisan League, 1915–1922* (Minneapolis: University of Minnesota Press, 1955); Seymour Martin Lipset, *Agrarian Socialism: The Cooperative Commonwealth Federation in Saskatchewan: A Study in Political Sociology* (Berkeley: University of California Press, 1950); David Laycock, *Populism and Democratic Thought in the Canadian Prairies, 1910 to 1945* (Toronto: University of Toronto Press, 1990).

35. The meaning, even the existence, of a "progressive movement" was questioned by Peter G. Filene, "An Obituary for 'The Progressive Movement,'" *American Quarterly* 22 (1970): 20–34. See also Daniel Rodgers, "In Search of Progressivism," *Reviews in American History,* December 1982, 113–31, and Stromquist, *Reinventing a "People."*

36. Nye, *Midwestern Progressive Politics,* 222–23.

37. On the origins of mugwump opposition to machine politics, see Seymour Mandelbaum, *Boss Tweed's New York* (New York: Wiley, 1965); John G. Sproat, *The Best Men: Liberal Reformers in the Gilded Age* (New York: Oxford University Press, 1968); and Martin Shefter, *Political Parties and the State: The American Historical Experience* (Princeton, N.J.: Princeton University Press, 1994).

38. The argument is developed in Paula Baker, "The Domestication of Politics," in *Women, the State,* *and Welfare,* ed. Linda Gordon (Madison: University of Wisconsin Press, 1990). For a particularly important biographical account of the new politics, see Kathryn Kish Sklar, *Florence Kelley and the Nation's Work* (New Haven, Conn.: Yale University Press, 1995). On the generational shifts in women's activism, see Carroll Smith-Rosenberg, *Disorderly Conduct: Visions of Gender in Victorian America* (New York: Knopf, 1985).

39. For accounts of these developments, see Robyn Muncy, *Creating a Female Dominion in American Reform, 1890–1935* (New York: Oxford University Press, 1991); Theda Skocpol, *Protecting Soldiers and Mothers: Political Origins of Social Policy in the United States* (Cambridge, Mass.: Harvard University Press, 1992); and Mina Carson, *Settlement Folk: Social Thought and the American Settlement Movement, 1885–1930* (Chicago: University of Chicago Press, 1990).

40. Central figures in articulating this democratic vision of reform were John Dewey and Jane Addams. See Robert Westbrook, *John Dewey and American Democracy* (Ithaca, N.Y.: Cornell University Press, 1991), and Jane Addams, *Twenty Years at Hull-House* (New York: Macmillan, 1910).

41. Useful accounts of La Follette's early political career may be found in David P. Thelen, *Robert M. La Follette and the Insurgent Spirit* (Boston: Little, Brown, 1976), and Robert M. Maxwell, *La Follette and the Rise of the Progressives in Wisconsin* (Madison: University of Wisconsin Press, 1956).

42. Robert M. La Follette, *La Follette's Autobiography: A Personal Narrative of Political Experiences* (Madison: University of Wisconsin Press, 1913), 5, 18–19.

43. Ibid., 138–62.

44. Roger Wyman, "Voting Behavior in the Progressive Era: Wisconsin, a Case Study" (Ph.D. diss., University of Wisconsin, 1970). For the parallel story of Republican Party factionalism in Iowa, see Mark Carlile, "The Trials of Progressivism: Iowa Voting Behavior in the Progressive Era, 1901–1916" (Ph.D. diss., University of Iowa, 1995).

45. The most compelling accounts of the settlement movement are still Addams, *Twenty Years at*

Hull-House, and *The Second Twenty Years at Hull-House* (New York: Macmillan, 1930). See also Allen F. Davis, *Spearheads of Reform: The Social Settlements and the Progressive Movement, 1890–1914* (New York: Oxford University Press, 1967).

46. Addams, *Twenty Years at Hull-House,* 158–61.

47. Ibid., 38–39.

48. Merrill D. Peterson, *Lincoln in American Memory* (New York: Oxford University Press, 1994), 279.

49. Quoted in ibid., 276–77.

50. Carl Sandburg, *Chicago Poems* (New York: Henry Holt and Co., 1916), 172; also quoted and discussed in Penelope Niven, *Carl Sandburg: A Biography* (New York: Scribner, 1991), 223–24. See also Blair Whitney, "The Garden of Illinois," in *Vision of This Land,* ed. Hallwas and Reader, 19.

51. Quoted in Douglas Wixson, *Worker-Writer in America: Jack Conroy and the Tradition of Midwestern Literary Radicalism, 1898–1990* (Urbana: University of Illinois Press, 1994), 359, 365, 425–26.

52. Meridel Le Sueur, "The Ancient People and the Newly Come," in *Growing Up in Minnesota: Ten Writers Remember Their Childhoods,* ed. Chester G. Anderson (Minneapolis: University of Minnesota Press, 1976), 17–18. Reprinted by permission of the publisher.

7 The Landscape Art of Jens Jensen

Robert E. Grese

Working out of Chicago at the turn of the century, Jens Jensen (1860–1951) was one of the first landscape architects from the Middle West to champion a style of design based on the distinctive qualities of the landscape found in the prairie states (Figure 7.1). His designs were a celebration of regional nature. He wanted people to experience the cycles and subtle beauties of the land. In the mosaic of savannas, prairies, wetlands, woodlands, and dunes found around Chicago, Jensen saw a diversity and quiet beauty that many other designers overlooked. His work featured

- The relatively flat or rolling topography of the prairie
- Slow quiet rivers and wetlands
- Interplay of sunlight and vegetation
- Expressions of the spatial quality of the landscape
- Textures of stones and vegetation
- Ecological patterns
- Seasonal changes

One of the major themes of Jensen's career was his attempt to awaken others to this beauty that was rapidly being lost. He noted that cities dulled people to the wonder and subtlety of nature. He wanted to inspire them to celebrate the peculiar qualities of the Middle West as well as to foster a spirit of conservation and stewardship.

Jensen was born in Dybbol, Denmark, in 1860. Many of his childhood experiences shaped his attitudes toward the landscape that later found expression in his design work. The low dunes of Denmark, with their broad view over the ocean, gave Jensen a feeling of unlimited space and freedom that he also found in the prairie region of the United States. Likewise, the favored plants of his youth, such as the hawthorn and wild rose, had complements in the Midwest. With his family and in his studies at the Danish folk schools, Jensen learned to celebrate the changes of the seasons and marveled at the legends and mysteries associated with the Danish landscape and its history. He felt that the United States had less developed cultural traditions associated with the landscape and sought to address that need through his design work and conservation activities.[1]

Jensen's schooling included no formal design training, but he did study horticultural arts at the Tune agricultural school in preparation for taking over the family farm. Two years in the German military in Berlin exposed him to the trends of urban park design, and he developed

Figure 7.1. Jens Jensen at the site of the Lincoln Memorial Garden, Springfield, Illinois. (Courtesy of Lincoln Memorial Garden)

strong preferences for naturalistic parks that provided a direct contrast to the city.[2]

In 1884, Jensen immigrated to the United States, working briefly on farms in Florida and Iowa before settling in Chicago, where he became a street sweeper for the West Parks. To support his young family, he worked for nurseryman Swain Nelson in the off-season and learned much about local nursery and garden practices in the Chicago area.[3] At the same time, he spent considerable time exploring the wilds around Chicago, wandering about the prairies, dunes, and woodlands much as he had as a youth in Denmark (Figure 7.2).[4] Gradually, he became expert in much of the native flora and was fascinated by the relationship of plants and their distribution to the geomorphology of the region.[5]

The turn of the century, when Jensen was beginning his career, was a time of rapid change in the United States. The nation was changing from an agricultural society run on horsepower to an industrial society based on fossil fuels and the automobile. Development was particularly rapid around the Chicago region and resulted in tremendous inequities of wealth and differential access to open space and other city resources. Chicago's leaders were clearly intent on making

Figure 7.2. Jensen's photograph of sand barrens in the Indiana Dunes. (Courtesy of Jens Jensen Collection, Bentley Historical Library, University of Michigan, Ann Arbor)

their city a regional and then an international center, and a number of social reformers, such as Jane Addams, were intent on acculturating recent immigrants and assisting the lower economic classes.[6]

A system of city park districts had been established in 1869, and leaders aspired to make Chicago into the "Paris" of the Midwest.[7] For the designs of the parks, the South Park District hired Frederick Law Olmsted, Sr., Calvert Vaux, and Horace William Shaler Cleveland. The Lincoln Park District hired local nurserymen Olof Bensen and Swain Nelson, and the West Parks engaged Chicago engineer and architect William Le Baron Jenney, who had studied in Paris.[8]

Each of the park districts had its particular challenges: low swampy ground and dry barrens in the South Park, sand dunes in Lincoln Park, and heavy clay prairie soils in the West Parks. Seemingly, the planners felt that the land had to be dramatically transformed to be useful as park scenery. Hence the "dismal monotony of original prairie and swamp" found in Washington Park would be transformed by Olmsted, Vaux, and Cleveland into a large meadow and bordering woods.[9] In Lincoln Park, the sands were transformed into lawns and open groves by bringing in topsoil from local farms. In the West Parks, Jenney followed both the Olmstedian and French picturesque traditions with formal gar-

Figure 7.3. "Pavilion in Humboldt Park." This scene clearly shows the character of the park as designed by William Le Baron Jenney. (From Alfred Theodore Andreas, *History of Chicago,* vol. 3, 1871–1885 [Chicago: A. T. Andreas, 1886])

dens at park entrances, dense plantings of trees and shrubs around park borders, picturesque stonework, and a variety of rustic chalets, refectories, pavilions, bridges, and other structures (Figure 7.3).[10]

Gradually, Jensen worked his way up the ranks within the West Parks and by 1888 was allowed to experiment with a redesign of a corner of Union Park that he called the "American Garden." Jensen featured locally native plants gathered from around the countryside and, through an idealization of the regional landscape, attempted to reconnect local people with their natural heritage, which was quickly being lost.[11] Through this forgotten garden, he established a theme of conservation that characterized his entire career. Like the other social reformers of his period—Jane Addams and the like—he also committed himself to promoting parks as a way of humanizing the increasingly

industrial city. As Jensen continued to demonstrate his abilities in administering and providing leadership in the parks, he was given increased responsibilities. In 1895, he became superintendent of Union Park and, in 1896, superintendent of Humboldt Park. His rise through the ranks came to an abrupt halt in 1900 when he was fired for having refused to participate in the graft then rampant in the park districts. His separation from the parks was to be short-lived, however, and in 1905 he was rehired as superintendent and landscape architect of all the West Parks when prominent businessman Bernard Eckhart was appointed chair of the West Park Commissioners and was charged with cleaning up the system.[12]

Jensen's brief interlude away from the parks forced him to broaden his career and allowed him to experiment with his evolving ideas about design in private commissions. Collaborations

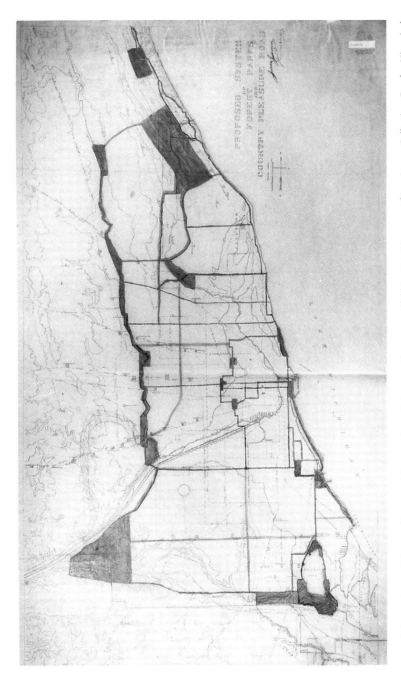

Figure 7.4. Jens Jensen, "Proposed System of Forest Parks and Country Pleasure Road[s]" (1903). (Courtesy of Jens Jensen Collection, Bentley Historical Library, University of Michigan, Ann Arbor)

with many of the young architects then establishing their careers in Chicago also helped him cultivate personal friendships and build a broader professional reputation among local designers. Working at his kitchen table, Jensen produced a balance of residential and commercial work throughout Chicago, particularly in the northern suburbs. Among these early collaborations was his work with Hugh M. G. Garden on St. Ann's Hospital in Chicago in 1899,[13] with George Maher on the Rubens estate in Glencoe in 1903, on Dwight Perkins's house in Evanston in 1904, and with Robert Spencer on the A. C. Magnus estate in Winnetka in 1904.[14] After his rehiring in 1905, Jensen had the unique opportunity to reshape Chicago's West Parks. The earlier designs by William Le Baron Jenney and engineer Oscar Dubuis had never been fully implemented, and much of the park district's facilities had fallen into disrepair.[15]

By this time, Jensen was extremely knowledgeable about the Chicago landscape through informal outings with his family into nearby wilds, through his involvement in local scientific organizations such as the Geographic Society of Chicago, and through his friendship with Henry Chandler Cowles and George D. Fuller of the University of Chicago, who were building a solid program on plant ecology.[16] Jensen himself even wrote scientific articles on plant distribution and soil types around Lake Michigan during this period.[17] In addition, he had served as a member of the Special Park Commission, which had been established in 1899 and charged with formulating plans for a regional park system for the Chicago area. Jensen's architect friend Dwight Perkins was the chair, and the landscape architect Ossian Cole Simonds was a member of the original commission. It is not clear when Jensen joined the commission, for his name is not listed among the members in 1899. However, his name appears in the 1904 report, and he is cred-

ited with having undertaken much of the field survey work. By 1903, he had produced a hand-drawn map of "Proposed System of Forest Parks and Country Pleasure Road[s]," which clearly served as the basis for the recommendations published by the commission in 1904 (Figure 7.4).[18]

Jensen's knowledge of the native landscape and his friendship with Chicago's Prairie School architects clearly shaped his redesign of the West Parks. Humboldt Park is a good example of his attempt at idealizing the native landscape. While the woodland plantings and open meadows repeated patterns used by Olmsted and Vaux in the South Parks, Jensen's wetland gardens were unique. He called the system a prairie river—celebrating native wetland plants in associations and patterns found in the wild (Figure 7.5). Park buildings were no longer the rustic creations used by Olmsted and Vaux or the elaborate Victorian structures typical of Jenney's work. Instead, they reflected the honest use of materials and simple geometric lines advocated by prairie architects. Jensen engaged his friend Hugh Garden to design Humboldt Park's refectory and distinctive lanterns, while he presumably designed other structures, such as the flower pavilion in the Rose Garden, himself.[19] In Garfield Park, Jensen attempted to produce a representation of the prehistoric prairie landscape in the lush gardens in the conservatory, which at the time was the largest conservatory in the world.[20]

In Columbus Park, which Jensen designed in large part from 1916 to 1920, he had a much freer hand in creating an idealized prairie landscape. He was able to suggest a sense of expansiveness, taking advantage of the large open spaces of the golf course to provide broad vistas for watching the interaction of land and sky and the beautiful sunrises and sunsets so characteristic of the prairie region. In Columbus Park, too, was a "prairie river," although more exten-

Figure 7.5. View of Prairie River in Humboldt Park, Chicago, with Jensen's flower pavilion in the distance. (Photograph by Frank A. Waugh, courtesy of Collection of the Department of Landscape Architecture and Regional Planning, University of Massachusetts, Amherst)

sive than the earlier version in Humboldt Park. While in most areas in the park the "openness" rather than the actual planting of prairie grasses was meant to capture the spirit of the prairie, along the "river" Jensen included a band of native prairie and wetland grasses and forbs.[21] Here, too, he planned a large outdoor theater space, which he called a players' green. The audience assembled near dusk to watch the setting sun to the west while the moon arose behind them and illuminated performances on the outdoor "stage" space. If the night were too dark, performances would be lighted by torches on either side of the "stage."[22]

In many of his small parks and playgrounds, Jensen experimented with innovations in children's play spaces. In places such as Franklin Park, designed in 1914, Jensen wanted to give city children a chance to play in wilder settings, much as he had on his family's farm in Denmark. Instead of a standard swimming pool, Jensen designed a naturalistic pool edged by horizontal layers of limestone. This gave the pool the appearance of being carved into the underlying bedrock, much like quarry pools found in the region or the river valleys cut through the limestone deposits of Illinois.[23] The nearby play area had none of the gymnastic equipment typical of most playgrounds, but instead provided a network of "wilder"-appearing outdoor rooms featuring native shrubs and trees that would attract birds and another naturalistic pool for wading. A dense planting was done around the perimeter of the small park (Figure 7.6).

For many parks and gardens, Jensen designed "council rings," modeled on Nordic and Native American traditions, as a special setting for outdoor social gatherings and cultural activities. A low stone seat encircling a central fire pit, Jensen's council rings brought people together at the same level and provided a milieu for storytelling, dance, drama, and simply gathering around a fire.[24] Jensen seemed to think that these features would stimulate much more imaginative play and a greater "bonding" with nature than was possible in more conventional playgrounds (Figure 7.7).

A Greater West Park System, presented by Jensen to the West Park Commissioners in 1919 and published in 1920, documents Jensen's holistic vision of a city with a network of parks, playgrounds, school sites, community gardens, agricultural land, large preserves, and linear parkways along streams, canals, and boulevards. He included specific suggestions for weaving a "prairie drive" through mixed neighborhoods of detached houses, apartments, and stores, all with access to the open meadow along the drive (Figure 7.8). Throughout the west side would be located a variety of "municipal kitchen gardens" for growing fresh fruits and vegetables and land for a "Technical University, Agricultural College and Art School" (Figure 7.9). Jensen's vision is a more human-scaled and community-oriented approach to city planning than that promoted in Daniel Burnham's earlier Chicago Plan and other "City Beautiful" proposals of the same period.[25]

During the same time, Jensen was actively working on a wide variety of other design proj-

ects. He kept an office in Steinway Hall, a building designed by Dwight Perkins, who leased the top floor and rented office space to many of his architect friends, including Jensen. He maintained this office until 1918, when he moved his design studio to his "summer" house in Ravinia (Highland Park) on a property he referred to as "The Clearing." Then in the early 1920s, he had the house winterized for the family of his son-in-law Marshall Johnson, who served as his office manager and chief draftsman, and built a small studio on the edge of the ravine.[26] Jensen is known to have been involved in 576 projects. These include 39 or 40 parks and playgrounds for Chicago parks as well as parks for the Illinois towns of Glencoe, Highland Park, Kenilworth, La Grange, Lombard, Oak Park, and River Forest; East Chicago and Hammond, Indiana; and Racine, Wisconsin. Jensen also did some of the very early planning to determine what lands should be included in the Cook County Forest Preserves and Lake County Forest Preserves.[27]

Throughout all his work, Jensen merged "design" with strong conservation values. He did this in various ways, emphasizing certain themes. His gardens and parks served as refuges for plants and animals as well as for people. He placed a special emphasis on creating bird gardens and wildlife habitats in the heart of the city.[28] Design features repeated in his projects included a hierarchy of spaces, a strong sense of movement, contrasts in light and shadow, careful handling of rock work and pools, and a clear emphasis on the native landscape and particularly on plants he thought to be symbolic. The hawthorn was one of them. With its horizontal branching structure, Jensen thought it represented the prairie, binding together prairie and woodland habitats (Figure 7.10).[29] The prairie itself was represented more symbolically than through an actual restoration of its flora. In the gardens designed for Henry Babson (house by

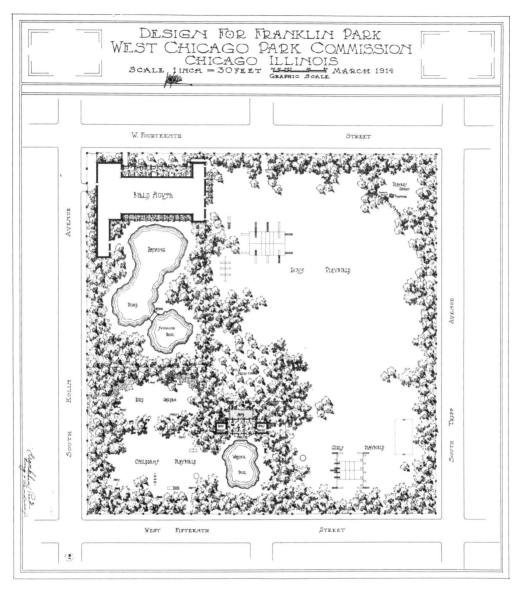

Figure 7.6. Jens Jensen, "Design for Franklin Park" (1914). The design of the playground illustrates Jensen's evolving thought about the more "naturalistic" play spaces used later in Columbus Park. (Courtesy of Special Collections, Chicago Park District)

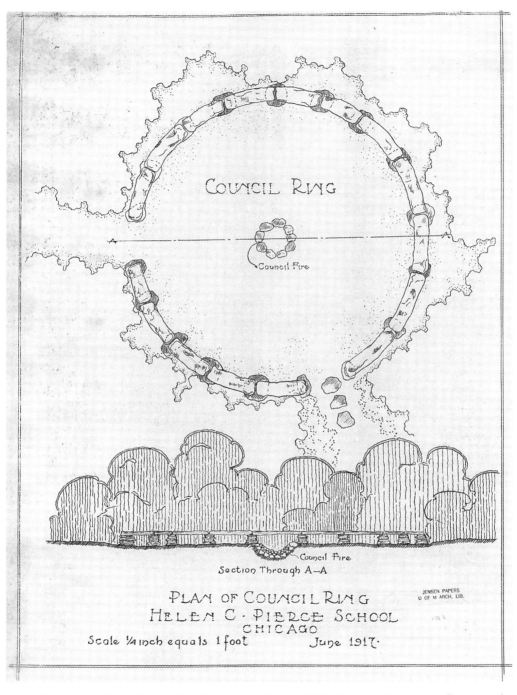

COUNCIL RING

Council Fire

Council Fire

Section Through A–A

PLAN OF COUNCIL RING
HELEN C · PIERCE SCHOOL
CHICAGO
Scale ¼ inch equals 1 foot   June 1917

Figure 7.7. Jens Jensen, "Plan of Council Ring, Helen C. Pierce School" (1917). (Courtesy of Jens Jensen Collection, Bentley Historical Library, University of Michigan, Ann Arbor)

Figure 7.8. Jens Jensen, a section of "Prairie Drive" (1919). (From Jens Jensen, *A Greater West Park System* [Chicago: West Park Commission, 1920]. Courtesy of Jens Jensen Collection, Bentley Historical Library, University of Michigan, Ann Arbor)

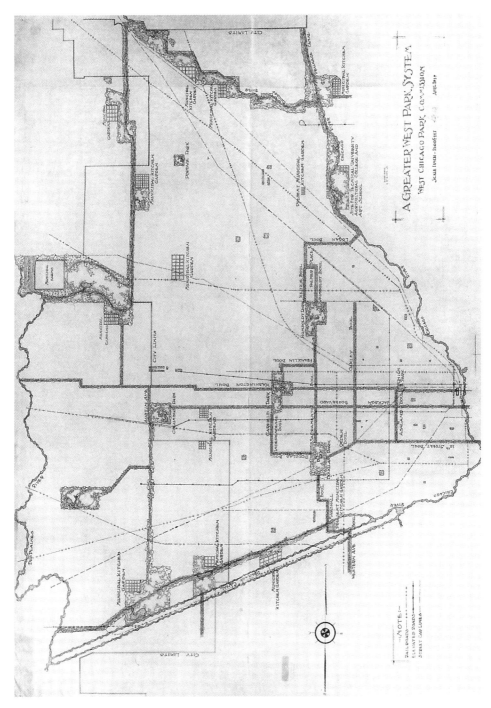

Figure 7.9. Jens Jensen, "A Greater West Park System" (1919). (Courtesy of Jens Jensen Collection, Bentley Historical Library, University of Michigan, Ann Arbor)

The "Illinois Way" of Beautifying the Farm

By WILHELM MILLER

This house is built on horizontal lines, to repeat the great horizontal lines of the prairie. See page 3

This is Circular 170 of the Agricultural Experiment Station, published
by the Department of Horticulture, University of Illinois, Urbana, 1914

COPIES FREE TO ANYONE IN ILLINOIS WHO WILL SIGN A PROMISE TO DO SOME
PERMANENT ORNAMENTAL PLANTING WITHIN A YEAR

Figure 7.10. The cover of Wilhelm Miller, *The "Illinois Way" of Beautifying the Farm,* showing the A. C. Magnus estate in Winnetka, Illinois, the gardens of which were designed by Jensen in 1904.

Louis Sullivan), Jensen labeled the large open space as a "prairie" with "violets and strawberries and other low growing prairie flowers" in the lawn. At the edges of bordering shrubs and trees would be planted a variety of prairie wildflowers, such as black-eyed Susan and purple coneflower. Along the "brook," he suggested such things as "spike rush, *Calamagrostis* [bluejoint grass], *Lobelia canadensis, Iris . . . Lobelia syphilitica,* Star of [Bethlehem, and] a few white water lilies on the edge of [the] brook" (Figure 7.11).

Gardens represented other themes as well. Jensen created a number of hospital gardens and clearly regarded gardens and parks as having a healing function in people's lives. From his early design for St. Ann's Hospital in Chicago, published by Jensen in 1901, to the designs for Decatur Memorial Hospital (1915–16) in Decatur, Illinois; Edward Hines, Jr., Hospital in Maywood, Illinois; and Henry Ford Hospital (1919–20) in Detroit, Michigan, Jensen showed great sensitivity to the needs of patients undergoing long recuperation periods, creating gardens that would change dramatically with the seasons and attract a variety of wildlife. At many of these hospitals, time in these "natural" gardens was a routine part of treatment.[30]

Jensen considered roadsides to be a potentially vital force for conservation, especially as people began to pursue motoring as a form of recreation. His design for the "Ideal Mile" of Lincoln Highway, with its emphasis on the native prairie and savanna habitats of northern Indiana, was intended to become a model for future highway construction.[31] Jensen also regarded gardens as a place that would merge art and nature in ways beyond the physical design of the space. In 1908, he helped mount an exhibition of public sculpture in Humboldt Park with his friends Lorado Taft and Charles Mulligan of the Art Institute of Chicago and the Mu-

nicipal Art League as a way of demonstrating how pictorial or allegorical sculpture appropriately sited in naturalistic environments could enhance appreciation of nature in the city.[32] Likewise, gardens were to serve as settings for a variety of activities that would create a tradition of celebrating in "natural" places. The aforementioned council rings were gathering points for these activities.

Lincoln Memorial Garden in Springfield, Illinois, designed by Jensen from 1934 to 1936, illustrated his mature thinking on landscape design. For this project of the Illinois Garden Club, he had limited resources, had to depend on volunteers, and had no nursery source for native plants. Rather than see these circumstances as limitations, Jensen used them as an opportunity to work with long-term landscape change and to create a sense of ownership and stewardship through volunteer participation in the entire process of restoring the land. Children collected acorns that were planted in a grand ceremony in 1936. Volunteers from the Springfield Chapter of the Illinois Garden Club worked with others from across the state to rescue plants from development sites, ship them to Springfield, and plant them in appropriate places in the garden. The planting of the garden was done over many years and in many phases, first planting trees and shrubs and later adding the groundlayer plantings (Figure 7.12).[33]

In addition to his professional design work, Jensen coordinated a number of formal conservation activities. As an attempt to build broader support for conservation, he helped found the Prairie Club and a more politically active group called Friends of Our Native Landscape. The Prairie Club grew out of an organization originally called the Saturday Afternoon Walking Trips, which was an extension of the Playground Association, intended to introduce people from the inner city to the wilds around Chicago. In

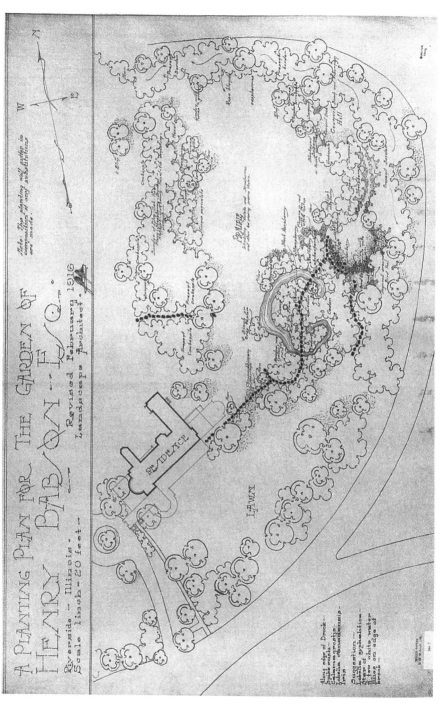

Figure 7.11. Jens Jensen, "A Planting Plan for the Garden of Henry Babson," Riverside, Illinois (1918). (Courtesy of Jens Jensen Collection, Bentley Historical Library, University of Michigan, Ann Arbor)

Figure 7.12. Council ring designed by Jensen in Lincoln Memorial Garden, Springfield, Illinois. (Photograph by Robert E. Grese)

contrast, Friends of Our Native Landscape was intended to lobby to protect important wilds throughout Illinois and, later, Wisconsin and Michigan, where subsequent chapters were formed. The first meeting of the "Friends" (as they became known) involved Avery Coonley, a businessman in Riverside, Illinois; Harold Ickes, who became Secretary of the Interior under Franklin Delano Roosevelt; Stephen Mather, the first director of the National Park Service; poet Harriet Monroe; architect Dwight Perkins; and Augusta Rosenwald, wife of Julius Rosenwald, the founder of Sears, Roebuck. Other important early members included ecology professors Henry Chandler Cowles and George D. Fuller and poets Vachel Lindsay and Carl Sandburg.

Important activities of these two groups included efforts to protect the Indiana Dunes and to set aside many of the eventual Illinois state parks.[34]

After his wife died in 1934, Jensen decided that he had had enough of city life and planned to retire to what had been the family's summer home since 1919 in Ellison Bay on Wisconsin's Door County peninsula.[35] He was not to rest on his laurels, however. He devoted his remaining years to establishing the school he would call "The Clearing." He described it as a "school of the soil" where students could get away from the hopelessly "confused" system of education in the existing schools and return to a simpler, more basic style of learning that combined stud-

Figure 7.13. Jensen photographed what he called "oak and friend aster." (Courtesy of Jens Jensen Collection, Morton Arboretum, Lisle, Illinois)

ies of ecology, horticulture, the arts, philosophy, and myriad related topics. During his lifetime, Jensen's school never attracted many students or had secure funding. After Jensen's death in 1951, his secretary, Mertha Fulkerson, continued the Clearing with the Wisconsin Farm Bureau. Its program evolved much to its present form, with an emphasis on a variety of classes in nature study, arts, crafts, and writing, but still in the spirit Jensen intended.[36]

It is a mistake to think of Jensen as belonging to an era of estate and park design that is long past. His work holds clues to designing the landscape in harmony with nature on a more sustainable basis. Rather than thinking of plantings as arbitrary selections, Jensen saw them as community groupings, associates, and friends (Figure 7.13). He did not think of landscape design as a profession, but as a craft. He said that land-

scape architects tended to get away from gardening as though the word smelled of "cabbage" and noted that "their fear of being classed with craftsmen rather than professionals had practically killed the art."[37] He disliked the term "landscape architect," but used it on many of his drawings. Some, like Ossian Cole Simonds, used "landscape gardener"; others, like Jensen's friend Frank Waugh, used "landscape engineer," but Jensen thought it sounded "metallic." Instead, he wished to be called a "maker of natural parks and gardens."[38]

A central feature of Jensen's work was providing places for people to enjoy and celebrate special events in the out-of-doors. Getting people to appreciate the physical forms of landscapes was only part of Jensen's goal; he also wanted them to appreciate the land with their hearts. Jensen seemed to know that watching the sunset on the summer solstice, marveling at a great blue heron fishing in Columbus Park, and experiencing the change of seasons creates lasting impressions on people and helps bond them to a particular place.[39] Jensen's emphasis on these things is probably one of the most important legacies of his work. In today's world, people are increasingly losing places to experience these wonders and are generally finding themselves too busy to take advantage of such simple pleasures.

Jens Jensen devoted his career to the problem of preserving and restoring a sense of the native landscape. His work serves as a model of merging conservation values with landscape design lifted to the level of art. In many places throughout the Middle West and around the country, development seems to be spiraling out of control, reducing the great beauty and diversity of the native landscape to a dull sameness. Unfortunately, it seems, few people have any sense of what is being lost. The clear value of Jensen's work is not so much as a nostalgic look to the past, but as an inspiration for a whole new ethic of land stewardship—preserving, managing, and celebrating the beauty and health of our natural landscape.

Notes

1. For discussion of the Danish folk school tradition and the impact it had on Jens Jensen, see John Christianson, "Scandinavia and the Prairie School: Chicago Landscape Artist Jens Jensen," *Bridge: Journal of the Danish American Heritage Society* 5 (1982): 11; Leonard K. Eaton, *Landscape Artist in America: The Life and Work of Jens Jensen* (Chicago: University of Chicago Press, 1964), 6–7; Malcolm Collier, "Prairie Profile: Jens Jensen and the Midwest Landscape," *Morton Arboretum Quarterly* 13 (1977): 50; and Robert E. Grese, *Jens Jensen: Maker of Natural Parks and Gardens* (Baltimore: Johns Hopkins University Press, 1992), 4–5.

2. Jens Jensen, *Siftings* (Chicago: Ralph Fletcher Seymour, 1939), 34–36.

3. Alfred Caldwell, interview with author, 17 December 1989.

4. Jens Jensen to Camillo Schneider, 15 April 1939, personal files of Darrel Morrison.

5. Jens Jensen, "Soil Conditions and Tree Growth around Lake Michigan," *Park and Cemetery*, April–May 1904, 24–25, 42; Grese, *Jens Jensen*, 65.

6. Jane Addams, *Twenty Years at Hull-House* (New York: Macmillan, 1910), 388–93; John C. Farrell, *Beloved Lady: A History of Jane Addams' Ideas on Reform and Peace* (Baltimore: Johns Hopkins University Press, 1967), 107–8.

7. Clarence Pullen, "The Parks and Parkways of Chicago," *Harper's Weekly*, 6 June 1891, 412–16, 423; Lois Wille, *Forever, Open, Clear, and Free: The Historic Struggle for Chicago's Lakefront* (Chicago: Regnery, 1972), 46–58.

8. Grese, *Jens Jensen*, 28–35; Daniel M. Bluestone, "Landscape and Culture in Nineteenth-Century Chicago" (Ph.D. diss., University of Chicago, 1984), 29–54; Chicago Park District, Office of Research and Planning, "Lincoln Park Restoration and Management Plan" (Chicago Park District Offices, Chicago, Ill., 1991), 7–12, 19–21; Julia Sniderman, "Bringing the Prairie Vision into Focus," in *Prairie in the City: Naturalism in Chicago's Parks, 1870–1940* (Chicago: Chicago Historical Society, 1991), 22–24; David Schuyler, *The New Urban Landscape: The Redefinition of City Form in Nineteenth-Century America* (Baltimore: Johns Hopkins University Press, 1986), 136–38.

9. Horace William Shaler Cleveland, *The Public Grounds of Chicago: How to Give Them Character and Expression* (Chicago: Lakey, 1869), 14–17.

10. Robert C. Turak, *William Le Baron Jenney: Pioneer of Modern Architecture* (Ann Arbor, Mich.: UMI Research Press, 1986), 84–97.

11. Jens Jensen and Ragna B. Eskil, "Natural Parks and Gardens," *Saturday Evening Post*, 8 March 1930, 19; Grese, *Jens Jensen*, 8.

12. Jens Jensen, "The Naturalistic Treatment in a Metropolitan Park," *American Landscape Architecture*, January 1930, 34; James Jensen, "Parks and Politics," *Sixth Volume of the American Park and Outdoor Art Association* 6 (1902): 12; Grese, *Jens Jensen*, 63–69.

13. James Jensen, "Plan for Hospital Grounds," *Park and Cemetery,* December 1901, 185; Grese, *Jens Jensen,* 104–6.

14. Grese, *Jens Jensen,* 94–98.

15. Reforms in the West Park System of Chicago," *Park and Cemetery,* August 1905, 329–30; Grese, *Jens Jensen,* 67–69.

16. Malcolm Collier, "Jens Jensen and Columbus Park," *Chicago History* 4 (1975): 225–35; Collier, "Prairie Profile," 51.

17. Jensen, "Soil Conditions and Tree Growth," 24–25, 42.

18. Dwight H. Perkins, *Report of the Special Park Commission to the City Council of Chicago on the Subject of a Metropolitan Park System* (Chicago: Special Park Commission, 1904); Grese, *Jens Jensen,* 64–67.

19. Mertha Fulkerson to Leonard Eaton, 9 February 1960, Morton Arboretum, Lisle, Ill.; Wilhelm Miller, "Have We Progressed in Gardening?" *Country Life in America,* April 1912, 26.

20. Thomas McAdam, "Landscape Gardening under Glass," *Country Life in America,* December 1911, 12–13; "The Biggest Park Conservatory in America," *Park and Cemetery,* June 1913, 74; Grese, *Jens Jensen,* 71–72.

21. Jensen, "Naturalistic Treatment in a Metropolitan Park," 37; Jens Jensen, "Report of Mr. Jens Jensen, Consulting Landscape Architect, on the Design of Columbus Park," in *Forty-Ninth Annual Report of the West Chicago Park Commissioners* (Chicago: West Park Commissioners, 1917), 16–18.

22. Jensen, "Report of Mr. Jens Jensen," 16–18; E. Genevieve Gillette, interview with Scott Hedberg, 27 March 1978; Grese, *Jens Jensen,* 82, 178–79.

23. Jensen, "Naturalistic Treatment in a Metropolitan Park," 37; Ruth Dean, "A 'Swimming Hole' in Chicago," *National Municipal Review,* May 1922, 138–39.

24. J. Ronald Engel, *Sacred Sands: The Struggle for Community in the Indiana Dunes* (Middletown, Conn.: Wesleyan University Press, 1983), 200–201; Grese, *Jens Jensen,* 176–78.

25. Jens Jensen, *A Greater West Park System* (Chicago: West Park Commission, 1920), 9–10; Eaton, *Landscape Artist in America,* 145; Grese, *Jens Jensen,* 87–94.

26. H. Allen Brooks, *The Prairie School: Frank Lloyd Wright and His Midwest Contemporaries* (Toronto: University of Toronto Press, 1972), 28; E. Genevieve Gillette, interview with Patricia M. Frank, 1973, transcript of tape recording, tape no. 16c, Bentley Historical Library, University of Michigan, Ann Arbor; Alfred Caldwell, interview with author and Julia Sniderman, 31 January 1987; Grese, *Jens Jensen,* 45, 137–38.

27. A listing of known Jensen projects is in Grese, *Jens Jensen,* 199–220.

28. Wilhelm Miller, "Bird Gardens in the City," *Country Life in America,* August 1914, 46–47.

29. Collier, "Jens Jensen and Columbus Park," 230–31; Wilhelm Miller, The *"Illinois Way"* of Beautifying the Farm, Circular no. 184 (Urbana: University of Illinois, Department of Horticulture, Agricultural Experiment Station, 1914), 9–10; Wilhelm Miller, *The Prairie Spirit in Landscape Gardening,* Circular no. 170 (Urbana: University of Illinois, Department of Horticulture, Agricultural Experiment Station, 1915), 17, 19–21.

30. Jensen, "Plan for Hospital Grounds," 185; "Jens Jensen, Consultant in General Landscaping," *Chevrons,* September 1929, Edward Hines, Jr., Hospital Archives, Maywood, Ill.; "Henry Ford Hospital Information for Patients," 1915, Henry Ford Hospital, Detroit, Mich., 18.

31. Lincoln Highway Association, "Ideal Section Nears Completion" [press release], 1 May 1923, Special Collections, University of Michigan Libraries, Ann Arbor; Grese, *Jens Jensen,* 106–10.

32. "The Sculpture Show in Humboldt Park, Chicago," *Park and Cemetery,* November 1908, 439–40; "Chicago's Park Sculpture Show," *Park and Cemetery,* October 1909, 127–30; Grese, *Jens Jensen,* 78–80.

33. Jens Jensen to Camillo Schneider, 15 April 1939; Grese, *Jens Jensen,* 113–20, 185–86.

34. Grese, *Jens Jensen,* 120–36.

35. Alfred Caldwell, interview with author, 12 November 1990.

36. Mertha Fulkerson and Ada Corson, *The Story of the Clearing* (Chicago: Coach House Press, 1972), 6, 32–65; Grese, *Jens Jensen,* 136–50.

37. Jens Jensen to Mr. and Mrs. Boardman, n.d., Morton Aboretum.

38. Frank A. Waugh to Jens Jensen, 8 April 1936 and 5 January 1938, Morton Arboretum; Alfred Caldwell, interview with Malcolm Collier, January 1981, transcript of tape recording, tape no. 2:4–5, Morton Arboretum.

39. Jensen, "Naturalistic Treatment in a Metropolitan Park," 37; Jensen, *Siftings,* 81–82.

8 Reimagining the Prairie: Aldo Leopold and the Origins of Prairie Restoration

Curt Meine

Our ancestors brought to the grasslands of the midcontinent the agents of transformation: bow and arrow, spear, spade, fire, horse, gun, trap, flatboat, treaty, Gunter's chain, seed, plow, rail, barbed wire, telegraph, lock and dam, automobile, agrochemical, center pivot, interstate. We continue to bring to the prairie new tools for the extraction, conversion, and distribution of its organic wealth and, increasingly, for *exemption* from its extremes of temperature, precipitation, space, and solitude. But we also build there an increasing, interest-bearing fund of cultural appreciation and expression: an accumulation of image and story, verse and song, historical narrative and scientific insight that may yet allow us to inhabit the place on its own enduring terms. We may yet recognize ourselves as transformed in the process.

Imagine the prairie. The act happens so subtly that we can hardly identify the original sources of our personal images. I cannot remember how I, like so many suburb-bound midwestern children, first came to conceive of the "prairie" as any patch of lamb's-quarter and velvetleaf tem-

porarily spared in the developer's master plan. At such sites throughout the Midwest, final demands on the prairie are issued. As the zone of contention pushes out to the latest "crabgrass frontier," the open spaces are encroached on, surrounded, staked with orange flags, and finally snuffed out. Some residual spirit of the native prairie survives even to the end—in the spontaneous arrival and dispersal of plants, in the surprising appearance of small mammals and red-tailed hawks, in the rasp of summer locusts and the tenacity of fall monarchs, in the very feel of openness itself. With imagination, we may read these signs as scholars of scripture read the Dead Sea Scrolls, reconstructing out of the oldest, tiniest, and most fragile fragments a view of the world, a knowledge of a place, a connection through time, an experience of enlargement and completeness.

Webster's offers this definition of the verb "imagine": "to form a mental image of (something not present)." The prairie is not and cannot be present except in its transformed and ever-changing state; the prairie that our ancestors experienced is gone. This is the blunt reality that history has bequeathed us, that we must acknowledge, and beyond which our ecological literacy must lead us. Yet the prairie is more than just what people have made of it over the past several decades, centuries, and millennia. The transformed prairie of the present cannot be understood apart from what it once was and what it might become. The prairie that our own descendants will find is now a-forming, and its creation reflects our imagination of it.

Imagination is not merely a quality we can possess, but a process in which we participate, individually and collectively. Our artists, musicians, poets, writers, teachers, historians, and scientists evoke the prairie for us—what it was, is, and might be. We are, in this sense, the imagination of the prairie, dwelling in the region, the region dwelling in us. The process of imagining the prairie has been unfolding for as long as people and space have interacted in the midcontinent, and that process will continue to unfold as both the people and the place inevitably change.

Within this broad context, we can understand prairie restoration as a revolutionary moment in the development of that relationship, when banishment of the native was replaced by encouragement, antipathy by renewal, and hubris by recognition. In that moment, one narrow and prescribed kind of imagination, which tended to deplete both the land and the human options upon it, began to evoke another kind of imagination, which aims literally to revive both.

Aldo Leopold knew and explored this territory where history, imagination, and prairie landscape came together.[1] His maturity as an interpreter and a reformer of American attitudes toward land was achieved on the northeastern fringe of the North American grasslands in Wisconsin, where tallgrass prairie and oak savanna

interpenetrate, melding northward into the upper Great Lakes forest. In this region of abutting biomes and gradual ecotonal shift, Leopold formulated and taught the fundamentals of modern conservation, and in his private life applied them on the sand county property he purchased in 1935 (Figure 8.1). In a few years, the Leopold farm, "first worn out then abandoned by our bigger-and-better society," became the locus of his literary imagination and the vantage point for his regional perspective.[2]

In our standard heroic American mythology, we imagine enterprising, westering pioneers peering out from dark eastern woods into the bright day of the welcoming prairie. Leopold might embody the actual experience of that landscape two generations later, stripped of its aboriginal landholders and biota, stripped too of illusion and deniability. Behind Leopold lay the northern forestlands, shorn first of the pines and then of the hardwoods; before him lay the midwestern grasslands, plowed through and through, skies brown with the dust of the High Plains, gullies eating back into the uplands from the watercourses, streambeds and river sloughs filling with sediment. Far from the landscape of democracy that Bryant and Whitman projected—the "very earthform of nondiscrimination," as Ed Folsom characterizes it[3]—the prairie landscape that Leopold observed was one of deterioration. It was a time and place that demanded reconsideration of one's natural and cultural inheritance.

For thirteen years, from 1935 until his death in 1948, Leopold divided his time between his home and office in Madison, Wisconsin, and the worn-out river-bottom land that he and his family worked to rehabilitate. In commuting between these poles of his devotion, Leopold regularly passed through former prairie country in Dane and Sauk Counties. Inhabited by native Sauk and Fox until their removal in the early

Figure 8.1. Aldo Leopold working at his "sand county" property in 1936. (Aldo Leopold Foundation)

1830s, and by Ho-Chunk (who retain lands nearby), these prairies were outliers of the continent's main arc of tallgrass. For early European explorers and missionaries following the water route from the Great Lakes, down the Wisconsin River toward its confluence with the Mississippi, they provided the first suggestion of the vast grasslands farther west.

Along Leopold's later automobile route lay a graveyard established by the region's first white settlers. And in one corner of it, Leopold found life (Figure 8.2). The cemetery, he noted in his essay "Prairie Birthday," was

extraordinary only in being triangular instead of square, and in harboring, within the sharp angle of its fence, a pin-point remnant of the native prairie

on which the graveyard was established in the 1840's. Heretofore unreachable by scythe or mower, this yard-square relic of original Wisconsin gives birth, each July, to a man-high stalk of compass plant or cutleaf Silphium, spangled with saucer-sized yellow blooms resembling sunflowers. It is the sole remnant of this plant along this highway, and perhaps the sole remnant in the western half of our county.[4]

Through all the years of Leopold's passing the graveyard, that lone stalk of silphium, secured deep in the loam alongside the late settlers, served as a checkpoint for his imagination. They were for him years of steadily expanding awareness of prairie ecology, and the "man-high" silphium provided a standard against which to measure that growth—and the cost of the prairie's loss.

Figure 8.2. The corner of the triangular Sauk Prairie Cemetery in Sauk County, Wisconsin, was replanted to native prairie plants by local conservationists in the early 1980s. (Photograph by Curt Meine)

Leopold concluded the paragraph with a comment both inspiring and profoundly chilling: "What a thousand acres of Silphiums looked like when they tickled the bellies of the buffalo is a question never again to be answered, and perhaps not even asked." Every summer, Leopold was able to observe the silphium, to ask himself that question, and to imagine an answer. In the process, he knew that he as an observer was as rare as the plant he was observing:

The Highway Department says that 100,000 cars pass yearly over this route during the three summer months when the Silphium is in bloom. In them must ride at least 100,000 people who have "taken" what is called history, and perhaps 25,000 who have "taken" what is called botany. Yet I doubt whether a dozen have seen the Silphium, and of these hardly one will notice its demise.[5]

At least one person did. In July 1947, Leopold drove past the graveyard and noted the silphium again in bloom. A week later, however, he passed again and found that the fence had been removed by a highway crew, and the silphium mowed over. "It is now easy to predict the future," he wrote; "for a few years my Silphium will try in vain to rise above the mowing machine, and then it will die. With it will die the prairie epoch" (Figure 8.3).

Figure 8.3. Roadside historical marker, Sauk County, Wisconsin. (Photograph by Curt Meine)

Leopold found in the loss of this singular plant a fit symbol for what we would now call the biodiversity crisis: "This is one little episode in the funeral of the native flora, which in turn is one episode in the funeral of the floras of the world. Mechanized man, oblivious of floras, is proud of his progress in cleaning up the landscape on which, willy-nilly, he must live out his days."[6] In a sentence that ranks among the most biting he ever wrote, Leopold added: "It might be wise to prohibit at once all teaching of real botany and real history, lest some future citizen suffer qualms about the floristic price of his good life."[7]

During these years, Leopold had come to realize fully the "price" of depleted floras and faunas.[8] His calculus included not only the loss of material benefits—the recreational and educational opportunities, the actual and potential genetic resources, the ecological functions and services—but also the loss of wild beauty, wonder, and mystery in the world. Like the silphium itself, those values were relegated increasingly to the most obscure and vulnerable corners of the landscape.

Leopold was in the final stages of preparing the manuscript that became *A Sand County Almanac* when he witnessed the prairie "funeral" and wrote "Prairie Birthday."[9] The timing could only have magnified the meaning for Leopold. And time has only magnified it further: when we lose populations, species, floras, faunas, communities, and landscapes, we lose our bearings and our reference points. We lose, too, the ability to ask certain questions, to formulate responses, to envision worlds. We lose in fact the context in which questions and curiosity and options thrive. We lose the very habitat of imag-

Figure 8.4. Prairie remnant, Sauk County, Wisconsin. (Photograph by Curt Meine)

ination. The result, to use Wes Jackson's apt phrase, is a "narrowing of the boundaries of consideration." [10] Over much of the North American prairie, that narrowing is visceral and visual: *"What a thousand acres of Silphiums looked like when they tickled the bellies of the buffalo is a question never again to be answered, and perhaps not even asked"* (Figure 8.4).

Leopold's observations of the midwestern landscape had intensified in the late 1920s, when he left the United States Forest Service to initiate his "Game Survey of the North Central States." [11] From July 1928 to January 1930, Leopold traversed the states of the upper Midwest, gauging the condition of game populations and habitat, and reviewing the effectiveness of the state con-

servation agencies. At the time, his interest in the region's native grasslands (such as it was) focused on their instrumental value in providing habitat for prairie chickens, rabbits, and other game animals. In his published report on the game survey, Leopold scarcely mentioned the prairie itself, and then only in the past tense. [12]

By the late 1920s, the demise of the tallgrass prairie (and much of the mixed-grass and short-grass prairie) was a fait accompli. Indeed, agriculture in the region was expanding, mechanizing, and intensifying through the 1920s, to the detriment of the fencerows, hedgerows, odd corners, and other fragments of vegetative cover that supported game animals and other "wild life." [13] Following Leopold's lead, the work of technicians in the emerging field of game management included the diversification of the farm landscape, to counter the accelerating trend toward monotonization and simplification. At this point, however, that work did not entail any specific concern with the restoration of the native flora and fauna in general.

Although Leopold paid scant attention to prairie per se in the course of the game survey, the experience did leave him with indelible impressions of the effects of the Midwest's epochal devegetation. His prolonged field work allowed him to see firsthand the full extent of land degradation throughout the region. Leopold's long-term interest in soil erosion and soil conservation, dating back over a decade to his days as a forester in the Southwest, resurfaced in his report on the game survey. Especially in the erosion-prone river breaks and bluff lands, he noted, "careless methods of cultivation," the "failure to conserve soil humus," and the "wholesale removal of brush, timber, and grass" had contributed to extensive rill and gully erosion. He pointed out "the necessity of restoring at least a part of [the] vegetation . . . for the production of game," and emphasized in the next sentence that the "restoration [of vegetation] is equally necessary for the conservation of the land."[14] He did not, however, specify *prairie* restoration. His concept of restoration did not yet embrace the notion of reestablishing native plant and animal communities.

Through the early 1930s, Leopold devoted himself primarily to summarizing his ideas on game management in a series of reports and in his landmark text, *Game Management.* In addition, he was preoccupied during those harshest days of the Depression with the basic challenge of securing a livelihood. With his appointment to the Chair of Game Management at the University of Wisconsin in 1933, both his ideas and his livelihood came to rest on more solid foundations.

The responsibilities that Leopold assumed in

his new position included his appointment as research director of the university's newly created arboretum. Since at least 1928, Leopold had been active along with other local civic leaders in the development of the arboretum. When plans for its establishment finally moved ahead in 1932, Leopold became more closely involved in defining its mission and methods. Organizers and supporters proposed contrasting approaches, envisioning the arboretum as a showcase for manicured gardens, for forest types from throughout the United States, or for plant specimens from around the world. As the arboretum was also intended to serve in part as a wildlife refuge, Leopold submitted in October 1933 a management plan for the area. He recommended that the arboretum lands be administered as a research area for university scientists, as a game-management demonstration site, as a refuge for dwindling native game species, and as a source area to help replenish local game populations.[15]

The months of the subsequent winter and spring evidently gave Leopold and the other arboretum organizers (especially Norman Fassett) pause to reconsider their overall mission. Destructive dust storms in Wisconsin's sand counties in the spring of 1934 may well have contributed to the change in emphasis.[16] In any case, by the time the arboretum was formally dedicated on June 17, 1934, a new vision for the place had taken hold (Figure 8.5). In his dedicatory address, Leopold called for a rejection of the "iron-heel mentality" that had destabilized the relationship between people and land. That attitude, he noted, "is . . . indifferent to what Wisconsin *was.* This is exactly the reason why the University cannot be. I am here to say that the invention of a harmonious relationship between men and land is a more exacting task than the invention of machines, and . . . its accomplishment is impossible without a visual knowledge of the land's history."[17] Accordingly, the

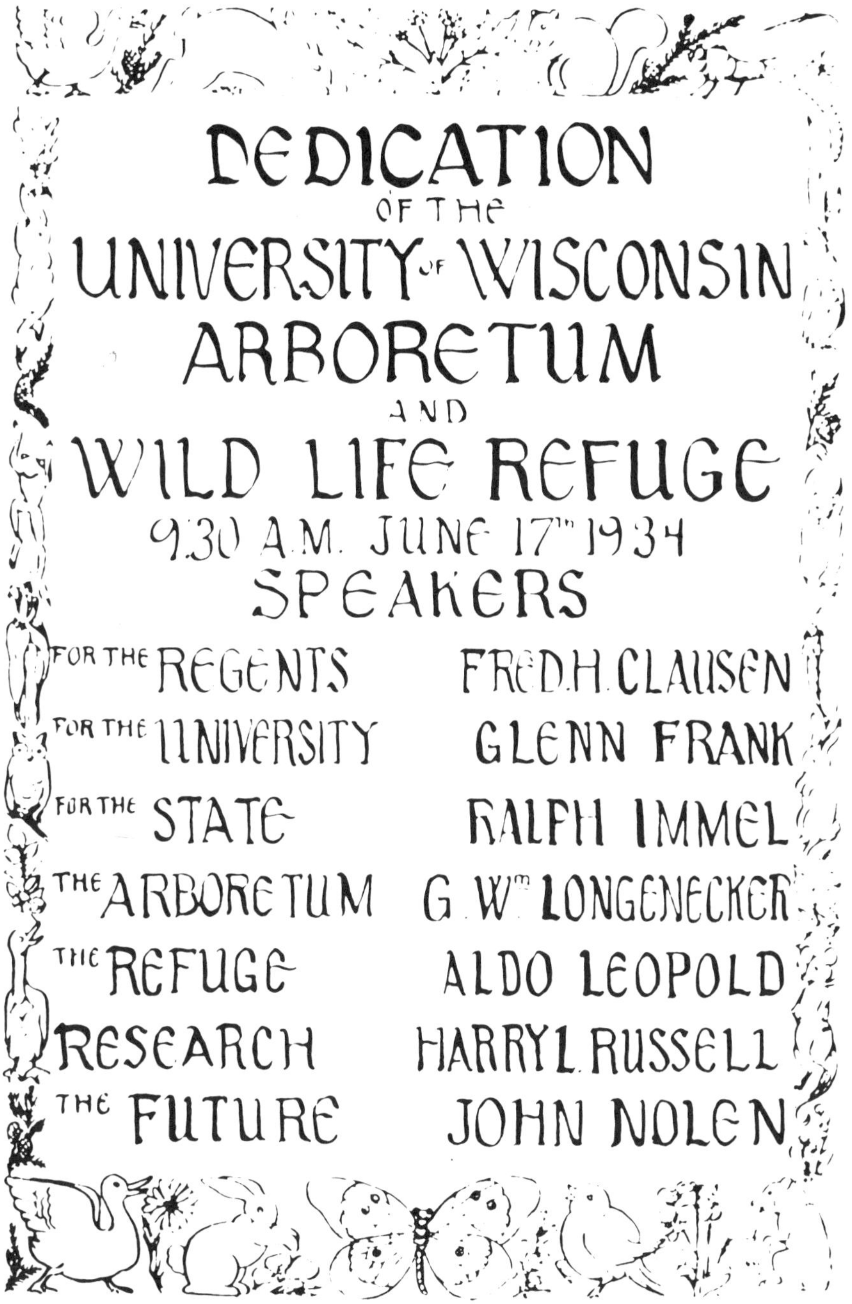
DEDICATION
OF THE
UNIVERSITY OF WISCONSIN
ARBORETUM
AND
WILD LIFE REFUGE
9:30 A.M. JUNE 17TH 1934
SPEAKERS

FOR THE REGENTS	FRED H. CLAUSEN
FOR THE UNIVERSITY	GLENN FRANK
FOR THE STATE	RALPH IMMEL
THE ARBORETUM	G. WM LONGENECKER
THE REFUGE	ALDO LEOPOLD
RESEARCH	HARRY L. RUSSELL
THE FUTURE	JOHN NOLEN

Figure 8.5. Dedication program of the University of Wisconsin Arboretum, Madison, Wisconsin. (University of Wisconsin Arboretum collection)

arboretum—belying the very term itself— would be not merely a site in which to display and cultivate trees, but a place in which to restore native plant and animal communities and, in so doing, cultivate an appreciation of history and possibility. In Leopold's words,

This Arboretum may be regarded as a place where, in the course of time, we will build up an exhibit of what was, as well as an exhibit of what ought to be. It is with this dim vision of its future destiny that we have dedicated a greater part of the Arboretum to a reconstruction of original Wisconsin, rather than to a "collection" of imported trees.[18]

Wisconsin's native landscape had included prairie; so, then, would its university's arboretum. In effect, Leopold and his colleagues were advancing a new branch of applied ecology and a new focus for conservation efforts. "The time has come for science to busy itself with the earth itself," Leopold concluded. "The first step is to reconstruct a sample of what we had to start with."[19]

In the months that followed, Leopold—in collaboration with university botanists Norman Fassett, John T. Curtis, and John Thomson; their students; prairie ecologist Theodore Sperry; and draftees of the new Civilian Conservation Corps—initiated the arboretum's prairie restoration program. They targeted a sixty-acre plot of degraded pasture on the arboretum grounds for their first restoration site. The summer and fall of 1935 were busy with preparation as the botanists and their assistants fanned out to the scant prairie remnants in and around Madison and gathered up the genetic legacy of coneflower, pasqueflower, bluestem, and puccoon. Planting began that fall and the following spring, and the Midwest's prairie began a partial and tentative return to the landscape and to the public consciousness[20] (Figure 8.6).

The idea of prairie restoration was not without precedent. Although the restorations at the University of Wisconsin Arboretum were the first undertaken, they built on the "prairie spirit" that had emerged in the work of the Prairie School architects and landscape architects, as well as midwestern writers and poets, in the first three decades of the century.[21] Robert Grese has written about the key contributions of Jens Jensen, in particular, during these years.[22] Jensen's work inspired the University of Illinois to publish Wilhelm Miller's *The Prairie Spirit in Landscape Gardening,* which called for the establishment of "prairie parks": "Every middle western state will make one prairie reservation before it is too late or *recreate one wild prairie* for the people to enjoy forever."[23] As an aesthetic, the prairie spirit would dissipate somewhat in the 1920s. However, the cultural current continued to flow, and at the arboretum it would merge with fresh concepts from the ecological sciences and from the conservation movement.

The idea of restoration had precedent, however inchoate, in Leopold's experience as well.[24] As a forester, he was familiar with reforestation efforts across the country and had contributed to them throughout his career as a forest ranger, researcher, administrator, and policy advocate. The restoration of game populations and habitats was a consuming interest of Leopold's from the mid-1910s on, and his thinking was marked by an ever-increasing infusion of ecological insight. After moving to Wisconsin in 1924, Leopold began to work with local farmers on several small-scale habitat restoration projects. He closely followed efforts in the late 1920s to reflood Wisconsin's great Horicon Marsh, perhaps the first large-scale wetland restoration effort on record. In the early 1930s, Leopold contributed substantially to similar wetland restoration projects in the vast marshes of Wisconsin's sand counties. At the same time, he served as an ad-

Figure 8.6. Members of the Civilian Conservation Corps contributed to the early prairie restoration experiments at the University of Wisconsin Arboretum. (University of Wisconsin Arboretum collection)

viser to the new Soil Erosion Service (later Soil Conservation Service, now Natural Resources Conservation Service) in its unprecedented, watershed-scale soil conservation project in Coon Valley in western Wisconsin.[25]

All these prior efforts involved restoration of a sort—of particular species, resources, habitats, and processes. At the University of Wisconsin Arboretum, however, the goal of ecological restoration was explicit from the outset and was tied to a broader historical understanding of landscape change. To read conservationist writings of the mid-1930s is to gain a sense of immediate crisis, but also of determined response. This was true even before the great dust storms began to blow; the dust-bowl experience only confirmed and deepened the response. "In the air" at the time was not only dust, but Hugh Hammond Bennett's zealous advocacy of stronger national soil conservation policies, Walter Lowdermilk's infusion of historical and religious perspectives on soil conservation, Jay "Ding" Darling's graphic editorial cartoons of wasted midwestern farm fields, the powerful photographic images of Dorothea Lange and Arthur Rothstein; Paul Sears's classic *Deserts on the March* (1935); Pare Lorentz's film *The Plow that Broke the Plains* (1936); and poems of Archibald MacLeish and ballads of Woody Guthrie.[26]

On the scientific front, these years also saw a weakening of classic Clementsian plant ecology, accompanied by a greater appreciation of (and debate over) the human role in altering grassland structure and function. Among the scientists whose work Leopold closely followed during this period was University of Nebraska botanist John E. Weaver, widely recognized as a leading student of prairie ecology.[27] Weaver's work on the adaptations of prairie plants, particularly their root systems, gave support to Leopold's emerging emphasis on the need to restore biological diversity to ecosystems that were intensively used and managed by people and to retain diversity within protected wildlands.

In his critical article "Why the Wilderness Society?" Leopold stressed the need to protect wilderness lands so that they could be compared with lands more intensively altered by human economic activity (Figure 8.7). For a case study, he turned to the prairies and to Weaver's fundamental work:

Weaver at Nebraska finds that prairie soils lose their granulation and their water equilibrium when too long occupied by exotic crops. Apparently native prairie plants are necessary to restore that biotic stability which we call conservation. . . . Here then is a new discovery which may illuminate basic questions of national policy. On it may hinge the future habitability of a third of the continent. But how shall it be followed up if there be no prairie flora left to compare to the cultivated flora? And who cares a hang about preserving prairie flora except those who see the values of wilderness?[28]

Leopold's choice of the prairie biome as an example in this article is significant. He might have been expected, in an article intended to define the aims of the new Wilderness Society, to extol the values of the "classic" American wilderness—unpopulated expanses of high mountain, canyonland, or northwestern forest. Instead, he turned to a region, and a biome, whose wildness had been extinguished along with the demise of the free-roaming bison herds and the subjugation of the Plains Indians. Leopold's rationale for wilderness protection was not merely recreational or scenic, but scientific, biological, political, economic, and deeply aesthetic.[29] The *imagination* of the prairie, he suggested, is essential to our own adaptation to and within it. With that, too, Leopold drew a direct connection between preservation of the wild and stewardship of the settled—and, in a broader sense, between the preservationist and utilitarian poles of the conservation movement.[30]

In the midst of these other activities, Leopold also embarked on the one for which he would become best known. It took an active imagination indeed to see anything more than waste in the eighty acres of exhausted sandy soil he purchased in January 1935. Leopold saw possibility—for himself, for his family, and for the land itself. "On this sand farm in Wisconsin," he would write in the foreword to *A Sand County Almanac,* "we try to rebuild . . . what we are losing elsewhere."[31] Inspired by the arboretum experience, and perhaps by the silphium standing alone in the roadside cemetery, Leopold and his family soon initiated their own efforts to bring prairie back to their land.

Again it is significant to note that *A Sand County Almanac,* as revered and influential a book on the American landscape as has been written, focused not on the sublime and dramatic—the more readily appreciated Yosemites and Grand Canyons and Yellowstones—but on the flat, mundane, pedestrian, and even degraded midcontinent. In this sense, *A Sand County Almanac* is itself a product of restoration. Its poignancy and its lengthy shelf life stem in part from its revelation of wonder amid the commonplace, its extraction of experience and understanding from landscapes known in the fullness of their evolutionary, ecological, and historical context. It is not merely Leopold's description, but his imagination, of these landscapes that brings them to life. That intention is made plain in the powerful words, also from his

Figure 8.7. Aldo Leopold photographed this eroding pasture in Sauk County, Wisconsin, in the late 1930s. (University of Wisconsin–Madison, Department of Wildlife Ecology)

foreword: "When we see land as a community to which we belong, we may begin to use it with love and respect. There is no other way for land to survive the impact of mechanized man, nor for us to reap from it the esthetic harvest it is capable, under science, of contributing to culture"[32] (Figure 8.8).

In "Prairie: The Forgotten Flora," an unpublished manuscript written in the midst of World War II, Leopold mused, "We can hardly understand our history without knowing what was here before we were."[33] The meaning of restoration, like the meaning of community, gained even deeper resonance against the background of the war. "Now that we must fight to maintain our national existence," he wrote, "one might presuppose a universal interest in the raw materials of and on which states were built. Yet I have never encountered, in any school or college textbook, an adequate description of prairie. Prai-

Figure 8.8. Curtis Prairie at the University of Wisconsin Arboretum. (University of Wisconsin Arboretum collection)

rie, to most Americans, is a flat place once dotted with covered wagons."

One long Cold War generation has passed, and conservationists continue to ask the question that Leopold framed in 1947: What kind of future can we imagine when we have lost our place and our past? The intervening decades have complicated the matter enormously. We are lodged so deeply in a way of experiencing the world and defining ourselves that the question seems almost quaint and fragile, a prairie remnant of the mind. The past seems so distant, the present so demanding, the future arriving so furiously fast—who has time to imagine a future? More frightening yet: Do we retain the *capacity* to imagine, or are we fatally bound by the "narrowing boundaries of consideration"?

There are surely no obvious answers to these questions and scant comfort in the solemn irony of Leopold's "Prairie Birthday." But against the fear we can rest the hope that if any landscape can evoke an enduring response to the "narrowing boundaries," the prairie can. One may hear it, for example, in Wallace Stegner's testimony from *Wolf Willow,* his premier act of prairie imagination. Stegner describes the Saskatchewan of his boyhood, where he had limited cultural opportunities, but unlimited prospects. In such country, he writes,

you become acutely aware of yourself. The world is very large, the sky even larger, and you are very small. But also the world is flat, empty, nearly abstract, and in its flatness you are a challenging upright thing, as sudden as an exclamation mark, as enigmatic as a

Figure 8.9. Contemporary view of the Leopold "shack" and adjacent restored prairie. (Photograph by Curt Meine)

question mark. . . . It was not prairie dwellers who invented the indifferent universe or impotent man. Puny you may feel there, and vulnerable, but not unnoticed. This is a land to mark the sparrow's fall.[34]

Such self-awareness, realistic but determined, may well be the prerequisite to the act of restoration. To seek to rebuild an ecological community, more than 99 percent of which has been lost, is not a job for the faint of heart—or vision (Figure 8.9).

Prairie restoration was born in a time of scientific revolution, economic upheaval, political uncertainty, and environmental crisis. It was, and remains, an act of defiance, of cultural evolution, and of commitment, aiming to reconnect people and landscape and to establish continuity among the past, present, and future.

It seeks to conserve not only the landscape, its inhabitants, and its processes, but also the deep sources of human curiosity and ingenuity. In this sense, the reimagination of the North American prairie has been both prelude to and product of restoration—not only of the land, but of ourselves within it.

Notes

1. For general biographical context, see Susan L. Flader, *Thinking Like a Mountain: Aldo Leopold and the Evolution of an Ecological Attitude Toward Deer, Wolves, and Forest* (1974; reprint, Madison: University of Wisconsin Press, 1994), and Curt Meine, *Aldo Leopold: His Life and Work* (Madison: University of Wisconsin Press, 1988).

2. Aldo Leopold, *A Sand County Almanac and*

Sketches Here and There (New York: Oxford University Press, 1949), viii.

3. Ed Folsom, "Walt Whitman's Prairie Paradise" (this volume, chapter 3).

4. Leopold, "Prairie Birthday," in *Sand County Almanac,* 45. Leopold's essay does not identify precisely the location of the cemetery. The family's usual route took them past several cemeteries in Dane and Sauk Counties. The Sauk Prairie Cemetery, outside Prairie du Sac, best fits the physical description in the essay. It is located, however, in eastern Sauk County, whereas Leopold twice mentioned that the cemetery in question was in western Dane County. If we assume that Leopold did not take poetic license with his county boundaries, several other local cemeteries conform to the clues in the essay. In the mid-1980s, local prairie enthusiasts replanted a "sharp angle" of the Sauk Prairie Cemetery with a mixture of cutleaf silphium, cup plant, big bluestem, Indian grass, Canada wild rye, and coneflower.

5. Leopold, "Prairie Birthday," in *Sand County Almanac,* 46.

6. Ibid.

7. Ibid.

8. For a discussion of the emergence of Leopold's appreciation of biological diversity in the functioning and conservation of natural systems, see J. Baird Callicott, "Whither Conservation Ethics," *Conservation Biology* 4 (1990): 15–20; Susan L. Flader, "The River of the Mother of God: Introduction," *Wilderness* 54 (1991): 18–22; and Curt Meine, "Keeper of the Cogs," *Defenders* 67 (1992): 9–17. See also Gary Paul Nabhan, "Sierra Madre Upshot: Ecological and Agricultural Health," in *Cultures of Habitat: On Nature, Culture, and Story* (Washington, D.C.: Counterpoint Press, 1997), 43–56.

9. The events that Leopold described in "Prairie Birthday" took place almost simultaneously with the preparation of the essay "The Land Ethic" and the original foreword to the manuscript of *A Sand County Almanac.* See Curt Meine, "Building 'The Land Ethic,'" in *Companion to* A Sand County Almanac: *Interpretive and Critical Essays,* ed. J. Baird Callicott (Madison: University of Wisconsin Press, 1987), 172; Dennis Ribbens, "An Introduction to the 1947 Fore-

word [to *Great Possessions*]," in *Companion to* A Sand County Almanac, ed. Callicott, 277; and Aldo Leopold, "Foreword" in *Companion to* A Sand County Almanac, ed. Callicott, 281. The first manuscript version of the essay "Prairie Birthday" is dated December 27, 1947. It was among the last of the *Sand County Almanac* essays to be written.

10. Wes Jackson, "Natural Systems Agriculture: The Truly Radical Alternative" (this volume, chapter 12).

11. Aldo Leopold, *Report on a Game Survey of the North Central States* (Madison, Wis.: Sporting Arms and Ammunition Manufacturers' Institute, 1931); Meine, *Aldo Leopold,* 259–81.

12. Leopold, *Game Survey of the North Central States,* 15–20. Leopold writes, for example, "The five [land] types in [the Midwest's agricultural] belt differ from each other in their proportion of original prairie, and in the origin of their soils. The prairie type contained no timber except along streams, hence its present upland timber is scanty. . . . Contrary to common belief, the cream of [the region's] game country was the prairie type, which is now the poorest. . . . The prairie type was the home of the prairie chicken. Parts of it now support pheasants, and parts a few quail."

13. Leopold focused on this trend in much of his pioneering discussions of game management in the late 1920s and 1930s. See, for example, Leopold, *Game Survey of the North Central States,* 59–67; "Progress of the Game Survey," *Transactions of the 16th American Game Conference,* (Washington, D.C.: American Game Association, 1929), 64–71; "Game Range," *Journal of Forestry* 22 (1931): 932–38; and *Game Management* (New York: Scribner, 1933), 304–23.

14. Leopold, *Game Survey of the North Central States,* 249.

15. The story of the founding of the University of Wisconsin Arboretum is told in Nancy Sachse, *A Thousand Ages: The University of Wisconsin Arboretum* (Madison: University of Wisconsin Arboretum, 1965), 11–28. Leopold's "University Arboretum Wild Life Management Plan" was submitted on October 25, 1933.

16. Thomas J. Blewitt and Grant Cottam, "History of the University of Wisconsin Arboretum Prairies," *Transactions of the Wisconsin Academy of Sciences, Arts and Letters* 72 (1984): 130–44; Michael Goc, "The Great Dustbowl: It First Came to Wisconsin," *Wisconsin Trails* 25 (1984): 20–24.

17. Aldo Leopold, "The Arboretum and the University," in *The River of the Mother of God and Other Essays by Aldo Leopold,* ed. Susan L. Flader and J. Baird Callicott (Madison: University of Wisconsin Press, 1991), 210.

18. Ibid.

19. Ibid., 211.

20. According to Sachse, three methods were used in the first planting: "Hay containing prairie seeds was spread over the ground, seeds were scattered broadcast, or whole sections of sod were transplanted in strips" (*Thousand Ages,* 50). Forty-two species were represented in this initial effort. See Theodore M. Sperry, "Analysis of the University of Wisconsin–Madison Prairie Restoration Project," *Proceedings of the Eighth North American Prairie Conference,* ed. Richard Brewer (Kalamazoo: Western Michigan University, 1983), 140–47; and Blewitt and Cottam, "History of the University of Wisconsin Arboretum Prairies."

21. Stephen F. Christy, "The Prairie Spirit," in *An Open Land: Photographs of the Midwest, 1852–1982,* ed. Victoria Post Ranney (Chicago: Openlands Project, 1983), 68–74. For a more developed discussion of the antecedents of modern restoration, see Marcus Hall, "Co-Workers with Nature: The Deeper Roots of Restoration," *Restoration and Management Notes* 15 (1997): 173–78.

22. Robert E. Grese, "The Landscape Art of Jens Jensen" (this volume, chapter 7).

23. Wilhelm Miller, *The Prairie Spirit in Landscape Gardening* (Urbana: University of Illinois Agricultural Experiment Station, 1915), quoted in Christy, "Prairie Spirit," 72. [Emphasis added] The extent of Jensen's influence on the development of the arboretum's restoration plans, and of his possible interactions with Leopold, awaits further exploration. Both were involved, for example, with the group Friends of Our Native Landscape.

24. For a commentary on Leopold's restoration activities, see Peter Losin, "A Restorationist Perspective on the New Leopold Biography," *Restoration and Management Notes* 6 (1988): 81–83.

25. Key publications by Leopold during this period include *Game Survey of the North Central States; Game Management;* "Helping Ourselves," in *River of the Mother of God,* ed. Flader and Callicott, 203–8; "Coon Valley: An Adventure in Cooperative Conservation," in *River of the Mother of God,* ed. Flader and Callicott, 218–23; and "The Wisconsin River Marshes," *National Waltonian* 2 (1934): 4–5, 11.

26. Donald Worster, *Dust Bowl: The Southern Plains in the 1930s* (New York: Oxford University Press, 1979).

27. John E. Weaver, *Prairie Plants and Their Environment: A Fifty Year Study in the Midwest* (1968; reprint, Lincoln: University of Nebraska Press, 1991). For a detailed history of the development of prairie ecology, see Ronald C. Tobey, *Saving the Prairies: The Life Cycle of the Founding School of American Plant Ecology, 1895–1955* (Berkeley: University of California Press, 1981).

28. Aldo Leopold, "Why the Wilderness Society?" *Living Wilderness,* September 1935, 6. Leopold may well have taken his cues from Weaver, who the year before had published similar thoughts in a paper written with Evan Flory, "Stability of Climax Prairie and Some Environmental Changes Resulting from Breaking," *Ecology* 15 (1934): 343. See Worster, *Dust Bowl,* 203.

29. Craig W. Allin discusses the evolution of Leopold's wilderness ideas in "The Leopold Legacy and American Wilderness," in *Aldo Leopold: The Man and His Legacy,* ed. Thomas Tanner (Ankeny, Iowa: Soil Conservation Society of America, 1987), 25–38.

30. Curt Meine, "The Utility of Preservation and the Preservation of Utility: Leopold's Fine Line," *The Wilderness Condition: Essays on Environment and Civilization,* ed. Max Oelschlaeger (San Francisco: Sierra Club Books, 1992), 131–72.

31. Leopold, *Sand County Almanac,* viii. Nina Leopold Bradley provides a personal account of the family's restoration work in "On the Land," *American Forests* 103 (1997): 26–29. See also Stephanie Mills,

"The Leopolds' Shack," in *In Service of the Wild: Restoring and Reinhabiting Damaged Land* (Boston: Beacon Press, 1995), 93–112, reprinted in *Wild Earth* 6 (1996): 56–59.

32. Leopold, *Sand County Almanac,* viii.

33. Aldo Leopold, "Prairie: The Forgotten Flora" (this volume, chapter 9).

34. Wallace Stegner, *Wolf Willow: A History, a Story, and a Memoir of the Last Plains Frontier* (Lincoln: University of Nebraska Press, 1955), 8.

Visual Prospects: Paintings and Photographs of the Contemporary Prairie

The following reproductions of work by sixteen of the twenty contemporary artists represented in "Plain Pictures: Images of the American Prairie" give a very broad, diverse sample of how the plains and prairies are seen and represented today. Intentionally, these works are, with two exceptions, different from those in the exhibition and from those discussed in "Sizing Up the Country," the summary of the artists' written answers to questions about their work. Here the "statements" are *visual*.

Robert Adams, *Nebraska State Highway 2, Box Butte County, Nebraska* (1978). Black-and-white photograph. (Courtesy Fraenkel Gallery, San Francisco)

Lee Allen, *Requiem for a Family Farm* (1997). Acrylic, 44 × 33 inches. (Courtesy of the artist)

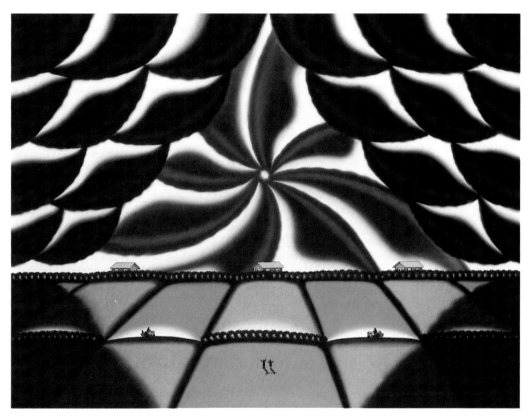

Roger Brown, *Approaching Storm* (1980). Oil on canvas, 54 × 72 inches. (Photograph by William H. Bengston; courtesy Phyllis Kind Gallery, Chicago–New York)

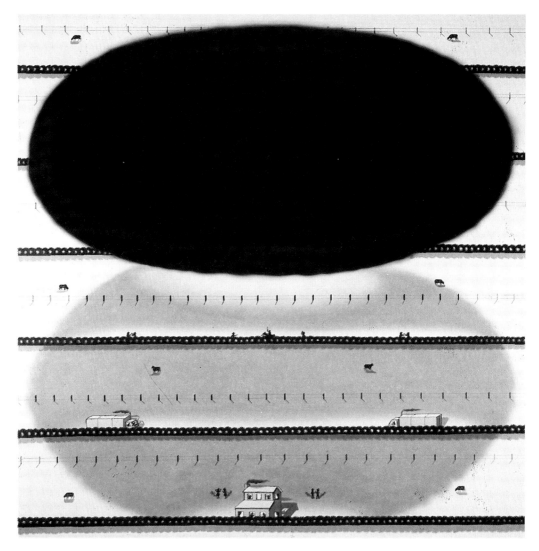

Roger Brown, *Home on the Range* (1980). Oil on canvas, 72 × 72 inches. (Photograph by William H. Bengston; courtesy Phyllis Kind Gallery, Chicago–New York)

James D. Butler, *Threshold* (1990–1991). Oil on canvas, 84 × 138 inches. (Courtesy of the artist)

Fred Easker, *Morning on Springville Road* (1995). Oil on canvas, 17 × 90 inches. (Courtesy of the artist)

Terry Evans, *Matfield Green Rest Stop on Interstate 35, Turnpike* (1994). Silver gelatin print, 42¼ × 41½ inches. (Courtesy of the artist)

Terry Evans, *Power Lines Intersecting the Flint Hills East of Matfield Green, Kansas* (1994). Silver gelatin print, 42¼ × 41½ inches. (Courtesy of the artist)

Harold L. Gregor, *Illinois Flatscape #38* (1989). Acrylic on canvas, 60 × 82 inches. (Courtesy of the artist)

Harold L. Gregor, *Illinois Landscape #143—A Late May Evening* (1997). Oil and acrylic on canvas, 5 × 35 feet. (The Art Collection of McCormick Place Convention Complex; courtesy Metropolitan Pier and Exposition Authority, Chicago)

Walter Hatke, *Corner of Elm* (1983). Oil on canvas, 19 × 27 inches. (Courtesy of the artist)

Walter Hatke, *Hillside* (1983). Oil on canvas, 22 × 36 inches. (Courtesy of the artist)

Stan Herd, *Iowa Landscape* (1996). Crop art, Cedar Rapids Airport. (Photograph by Jonathan H. Van Allen)

Harold D. Holoun, *Prairie Dawn* (1988). Oil on canvas, 50 × 78 inches. (Courtesy of the artist)

Harold D. Holoun, *Omaha Skyline 2/2/97* (1997). Oil on paper, 18 × 22 inches. (Courtesy of the artist)

Keith Jacobshagen, *Cooling in July* (1997). Oil on canvas, 30 × 34 inches. (Courtesy of the artist)

Gary Irving, *Edge of the Pasture, Nebraska Panhandle* (1995). Color photograph. (Courtesy of the artist)

Gary Irving, *Trees at Dawn, Ogle County, Illinois* (1989). Color photograph. (Courtesy of the artist)

Stuart Klipper, *Minnesota #68, Winter 1997*. Color photograph. (Courtesy of the artist)

Stuart Klipper, *Minnesota #8, Fall 1993*. Color photograph. (Courtesy of the artist)

Genie Patrick, *Curving Rows* (1996). Oil on paper, 22 × 30 inches. (Courtesy of the artist)

David Plowden, *Westbound Freight Train West of Havre, Montana* (1971). Black-and-white photograph. (Used by permission of David Plowden and Sterling Lord Literistic, Inc., copyright © 1971 by David Plowden)

David Plowden, *Farm by Chicago & Northwestern Tracks, Mechanicsville, Iowa* (1986). Black-and-white photograph. (Used by permission of David Plowden and Sterling Lord Literistic, Inc., copyright © 1986 by David Plowden)

James R. Winn, *A Tuesday Evening* (1986). Acrylic on paper, 19 × 38 inches. (Courtesy of the artist)

James R. Winn, *Dusk: #37* (1995). Acrylic on paper, 20 × 46 inches. (Courtesy of the artist)

9 Prairie: The Forgotten Flora

Aldo Leopold

On Sept. 3, 1763, a decade before the Revolution, Captain Jonathan Carver left Mackinac for the wilds of "Ouisconsin." He wanted to prove that the French explorers, while they had covered a lot of ground, had not kept their eyes open. He, an Englishman, was going to show them how to make and record observations in new [lands].

To [this] little circumstance we probably owe the explicit descriptions of our state recorded in Carver's *Journal*.[1]

Proceeding to Green Bay and up the Fox, he arrived at Fond du Lac, and on Sept. 10 continued his ascent of the river toward "the carrying place," or Portage. (His disdain of everything French apparently included place-names).

About twelve miles before I reached the carrying place, I observed several small mountains which extended quite to it.

These, I suppose, were the moraines north of Portage.

Carver remarks of the Fox as it approaches Portage:

I cannot recollect anything else that is remarkable in this river, except that it is so serpentine for five miles as to gain (only) one quarter of a mile.

Mrs. Kinzie later noted this same circumvolution.

The Carrying Place between the Fox and the Ouisconsin Rivers is in breadth not more than a mile and three quarters, though in some maps it is delineated as to appear to be ten miles.

Carver here digresses to suggest that French geographers twist or omit their rivers, and even run them uphill, in order to mislead the English. Having demolished the incompetents, he returns to Portage:

Near one half of the way, between the rivers, is a morass overgrown with a kind of long grass. [Doubtless the marsh between Portage and the Agency House.] *The rest of it is a plain with some few oak and pine trees growing thereon.*

Here, then, is an assertion, by a competent Englishman (no less), that the original landscape surrounding the Agency House was prairie, bearing only scattered oaks and pines.

Mrs. Kinzie, arriving at Portage in 1831, confirms Carver's description in many passages of *Waubun*,[2] but she adds that a "thickly wooded ridge" lay to the north. This, I suppose, was one of the moraines.

The wide prevalence of prairie in the region is attested by Carver's description of the view from Blue Mounds:

For miles nothing was to be seen but lesser mountains, which appeared at a distance like haycocks, they being free from trees. Only a few groves of hickory, and stunted oaks, covered some of the vallies.

What is prairie?

There is irony in the question. Half of southern Wisconsin was once prairie. Now that we must fight to maintain our national existence, one might presuppose a universal interest in the raw materials of and on which states were built. Yet I have never encountered, in any school or college textbook, an adequate description of prairie. Prairie, to most Americans, is a flat place once dotted with covered wagons.

Prairie was, in fact, a community of plants and animals so organized as to build, through the centuries, the rich soil which now feeds us.

The plants included not only grasses, but also herbs and shrubs, to a total of 50 or 75 species. This plant community was adapted, with extraordinary precision, to the vagaries of drouth, fire, grazing mammals, and Indians. The more the Indians burned it, the more legumes it grew, the more nitrogen they pulled out of the air, and the richer it got. So, even among plants, we encounter the "uses of adversity."

Many prairie plants bore flowers of singular beauty, and nearly all colored in fall like a maple in the woods.

Some of the prairie plants are now nearly extinct; many have become uncommon; none retain their original dominance (save only ragweed, which was adapted to ground torn up by buffalo, and now finds ground torn up by Mr. McCormick to be just as good). Most of the prairie flora has disappeared from view, partly by reason of plow and cow, and partly by reason of competitive Asiatic and European weeds and grasses. None of the grasses now dominant in southern Wisconsin is native. Roadsides, the natural refuge for prairie, are becoming more and more untenable for anything save sweet clover, quack, and blue grass.

The old flora, like an old book, should be preserved for its historical associations. We can hardly understand our history without knowing what was here before we were.

The practical question is: where, and by whom, shall the prairie flora be given a roothold on some odd bits of its former domain. The University is giving it some hundred acres of the Arboretum. An equally suitable place is the Agency House at Portage.

We have here restored, at great pains, the architecture and furniture of an 1830 household, and then set it in a landscape monopolized by stowaways from Asia. It is only what we don't know about plants that prevents such an incongruity from hurting us.

A roothold for prairie is not to be achieved by wishing it; aggressors are hard to dislodge, particularly quack. There are many prairie species, requiring a considerable range of cultural methods. These methods were unknown a decade ago; they are now being worked out, at the Arboretum and elsewhere. While the reestablishment of prairie requires much skill and some expense, its maintenance fortunately requires nothing but an occasional burn.

Stock of a dozen prairie plants still exists on the unplowed parts of the Agency property: turkey-foot bluestem, little bluestem, prairie clover, lupine, spider wort, lead plant, flowering spurge, puccoon, Indigo-plant, lespedeza, anemone cylindrica, blazing-star. Seeds of many more are to be had for the gathering, if one knows where to look.

I urge that a prairie be reestablished as the necessary and logical environment of the Agency House.

Notes

This hand-written manuscript was dated November 6, 1942. There is no notation about the circumstances of its composition. In it, Leopold promotes the idea of prairie restoration at the Agency House Historic Site in Portage, Wisconsin. The manuscript is in the Aldo Leopold Papers, Series 9/25/10–6, Box 18, University of Wisconsin–Madison Archives, and is published with the permission of the Aldo Leopold Foundation.

1. Captain Jonathan Carver, *Three Years' Travels Through the Interior Parts of North America* (Philadelphia: Key and Simpson, 1796).

2. Mrs. John H. Kinzie, *Waubun* (Menasha, Wis.: Banta, 1930).

10 The Phoenix People of Sod Corn Country

Pauline Drobney

The first time I remember seeing a prairie was during my sixteenth summer. I had earned my driver's license and was eager to hone my new skill. My aging grandfather, meanwhile, was no longer able to drive and needed to visit the nearby town of Manson to buy clothing ample enough to accommodate his generous build, and so we struck a deal. I happily drove him to Manson, and he purchased a couple of pairs of striped coveralls.

On the way back to Pocahontas, Grandpa looked at me and asked, "Did you ever see that piece of land they never plowed?" I had not. "Would you like to?" he asked. My affirmative answer had more to do with humoring Grandpa than it did with any interest in or curiosity about this unplowed place. But in a little while, he and I stood on a gravel road, the grand, heavy, wooden Kalsow Prairie State Preserve sign creaking in the breeze on the corner of a country crossroads (Figure 10.1). I looked across the prairie and gave it as fair a chance as I knew how. I tried to attach some significance that would register in my own life, tried to imagine my ancestors in covered wagons crossing endless grasslands like this. In the end, the place just looked like a bunch of weeds.

But this memory has become precious to me. The image of my grandfather, in old age and wisdom, standing with me, in youth and inexperience, on that gravel road separating the ancient black-soil prairie on one side of the road from the modern cornfield on the other has great personal symbolism for me. Yet at the time, prairie was unknown and unknowable to me. How could I know it? It was not a part of my life.

To know prairie, one must be immersed in it in some way. You don't come to know prairie by standing at its edge and looking in; you must be *in* prairie and let it get into you.

I grew up in the flatlands of Pocahontas County in northwestern Iowa. I knew my agricultural heritage. It was evident everywhere, for surrounding the little farm town of Pocahontas were fields of corn and beans. One of my earliest jobs as a child was bean walking. Whenever I mention this to someone, I know immediately if they have ever been a bean walker by the knowing smile that appears on that person's face. It is hard, hot work—hoeing, chopping, or pulling thistles, cockleburs, and other weeds from within the rows of beans—but I liked it. As I walked, and the sweet black

Figure 10.1. Roadside marker at Kalsow Prairie State Preserve, Pocahontas County, Iowa. (Photograph by Carl Kurtz, St. Anthony, Iowa)

soil oozed between the toes of my bare feet, I knew I was a part of a proud farm people, but I had no idea that this soil was the legacy of prairie.

Growing up with my five siblings and a menagerie of wild animals both inside and outside our house, I was unknowingly exposed to parts of prairie, for in my hometown, our house was considered the nursery for injured and orphaned animals in a time and in a place where such activities were considered acceptable. Pretty wildflowers were transplanted to our gardens from roadsides, and every year, we all piled into the family station wagon and "hunted weeds." My mother later made arrangements of the dried pods and seed heads of plants that we collected during our roadside sojourns and

hung from strips of ripped rags tied to the garage rafters.

These were among the dormant kernels of prairie that were planted in me in early youth and that I carried to adulthood. When I entered college at the University of Northern Iowa after high school, my interest in field biology increasingly drew me away from the special-education major for which I had registered. And when I enrolled for two sessions at Iowa Lakeside Laboratory, a biological field station at Lake Okoboji, I was thrilled by the diversity and wonder of prairie. I had no idea that such a thing was out there. Had no idea that there was so much variety in a state so often scorned for a monotonous dominance of corn and beans on its landscape. This only served to set my roots deeper in the black soil of Iowa, for if such things could be discovered in ten short weeks at a biological field station, what else could be learned in a lifetime, and what had these little prairies been a part of? The seeds planted in me by Grandpa and the rest of my family germinated in that summer after my sophomore year.

Returning to Pocahontas after my epiphany, and before the fall semester called me back to school, I set out on my bicycle, searching the roadsides for a kind of plant that my mother told me she remembered had been carefully cultivated beneath my grandmother's lilac bush. It was a special plant that Grandma had called prairie tea and that made a good soothing brew. As I searched, I was impressed and disappointed that in this agriculturally rich area, there were generally not many species in the roadsides and that there were large spaces between prairie plants. Still I brought back small pieces of several kinds of plants to my mother, and, finally, I produced a plant to which she exclaimed, "That's it!"

Prairie tea. I like the name and think it seems more appropriate than the name "mountain mint" usually given it in books. Finding prairie tea for my mother, getting her a start of it, and later growing it in my own gardens directly connected me to prairie in a new way. I commonly saw prairie tea in prairies, both wet and dry. It is a plant that was used by my ancestors and by Native Americans, and that I use. I became more a part of prairie, less a spectator.

It occurs to me that in the English language in this country, we think of prairie as being very dimensional. We enter a prairie and leave a prairie, can drive up to it and pass it or go to another prairie. A prairie is a thing we can put a fence around and define in terms of size because it is surrounded by something else, usually cropland or bromefields. But I think that this is a concept born of fairly new assumptions.

I suspect that a couple of hundred years ago,

among native peoples of the prairie region, reference to "a prairie" might not have made sense. I suspect that there was a concept or word that meant simply "prairie," the landscape, not "a prairie," a circumscribed parcel of land. In those days, one would have been surrounded by and immersed *in* prairie. People probably thought of themselves as somehow being a part of prairie. There may have been words for many kinds of prairie, such as wet prairie, dry prairie, or prairie where the buffalo had been.

I mention this because it seems that the uses and concepts attached to the word "prairie" provide insights into our habitation of the land and our rapid loss of memory of the prairie landscape that our ancestors settled. The change wrought on the natural landscape came so quickly that today's descendants of agrarian European pioneers, who themselves had no context for prairie, have little cultural memory of what was once a major ecosystem of the North American continent.

Several years ago, I met the last surviving sibling of the grandfather who had introduced me to prairie. Anna, who still lived on the farmstead where my family had settled, was in her late nineties and had failing eyesight. She told me stories of the wet sloughs near the house and of the native "blue lilies" that she and her family had transplanted and grown in their gardens. I imagine the blue lilies to have been the spiderworts of moist prairie in mid-spring. The thing Anna's opaque eyes missed most were her gardens.

When Anna died a couple years later, I realized that an incredible history of my family was recorded in the artifacts preserved on this farm. This history ranged from letters written in Bohemian and the skirts worn by my great-grandmother on her journey from her motherland to America, to the bags of white goose feathers and dill weed hung by Anna above her big loom with a work in progress. All these things were like a thread I longed somehow to follow back to a time of prairie on the land. If I could read the clues, perhaps I could "know" prairie better.

When most of the possessions of my grandfather's people were sold at auction, I bought the single-bottom, horse-drawn plow. Sometimes, on a summer evening, I lay my ear against the steel and imagine a sound like shoestrings popping, described by European settlers as the sound that leadplant roots made as they broke under the plow. I sometimes imagine ways to run old breaking plows backward, zipping intact prairie back into black furrows like an old movie run backward. For the paramount lesson I have learned in the past twenty years, which I have spent working to reconstruct prairie on plowed ground and working to repair and manage prairie remnants, is that it is easier to preserve and nurture remnant prairie than it is to rebuild prairie from scratch.

The pieces of Iowa's ancient ecosystems are typically small and hidden (Figure 10.2). Tucked away in isolated farm parcels inaccessible to the plow, on steep limestone outcroppings, in deep dry loess soil deposits, or in wet spots, there still exist fragments of the once-vast and -variable natural landscape. It was a wild place, as wild and special as any tropical rain forest, misty fern-bedecked old-growth forest, or island atoll. For in Iowa there once existed a vast grassland from the Missouri River to the Mississippi River, punctuated by occasional groves of open-grown oaks. These oak groves, with their grassy understory, were called savannas, openings, or oak barrens. The open prairie—dominated by tall bunchgrasses, native sunflowers, and wild asters —was studded with such floral gems as shooting star, prairie smoke, white-fringed prairie orchid, and prairie lily.

And thriving in sun-dappled understories of horizontally branched centurion oaks among the grass and the grasslike sedges, there grew wildflowers blooming in succession from spring until killing frost. Here was a peculiar mix of what we think of as prairie species growing among others we often consider to be forest species. Blazing star, yellow lady's slipper, and leadplant mixed with columbine, mayapples, and jack-in-the-pulpits. There were some species that thrived neither in full sun nor in deep shade, but under the limbs of oaks. These were the signature plants of the sun-filtered savanna, including purple milkweed, creamy gentian, and the delicate, blue, vining leather flower.

This place, now named Iowa, also teemed with wildlife. Prairie chickens whirled wildly in misty, morning, spring courtships. Herds of bison thundered across the prairie, and elk browsed beneath branches of ancient oaks. Complex relationships existed among the species of plants and animals: the bluebirds, the bugs, the blazing star, the bison, and the big bluestem all depended on one another and the physical environment of the prairie to survive and thrive.

And through time and with the passing of thousands of generations, the genetic character of a species with limited mobility in one area probably became subtly different from that of the same species in another area, as populations responded to conditions in their respective local environments. Such genetic differences were likely to be most pronounced among populations of species occupying areas with notable differences in topographic, soil, and moisture conditions as are found in geologic landforms. Those occupying the steep limestone bluffs of northeast Iowa developed a genetic memory of how best to survive in this rocky, xeric local environment in association with other species of plants and animals living there. The genetic memory of the same species in the glacier-flattened prairie pothole region of northwest Iowa, was allied to organically rich, soggy soil

167

Figure 10.2. Virginia wild rye at sunset in eastern Story County, Iowa. (Photograph by Carl Kurtz, St. Anthony, Iowa)

with a characteristic association of species of plants and animals likewise locally adapted.

In addition to genetic differences, these areas had distinctive mixes of species. The steep-sided loess hills along the Missouri River, formed by the action of glacial winds, with loess soil deposits sometimes as deep as 200 feet, were dry and supported yucca and skeleton weed, which are typical of the drier mixed-grass prairies to the west of the Missouri River, but are rare in most of Iowa.

Prairie cordgrass prevailed as a common species in the prairie pothole region, but was poorly adapted to dry loess hills uplands. Creamy gentian and purple milkweed were at home in the open savannas of the gently rolling hills in southern Iowa, but occurred more rarely in northern Iowa. Conversely, pasqueflower, shooting star, and prairie smoke were more common in the open prairies of northern Iowa.

The primeval prairie landscape was not devoid of people. The Native Americans who inhabited the prairie and savanna landscape were crucial to the survival of the ecosystems they occupied, for they lit the fires necessary to the proliferation of native ecosystems. These fires go back to antiquity; the North American prairies originally developed in response to long periods of hot dry climate prone to fires, an environment hostile to trees. Although the climate eventually became cool and moist enough to allow the landscape to readily support trees, the vista that greeted the first Europeans in what is now Iowa and the surrounding region was not the arboreal forests to which they were more accustomed.

Grassland, including savanna, survived because fires periodically swept the land. There is evidence that most of the fires were not accidental lightning strikes, but intentionally set, probably annually by Native Americans in order to more easily hunt wild game, to aid in travel, and

to protect themselves or harass enemies. These fires kept trees at bay in the prairie and prevented savannas from being choked by woody encroachment. Fire in the prairies and savannas of Iowa was as necessary as sunshine and rain.

To the European farmers who began to settle in Iowa in the mid-nineteenth century, however, the nearly treeless prairie was a foreign place, and fire was a terrifying force to be conquered. But the American prairie was huge, occupying 240 million acres,[1] parts of twelve states, and a portion of Canada. When it was discovered that the rich black soil of the tallgrass portion of these grasslands was ideally suited to agriculture, the tallgrass prairie landscape was rapidly settled. To the pioneers, prairie seemed boundless, its bounty endless. Iowa figures prominently in this picture, for tallgrass prairie dominated a larger proportion of what is now Iowa than of any other state. Iowa was the heart of the tallgrass prairie.

The lure of available land and good farm soil was so intense that within ten years of settlement of any given area in Iowa, the natural landscape was, in essence, completely converted to an agricultural landscape.[2] The patterns of settlement and demise of tallgrass prairie in Iowa were typical of those in other parts of the tallgrass prairie region, and within a span of a mere sixty to seventy years during the latter half of the nineteenth century, most of the ecosystem was gone.[3]

With the difficult work of turning the prairie sod came the practice of growing sod corn. In some cases, this consisted of nothing more than planting seed in an upturned clump of root-laden soil chopped out of the sod. In other cases, it involved planting corn in newly turned furrows of prairie sod. As the upturned roots of prairie sod died, they supplied abundant nutrients to the planted corn.

The planting of sod corn represents a profound turning point in Iowa history, as prairie was rapidly supplanted by crops. The term "sod corn" both expresses the irreversible transition from native "sod" to exotic "corn" and forever links tallgrass prairie with the new agricultural people. Iowa's farm economy is symbolically rooted in those first corn rows nourished by the decaying prairie sod. Even now, midwestern farming is directly dependent on ancient prairies, for it was the continual cycle of growth and decay of prairie plant roots that was responsible for the accumulation of richly organic soil.

As an agricultural people, therefore, we Midwesterners are a prairie people, whether we realize it or not. But our prairie heritage is difficult to appreciate, since the tenure of prairie under Euro-American stewardship was brief and the remaining prairie changed drastically.

In the brief time that the term "sod corn" was coined, used, and forgotten, European settlers left their impressions of the native landscape of the Midwest in place names of forgotten origin. Towns called Prairie City, Pilot Grove, Plover, and Buffalo Center, Iowa; Blooming Prairie, Minnesota; Pretty Prairie, Kansas; and Golden Prairie, Missouri are like faint echoes of a lost landscape. The use of the word "prairie" has shifted from describing a lush, grassy native meadow, to describing flat land. We are more likely to use the word "prairie" as an adjective in identifying a "prairie farm," "Prairie Estates," or "Prairie Pork." There seems to still be a vague sense of place attached to the word, but little or no knowledge of the ancient grasslands. This is no wonder, for the focus in settlement was on "civilizing" the land.

With settlement, plowed land and roads effectively created fire breaks in remaining prairie. In Pocahontas County, in slough country, settlement was impeded by wet sloughs given names like Devil's Island, Purgatory, Muskrat, and Sixteen-Mile Slough, which are clues to pioneers' attitudes about them.[4] A history of Pocahontas County, Iowa, noted, "These were great places for muskrats and ducks and gave rise to the familiar proverbs that 'a flat-boat should be included in a farmer's list of apparatus necessary for cropping here' and that 'a man became web-footed after living in Pocahontas County a year.'"[5] But even though settlement was slowed in this wet country, fire was intentionally and creatively prevented. In Pocahontas County, there is a record of cattle being sent to prairie in spring to graze so that by fall, there was nothing to fuel a prairie fire.[6]

With the planting of crops and the prevention of fire, unbroken prairie became a thing of the past, and surviving remnants began to degrade. Parcels of prairie became smaller and smaller and were increasingly isolated from one another. Many animals were gone from the prairies. In my home county, the last free-ranging bison was reported to have been shot, amid much commotion, in 1863.[7] My grandfather recounted remembrances to my brothers of prairie chickens booming their early-morning courtship calls. I have never seen a prairie chicken in Iowa. In the span of two generations, we lost an important prairie species. The losses we recount to our children or grandchildren, if we are attentive and observant enough to be aware of them, will be of less conspicuous but nonetheless important species. The loss of even one species of endemic butterfly is a loss of an element of interdependence so important in prairies.

Prairie remnants have degraded in several other ways. In addition to loss of native species, there have been additions of exotic species brought, intentionally or unintentionally, to the area by human inhabitants. They compete with native plants and animals for space, light, and food. Agricultural erosion, pesticide drift or overspray, runoff of chemicals used on roads in winter to melt snow, and dredging of roadside ditches for drainage strain the ability of prairies to persist.

Another threat to the uniqueness and stability of the ancient grassland ecosystem is the loss of genetic exchange. In the large, unbroken expanses, genetic exchange flowed naturally; if a species was extinguished in one area, the population possibly could be reestablished by members of another population that had survived elsewhere. The prairie today is highly fragmented, and the survival of some semblance of grassland ecosystems may depend on finding ways of reconnecting these remnants. If a small population of organisms exists in a very small area for many generations and there are only a few organisms to breed with, the potential for inbreeding is obvious. With inbreeding comes decreasing species vigor and increasing genetic degradation. And if a population existing on a remnant is extinguished, the possibility for reestablishment from another remnant is almost nonexistent because remnants are distant and isolated from one another.

Many of the problems of prairies are also common to savannas, but these ecosystems face special challenges simply because they include trees (Figure 10.3). You could say that we could not see the savannas for the trees, and thus mistook them for forests. Because we did not understand the character of historic savannas and open woodlands until the past several years, we thought that these densely wooded areas were forests and encouraged fire prevention. Actually, they were languishing savanna remnants dying from lack of light. Without fire, the openings among the oaks became heavily overgrown with fire-intolerant trees and shrubs. Oak seedlings do not survive in deep shade, so only those trees large enough to compete for sunlight remained,

and the composition of woody species shifted. This is why it is common in overgrown savannas to see a few large oaks, often with their lower limbs dying or dead from lack of light, surrounded by a dense stand of rather uniform younger trees.

The diverse understory in these dark woodlands languished, except sometimes along trails, at woodland edges, or in areas where enough sunlight still reached the ground to support the light-loving herbaceous vegetation. Because we have known nothing else, we have come to think that woodlands support only spring-blooming wildflowers and none that open later in the season. The simple reason that wildflowers can bloom in the spring is that they complete the critical pulse of their life cycle when there is ample sunlight before the trees leaf out. As the season progresses in densely overgrown savannas, however, the ground becomes so dark that wildflowers that should be blooming cannot thrive. After several years, the weakened populations of plants finally die.

In Iowa, most of the historic woodlands were open, and forest communities were uncommon. We have misnamed most of the remaining savanna communities in Iowa, as in most of the Midwest, as forests. In so doing, we have locked them into a fatal cycle of forest management, whereas they need open-woodland management. Dying savannas can be recognized by the presence of characteristic flower, grass, and grasslike species growing in brighter pockets of the woods and, often, by the presence of oaks with horizontal limbs, for only an oak grown in full sun will have this kind of characteristic branching pattern. Prairies and savannas without rejuvenating fires grow rank in vegetative debris and dense with brush and trees. Because of the severe effects of deep shade on the savanna plant community, the opportunity for successful restoration of light-starved wood-

Figure 10.3. Prairie savanna with old bur oaks, shooting star, hoary puccoon, and columbine at Rochester Cemetery, Cedar County, Iowa. (Photograph by Carl Kurtz, St. Anthony, Iowa)

lands perhaps is limited to only the next several years.

Both prairies and savannas, therefore, need human stewardship, and there has been a great shift in philosophies of management. As late as the early 1960s, prairie managers thought that the best way to preserve the remaining fragments was to put fences around them to keep people out. People had done enough harm, and nature would know how to heal itself. The fatal flaw in this approach is that one key species is missing, but is critical to the survival of even small prairie and savanna remnants. That species is us. Show me a black-soil prairie remnant in good condition, and I'll show you an attentive prairie steward.

Lending fire to grass duff connects us to aboriginal people living on prairie hundreds of years ago. With the reenactment of that ancient ritual, the prairies and savannas respond.

A prairie scientist from Illinois named Gerould Wilhelm, who had an interest in Native American language and culture, noted that many native peoples had a term for themselves that meant the "Human Beings" or the "One True People," as opposed to others or outsiders.[8] He had thought that these references were a "quaint chauvinistic notion" until he heard the following story.

In 1795, the Shawnee people, half of whom were being displaced from their homes in Ohio, were seeking a new home, so they sent their shamans—their wise people, the people who knew the sum total of their history—to Illinois to see if they might be able to make a home there. So the shamans, who knew the ways of the plants and animals and who knew the landscape of Ohio, went to Illinois. They observed the plants and animals and the ways the people who lived there used them. The shamans saw that the ways of the people of Illinois and the land itself were different from their own ways and land. So they returned to their people and told them that the Shawnee could not go to Illinois to live because they were not the True People of that place. After that, the Shawnee dispersed along the trails, and the True People of Ohio disappeared from the face of the earth.

I have heard people say that the survival of tallgrass prairies lies in making them economically valuable. I reject this way of thinking. The dollar is a fickle thing, and what is worth lots of money today is valueless tomorrow. I think that the preservation of tallgrass prairies and savannas lies in the connection of the people of a landscape with the native ecosystems. Only if prairie and savanna become a part of the language and tradition of the people who live on the land is there possibility for long-term survival of these local ecosystems.

How does a people begin to develop a language and a tradition of an ecosystem? As I muse on this, I look down at my young son, not yet two years old. He is hungry for the outdoors. When I come home from work, it is not unusual for him to run to me and say, "Boots!" and point to his feet. He wants me to take him out into the snow to explore and discover. He is hungry for nature. It comes naturally to kids. Ian hears crows call and calls back. Chickadees, willow sticks, ice crystals—all delight him. As he gets down on all fours and happily munches snow by scooping it up with his mouth, I realize that he is still wild. This wildness is inborn and should be nourished, for in it is creativity, problem solving, coping, and knowing one's place on the earth.

I go to a hill and watch a hawk, chased by crows, fly from the treetops of one of those dying Iowa savannas. Looking across a bromefield to the trees beyond, I dream. Over the hill is a beautiful, although damaged, little prairie. I've walked this prairie in full sun and in full moonlight. In the light of a full moon, where the prairie meets a wet woods, I found the largest Michigan lily I have ever seen. It was a full six feet tall, growing in a moist area, in partial shade. So much is here. Based on experience, I feel certain that there is much more on this 100 acres than I can possibly know without living with it and nurturing it.

This is a piece of land I dream on. I have looked for a prairie remnant that I could manage, where I could apply unfettered what I think I have learned. I dream of owning this piece of land with my family. It is a place where Ian can learn things not taught in any school and where his father and I can continue to learn. I want to own this prairie so that it can own me. I want to be one of the True People of this place.

The prairie and savanna pieces on the land I dream on are minuscule compared with the 30 million acres that once existed in Iowa, but they are important, not only to me, but in the grandest scheme to preserve these ecosystems. Aldo Leopold said that the first rule to intelligent tinkering was to preserve every cog and wheel.[9] Well, here is a cog, and there is a wheel. This prairie and this savanna hold the memory of this particular place. They are the toolboxes for large, landscape-scale restoration that might afford the best possibility for our grandchildren's grandchildren to experience the ecosystems of Iowa.

For the 100-acre parcel of land I dream of owning, I have begun to try to understand what was there in the nineteenth century. I have studied surveyors' notes and maps from the nineteenth century available from the County Recorders office in the court house. This is a good starting point. I see where the historic savanna was, where prairie was. The surveyors noted the kinds and sizes of trees they marked; these species are still on the landscape. I see that the nearby river had twists and turns that were

straightened when its course was altered. Some aerial photographs available through the Natural Resource Conservation Service provide me with further information. It appears that there is a ghost of an oxbow near "my" land.

Each of the remnant prairies and savannas nearby, regardless of size or condition, is like a history book. No two are the same. Diverse fragments keep the secrets of the past for those who learn to read them. By comparing remnants, I can better understand what my goals of restoration should be. But alone, these small remnants may not survive for the long haul. Landscape-scale ecological restoration on former farmland may be the best opportunity to preserve ecosystems in intensely agricultural parts of the Midwest like Iowa.

The first flicker of this realization came with the Fermilab Project, in Batavia, Illinois. Under the guidance of Dr. Robert Betz, seeds were harvested from local prairie remnants and planted parcel by parcel, over a decade, on approximately 1,000 acres of land. Despite early skepticism, it became clear that wild seeds can be harvested and planted, and will germinate and grow using modifications of agricultural practices and application of fire. The Fermilab Project also demonstrated that a developing prairie matrix eventually displaces weedy species, including thistles, despite an early dominance of exotic annual and perennial weedy species. Betz has postulated that the planted prairie community develops a matrix of fast-growing opportunistic species that establishes early. This matrix eventually creates conditions that allow some of the long-lived perennial species typical of good-quality prairies to establish. At Fermilab, this process takes about a decade.

Despite the pioneering work at Fermilab and the popularity of the walking tour and interpretive program, the focus at this site is research in physics, and prairie reconstruction is performed by a dedicated grounds-keeping staff when they are free from other tasks. Thus the ability to answer many of the important questions about the relationship of management to the development of a planted prairie community is in some ways impeded. In addition, even 1,000 acres is small, in terms of the scale of the ecosystem and the needs of organisms once typical of it. Something larger was needed.

Over the past ten years, Carl and Linda Kurtz, private landowners in central Iowa, have benefited from the information gained from the efforts at Fermilab. The Kurtzes have been harvesting seeds from a good-quality local prairie they rent and planting this seed on the family farm. To date fifty acres have been planted using a fertilizer spreader, and the acres of corn and beans have diminished annually as the acres of prairie have increased. Carl and Linda are keen observers and hard workers, and it would not be unusual to see them grubbing out weeds in their prairie planting or sitting at a sunny dining-room table during the long winter, sorting through a sample of seed, separating one species from another, counting them, and evaluating the success of the previous fall's harvest.

Carl and Linda Kurtz have made some important observations on their prairie plantings. They noticed that a prairie parcel dominated either by grass or by forbs does not seem as vigorous through time as one that has a balance of forbs and grass. It also seems that the more species diversity in the planting, the greater the stability of the community.

In working with prairie, it helps if you can think like a prairie. Carl and Linda have understood that early in the life history of the prairie plant, most of the available energy is directed to the root, and the shoot remains small for at least a year or two. Without enough light, the prairie seedlings are less vigorous and can die.

Soil used to grow crops has abundant weed seed, so weeds are plentiful in early prairie plantings on such land. In the first year, weeds are mostly rapid-growing annuals that produce deep shade and copious amounts of seed. The Kurtzes reasoned that periodic mowing during the first growing season in a prairie planting could help reduce competition for light, space, food, and water and greatly reduce the production of weed seeds. Many of the species that appeared in the Fermilab prairie planting only after a decade of development and with additional planting were growing in Carl and Linda's prairie in three to five years from a single initial planting. This practice proved important to a landmark project that is located, appropriately enough, near Prairie City, Iowa.

Walnut Creek National Wildlife Refuge (NWR), now called Neal Smith National Wildlife Refuge and Prairie Learning Center, began in 1991 with a congressional appropriation initiated by former representative Neal Smith. Ecologically, the goal is to emulate historic natural ecosystems, ultimately on 8,600 acres, and so all the seed used at the refuge originated from local remnant prairie sources. Many animals that are absent from prairie and savanna remnants or that are becoming rare are being reestablished at Neal Smith NWR, including bison, elk, jack-rabbits, regal frittilary butterflies, and, perhaps someday, prairie chickens. This is the first landscape-scale attempt to reconstruct historic natural ecosystems on former farmland, and, as such, it is a prototype. Research is used by refuge staff to understand the condition of the developing natural landscape much as a thermometer is used by a doctor to understand the health of a patient. Studying the plant and animal community and the water and soil conditions indicates whether the refuge is progressing toward its ecological goals, so that changes in management can be made if necessary.

In this restoration of historic natural systems

at Neal Smith NWR, people are vitally important. Volunteers help staff collect and plant seed, observe and make changes in plant and animal populations, and celebrate successes in restoration. A commitment has been made to environmental education programs, so that children can, as a part of their school experience, become immersed in prairie, at least for a day. A prairie curriculum is being distributed so that teachers in Iowa can integrate prairie into a regular school program. Among other things, students help collect, clean, and plant prairie seeds and, thus, become a part of the restoration effort. Often they bring their parents. In the years to come, students, parents, and volunteers can return to the refuge, witness change on the landscape, and know that their efforts made a difference. And when a person contributes to the restoration of the native ecosystems by planting some seeds, for example, that person begins to "own" that prairie. A local prairie tradition and vocabulary begin to develop.

Other projects are being undertaken throughout the tallgrass prairie region that are tailored to the local needs. Stephen Packard, a restorationist working for The Nature Conservancy in Illinois, has provided leadership in discovering the existence of rare savanna ecosystems and in learning how to manage them. The Volunteer Stewardship Network helps to heal damaged savannas and prairies on privately and publicly owned natural areas in Illinois. Several agencies and organizations have joined to form the Chicago Wilderness Project, designed to protect and steward several significant natural areas within the Chicago area.

The Iowa Prairie Network offers people an opportunity to learn about, enjoy, and steward local prairie and savanna communities. Local chapters set their own agendas, but are linked to a statewide network for sharing information and responding quickly with a unified voice to

protect a threatened natural community. A similar grassroots network called the Southwest Wisconsin Prairie Enthusiasts has in recent years begun to purchase land and steward it. The Missouri Prairie Foundation has as its major goal the purchase and preservation of prairie remnants.

In the past several years, several roadside prairie projects have developed in the tallgrass prairie states, including Wisconsin, Minnesota, Iowa, and Missouri. They are spearheaded by departments of transportation and other organizations, including the Integrated Roadside Vegetation Management Office in Iowa, and are providing ways to plant prairie species along roadsides. In addition to aesthetic value, roadside plantings have the potential to connect remnant and planted prairies otherwise isolated from one another, creating a corridor for genetic and species exchange.

Recently, producers of prairie seed have begun to respond to the need for local ecotype seed of both forbs and grasses. Innovative projects like the Iowa Ecotype Project have sought to assist commercial growers by developing a genetically diverse seed base of local origin and making it available to growers. Even backyard gardeners can contribute to the preservation of native ecosystems by using responsibly obtained seed of wild plants from their local area in their flower gardens.

Our technology affords us an instant view of tropical rain forests half a world away. Our concern about the decimation of rain forests is registered in school programs, popular literature, and even the sale of items that relate to tropical rain forests. Midwestern tallgrass prairies and savannas, though, are seldom granted the status of pristine wilderness because they are mostly small and degraded. We in the Midwest exist somewhere in the middle of two extremes. The extensive pristine wilderness typical of the pre-historic ecosystems of our highly fertile agricultural regions are neither completely extant nor totally gone, as are the preagrarian landscapes of England.

Approximately 3 percent of the original tallgrass prairies still remains in midwestern America.[10] In Iowa, however, the estimate of extant prairie drops to less than 0.1 percent and most remnants are severely damaged.[11] But fragments of ecosystems *do* still exist. These are the ecosystems that have shaped our history, our economy, our quality of life. They may, indeed, hold the key to answers we could need in the future. Furthermore, if we as a people decide that tallgrass prairies and savannas, like tropical rain forests, must not pass from this earth, then we must boldly and creatively act not only to preserve and restore the remaining pieces, but also to rebuild examples of them in areas where they no longer exist.

If Iowa, once the epicenter of tallgrass prairie, is now the most decimated state in terms of loss of native ecosystems, as many suggest, then why not make it a center of healing, of learning about rebuilding and repairing these nearly lost native ecosystems? Although we cannot turn back the clock and exactly duplicate historic ecosystems, we can choose to value, preserve, and restore representations of them before the last remnants are gone. Critically important in this work is the inclusion of people within these examples and remnants of the native landscape.

Like the species mixes and genetic memories of species in local ecosystems, the people who steward a place will, through time, come to understand the ways and needs of the area better than anyone else. They will have a local knowledge. In Iowa, the True People along the limestone river bluffs near Harper's Ferry will have knowledge and ways different from those of the True People of the seepy loess-capped hills of

Leon in south-central Iowa. And the True People of the great sand deposits of Muscatine in southeast Iowa will have knowledge and ways different from those of the True People of the deep black-soil prairies of Pocahontas in northwest Iowa. In other states, there will also be local True Peoples. Like the phoenix rising from the ashes, the descendants of sod-corn farmers will know their place in the ancient ecosystems and begin to plant new seeds on the land. And the land will respond.

Notes

1. Daryl D. Smith, "Tallgrass Prairie Settlement: Prelude to Demise of the Tallgrass Ecosystem," in *Proceedings of the Twelfth North American Prairie Conference,* ed. D. D. Smith and C. A. Jacobs (Cedar Falls: University of Northern Iowa, 1992), 195.

2. Daryl Smith, "Iowa Prairie—an Endangered Ecosystem," *Proceedings of the Iowa Academy of Science* 88 (1981): 7–10.

3. Smith, "Tallgrass Prairie Settlement," 195.

4. Robert E. Flickinger, *The Early History of Iowa and Pioneer History of Pocahontas County, Iowa* (Fonda, Iowa: Times Press, 1904), 142.

5. Ibid.

6. Ibid., 263.

7. Ibid., 221.

8. Gerould Wilhelm, "The Human Beings of the North Branch—a New Chapter to an Old, Old Story," *Prairie Projections* 6 (1993): 1–15.

9. Aldo Leopold, *Round River, from the Journals of Aldo Leopold,* ed. Luna B. Leopold (New York: Oxford University Press, 1953), 147.

10. Smith, "Tallgrass Prairie Settlement," 195.

11. Ibid.

11 *Tanji na Che:* Recovering the Landscape of the Ioway

Lance M. Foster

Baxoje min ke. I am an Ioway, a member of the Iowa Tribe of Kansas and Nebraska, located near White Cloud, in northeast Kansas. The state of Iowa owes its name to our ancestors, who lived in the lands that became Iowa before their removal to Kansas through the Treaty of 1836. We are legally known as the Iowa, although we pronounce it "Ioway."

When I came to Iowa to attend graduate school, I hoped to see a land that breathed the stories of old times. Maybe I expected too much, since I was raised in Montana, where so much of the land is as the Creator made it. When I came to Iowa, I could taste the chemicals that ensured the monoculture of corn and soybeans that swept from horizon to horizon. Iowa, I learned, is the state that has been most transformed from its primeval condition. Almost all its wetlands have been drained, its forests decimated, and its animals eradicated, and less than 0.1 percent of its prairies is left. Thus the pastoral countryside of Iowa is not native, and my ancestors would hardly recognize it.

However, I was determined to understand this place, this Iowa I found, and to discover the sleeping form of the Iowa past under the monotonous blanket of the present. Our landscape and culture was like a great and graceful earthen vessel, molded over ages by loving hands, that was shattered by an angry visitor into a thousand pieces. My time has been one of searching for the scattered shards of memory and place. Some shards have been recovered and assembled by specialists in new ways—as literature, archaeology, history, or mythology. But I believe that the essence is still there. Sitting Bull, the Hunkpapa Lakota, once said that whatever you have lost, if you go back and look hard enough, you will find it. Some shards may be disguised as an old story; some, buried at an archaeological site; some, hidden in an archaic phrase. Some pieces may even be in the song of a meadowlark or in the swirl of snow that comes in as you shut the door. As my uncle Herman Bear Comes Out, of the Northern Cheyenne, once told me, all the answers are still out there, in the Land, where they came from in the first place. So I have come to discover *Tanji,* the prairie.

Ioway to Iowa

Historically, the state of Iowa got its name from the Iowa Territory; the territory, from the Iowa River; and the river, from the Iowa who lived on it (Figure 11.1). But contrary to various non-Indian speculations, the word does not mean "Beautiful Land" or "This is the Place." "Iowa" comes from our neighbors and cousins the Dakota, who called us *Ayuxba* (AH-you-khbah), the "Sleepy Ones." According to some Dakota I have talked to, it was a way to tease us about how we acted tired to get rid of them when we felt they had overstayed their welcome during long intertribal visits. Some of our Algonquian-speaking neighbors like the Illini and the Meskwaki borrowed the word and transformed it to *Ayuway,* which the French, in turn, took and passed on to English speakers. Ultimately, it came to be spelled "Ioway." [1]

We called ourselves *Baxoje* (BAH-khoh-jay), another teasing name given to us by our brothers the Otoe. It comes from an ancient incident in which, while the People were camped together on a sandbar, the Ioway camp was covered with ashy snow blown onto it. Thus we became *Baxoje,* the "Ashy-Snow-Heads." In return, we called the Otoe the *Watodatan,* the "Ones Who Always Copulate," because of an illicit affair between one of their young men and one of our young women. But both the Otoe and the Ioway had other names for ourselves. The Otoe said *Chiwere,* and the Ioway said *Chikiwere,* both words meaning "The People Who Are From Here," the Original People of this place. [2] Tribal stories also say that we came from this place.

Archaeology and "the Great Nation"

According to tribal tradition, the ancestors of the Ioway Indians united as a people ages ago. The clans had come together and agreed to become a People, the *Honga,* the Great Nation. Some clans had come from the Great Lakes. Others had come from the north, from a land remembered as very cold. Yet others had come from the western prairies or the eastern woodlands. Some of the ancestors had made great mounds in the shapes of animals and birds along the bluffs of the Great River. Others had traded down the river to the great southern mound cities and returned with new ceremonies, new beliefs to add to the older ones.

This development of the clans into one Nation is traced in the ancient stories and traditions of the Ioway and their brothers: the Otoe, Ho-Chunk (Winnebago), and Missouria. Other relatives of these peoples also seem to have been part of this Great Nation, including the Omaha, Ponca, Kansa, Quapaw, and Osage. Stories recall a time when they were all one People and when all the land of this Middle Place was theirs. These stories seem supported by archaeological research. The culture is called Oneota, after a rock formation along the Upper Iowa River in northeastern Iowa where certain types of pottery fragments that characterize this culture were first found. [3]

The Oneota appear to have developed from indigenous Woodland peoples of the upper Mississippi River Valley and surrounding areas by about A.D. 1000. [4] The Oneota left hundreds of sites across the Midwest—in Wisconsin, Iowa, Minnesota, Illinois, Missouri, Kansas, Nebraska, Michigan, and South Dakota. [5] Their culture was oriented to the rivers and wooded valleys of the tallgrass prairie, with present-day Iowa at its heart. Oneota was a flexible culture that survived changing climate and resources. The people hunted when there was game, farmed when growing conditions were good, and intensified the gathering of wild plants when times were lean. [6] In that way, the Oneota flourished here until the seventeenth century, when contact with advancing European culture and its attendant diseases and trade wars splintered the Nation into smaller nations, and fragments coalesced into the nations we know historically as the Ioway and their brother nations, like the Otoe. [7]

Figure 11.1. The Upper Iowa River was named for the Ioway, who occupied a series of villages on it from prehistoric times until the late seventeenth century. They later lived on another prairie river farther south that was also named for them, the Iowa River. Iowa Territory, and subsequently the state of Iowa, derived their names from these rivers and from the Iowa Tribe. (Photograph by Lance M. Foster)

Reimagining the Prairie: *Tanji*

The tallgrass prairie was not a featureless expanse of grass to the Ioway. Here and there, features natural and cultural marked a land that was familiar and comforting. The lands were under the great dome of the Sky, which was conceived of as the roof of the Earth-Lodge, with the Island-Earth as its floor and the Four Winds as the Protectors and Earth-anchors.[8] The Directions were named by the Winds: *Byuwahu,* the East, "The Sun Comes from There"; *Mansje,* the South, "Warmth"; *Byuwari,* the West, "The Sun Goes There"; *Umeri,* the North, "The Cold Side." The South Wind was considered beneficient, while the rare Northeast Wind brought killing blizzards and was thought to be maleficient.

The other great Powers, besides the Winds, were the Day, the Night, and the Winter. Although the Big Male Winter, the time of glaciers, had been killed by Mischinye, the Great Hare, long ago, the land still bore the scars of that glacial age, and the Small Female Winter returned every year with her bitter winds.

The cycle of the year was marked by events occurring during the months. There were variations, but the cycle collected by anthropologist Alanson Skinner is the most widely known today.[9] The new year began in March, with the greening of the land, encouraged by the singing of the frogs; thus March was called the Frog's Moon (*Pesge etawe*). April (*Mak'anye,* Cultivating Moon) and May (*Bi wa'un nyinge,* Nothing-to-Do Moon) marked the beginning and end of preparing the fields for corn. The changes in the appearance of the landscape as summer approached were noted in the names of June (*Wixra shuwe,* Little Flowers) and July (*Wixra xanje,* Big Flowers). Late summer, fall, and winter were the time of hunting. August was the Buffalo Rutting Moon (*Che Kiruxe*); September,

the Frost in Animal Beds Moon (*Doxina Gremina*). The bugling of the bull elk as he gathered his harem gave October its name, the Elk Whistling Moon (*Huma Yochinya*). November was the Deer Rutting Moon (*Ta Kiruxe*); December, the Raccoon Rutting Moon (*Mingke Kiruxe*). January and February were, respectively, Little Bear Jumping (*Munje'tawe Shuweinye*) and Big Bear Jumping (*Munje'tawe Shuweinye Xanje*). The names reflect the growing size of bear cubs as they emerge from their dens on the warmer days of winter.

The summer was also a time of the Thunderers and tornadoes. Tornadoes were called *t'at'anwe,* which described the incessant and erratic jumping movement they made while skipping along their path of destruction. I have heard some nations call them the Finger of God. The Thunderers traveled the river valleys during fierce storms, skimming along the bluffs and stopping to rest on mounds that marked their routes or on cedar trees, which they had great affinity for. Sometimes the Thunderers fought the Underwater Spirits, the Ischexi. The allies of the Thunder in their status as Guardians of the Sacred were the Cedar and the Snakes.

The larger rivers provided regular travel routes between the large summer villages, near their mouths and junctures, and the dispersed winter hunting camps, at the headwaters and in sheltered valleys. For example, a string of familiar seasonal homes and campsites were established along the course of the Des Moines River, called *Mingke Ni,* the "Raccoon River" (the name survives as one of its tributaries). Indeed, although the Ioway knew the prairie lands, the river valleys were their primary homes, full of timber, game (especially in the winter), rich river terraces for garden plots, and protection from winter storms (Figure 11.2). Every large Oneota village site is located near a river. Large summer village sites full of storage pits were found along the lower reaches of the Des Moines

Figure 11.2. Prairie river terrace on the Watá (Feel-the-Depth/Little Sioux River) is an example of the type of landscape the Ioway chose for the location of their garden plots and villages. Behind, rising hills provide protection from harsh prairie winds as well as a place to bury the dead. Sites of villages from the Oneota culture, ancestral Iowa and Otoe and others, are located all along the terraces of the Watá. (Photograph by Lance M. Foster)

River in what are now areas of Red Rock Reservoir[10] and Iowaville, near Selma.[11] Other villages were on the Iowa and the Upper Iowa Rivers, the Mississippi, and the Missouri. Even today on their reservation lands, the Ioway maintain this attachment to rivers, with the Ioway of Kansas on the Nemaha and Missouri Rivers, and the Ioway of Oklahoma on the Cimarron River.

Cultural evidence also abounds for the Ioway attachment to wooded river valleys. For example, the woodlands were the home of the Little People, longtime friends of the Ioway. Trees were benevolent beings that sometimes captured evil spirits. Dead standing trees were known as "witch trees." The evil in them would twist, gnarl, and then kill them. No one dared cut down a standing snag, since that would release the spirit. Instead, the "witch trees" were left for the Thunder to strike and destroy.

Ioway stories also contain knowledge of the proximity of certain tree species to water. For example, in one of the stories Trickster, Ishjinki, is blinded when he falls into a pile of excrement and his eyes are glued shut:

He went along until he bumped into a tree and asked, "What kind of tree are you?" The tree replied, "An oak" (*Butu*). So Ishjinki said, "Oh, I know where you grow, on the dry highlands." He went on to another, and asked what it was. It replied, "A walnut" (*Tóku*).

He proceeded until he came to another tree and asked it what kind of tree it was. It said, "An elm" (*Éhu*). "Oh," said Ishjinki, "you're near the bank." He went on and came to another and inquired what that was. It replied, "Hackberry" [*sic*]; then he came to the cottonwood (*Baxré*). "Oh you are right on the bank," said Ishjinki. He went on and came to another and asked what it was. It said, "Willow" (*Uxristun'a*). "Oh," said Ishjinki, "I am at the water's edge," and he leaped right into the water and washed his eyes open.[12]

Although hunting camps are not as easy to find and recognize as large villages, they can be identified by evidence that game was killed and butchered; by game-watching stations, located at good vantage points and marked by lithic debitage (the leftover stone chips from making artifacts); and by campfires. Ceremonial areas are often recognizable on upland ridges with burial mounds or at unique landforms, such as isolated boulders with petroglyphs. Up in the headwaters of the Des Moines River, in the prairie pothole country of the Des Moines Lobe, there were undoubtedly winter muskrat and beaver camps. In warmer months, waterfowl (*mixe*) were hunted there, as revealed by many legends about them.[13] In one, Ishjinki the Trickster fools some waterfowl into dancing around him with their eyes shut while he knocks them over their heads and stuffs them in his bag. He sings, "Whoever looks will have red eyes." It is the coot that first peeks and then warns his brothers about what is happening. That's why the coot, or mudhen, has red eyes and is the most watchful of all waterfowl.

The wetlands and marshes that covered roughly 20 percent of the present state of Iowa were places left from earliest creation, remnants of the time of the Flooded-Earth from which Trickster had created the present Earth-Island, with the assistance of Muskrat. Muskrat was instructed to dive to the bottom of the Flood and to bring up mud, which Trickster spread around to make this Earth-Island. The Marsh (*Jegixe*),

with its swarm of invisible and visible life, was the still-powerful remnant of Creation, and the prairie pothole region continued to be a part of the process of ongoing Creation. In fact, some of the burial mounds built high on river bluffs and prairie knolls have rich marsh earth added to them. This may be symbolic of the connection between the rebirth of the dead through the mound and the energy of creation, issuing from the primal marsh.

During the fasting or vision quest, other sacred places included canyons, bluffs, caves, and isolated high hills and rock formations and glacial erratics, some with inscribed petroglyphs. Over the years, I have heard elders tell stories of haunted and mysterious places on the prairies of northwestern Iowa and southwestern Minnesota. Oceyedan Mound was avoided by all tribes as the home of a race of small and angry spirits. Pilot Knob was said to be haunted by the spirits of Ioway and Sioux warriors who died there. Spirit Lake was the home of one of the Ischexi, the Underwater Deities that ruled the Underworld. The Loess Hills were said to occasionally have a "Sun Bridge," which was a jumping-off place for the dead in their travel to the west and the Land of the Dead.[14]

Bordering the Big Sioux River in northwestern Iowa and southeastern South Dakota, Blood Run was a large ceremonial site at which oral tradition says many tribes—including Ioway, Omaha, Ponca, Otoe, Arikara, and Dakota—camped together. Tradition also holds that this was where the Arikara introduced the intertribal adoption ceremony known as the Pipe Dance to the other tribes.[15]

The great rivers were connected by overland trails through the upland prairie, with villages and sacred places at their meeting points. The Ioway chief No Heart of Fear prepared a map in 1837 to defend the Ioway's claim to aboriginal possession of the lands that would become Iowa (Figure 11.3).[16] The map reveals the rivers,

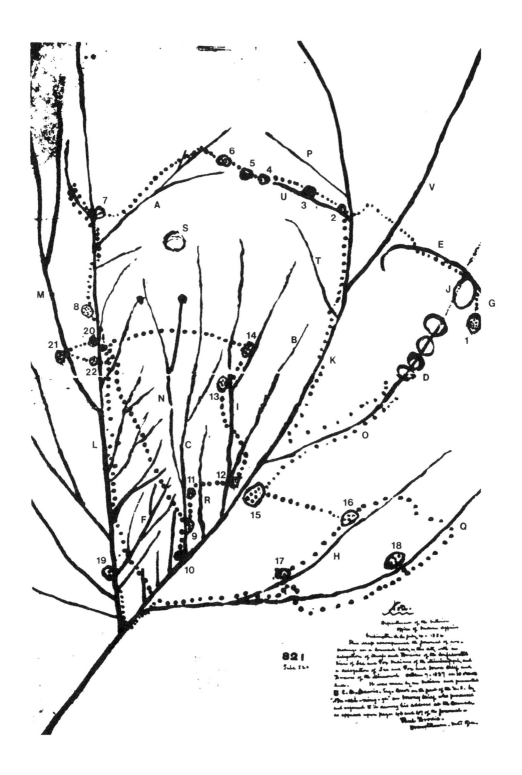

villages, trails, and migration routes of the Io-way across their homelands.[17] In marshy country, the glacial eskers and ridges provided relatively dry travel for people and buffalo. The Ioways were known as great walkers, and many of their names contain the word *mányi,* which means "to walk or go along."[18] When the French explorer Nicolas Perrot first met them in 1685, he noted that they often killed deer or buffalo while running after them.[19]

Moreover, the Ioway language reveals a great familiarity with overland travel through the prairies and, at the same time, the difficulties encountered from the varying vegetation. For example, *nathdáge* means "to leave a path while walking through tall grass." *Wahánré* means "to walk under and through brush or tallgrass while pushing it aside." *Wathánje mányi* means "to walk through brush or a thicket, shaking it," and *waxrán mányi* means "to walk through brush where there is no path."[20]

Most of the great trails in Iowa that were later used by the Sauk and the Europeans were made by the Ioway and their ancestors. One such trail that is recorded in historic French maps led from the Ioway villages on the Upper Iowa and Mississippi Rivers, across the marshy glacial plain of northern Iowa, to their villages on Oko-boji and Spirit Lakes, and thence through the Loess Hills to their village on the Missouri River.[21] Although a detailed study has not been made of this route, I strongly suspect that it followed glacial landforms such as eskers, which provided relatively dry passage across marshy terrain.

The prairie in a very real sense defined the Ioway as a people, and they, in turn, helped define and maintain the prairie. By contrast, when a group of Huron and Ottawa fled from Iroquois aggression and sought refuge in the prairie lands of the welcoming Ioway, they felt vulnerable and dismayed by the endless open expanses. They were a woodland people and feared the overwhelming spaces as much as the European settlers did two centuries later. The Huron and Ottawa returned to the eastern forests and meadows. They preferred to face the wrath of the Iroquois rather than the loneliness of the treeless lands.[22]

The magnet that drew the Ioway away from their rivers and bluffs to the open prairie was *Che,* the Great One, the Buffalo, although at the same time increasing pressures from other native populations to the north and east began pressing the Ioway to the west and south.

Figure 11.3. Nasjeninga (No Heart of Fear) drew this map during treaty negotiations in 1837 to support Ioway claims to ancestral territories in what would become Iowa and portions of surrounding states. The main branch leading from the lower left to the upper right is the Mississippi River (Nyitanga, Great River), and the large vertical branch to the left is the Missouri (Nyisoje, Smoky River). William Green, the state archaeologist of Iowa, has added the letters and numbers in order to expand on the captions in the lower right and identify the rivers (solid lines), lakes and villages (circles), and travel routes (dotted lines): (A) Big Sioux River, (B) Cedar River, (C) Des Moines River, (D) Four Lakes (Madison, Wis.), (E) Fox River, (F) Grand River, (G) Green Bay or Lake Michigan, (H) Illinois River, (I) Iowa River, (J) Lake Winnebago, (K) Mississippi River, (L) Missouri River, (M) Platte River, (N) Raccoon River, (O) Rock River, (P) Root River, (Q) Sangamon River, (R) Skunk River, (S) Storm Lake, (T) Turkey River, (U) Upper Iowa River, (V) Wisconsin River; (1) eastern Wisconsin, 1500s–1650?, (2–3) Upper Iowa River sites, ca. 1650–85, (4–6) northern Iowa Lakes sites (Milford, Gilett Grove), ca. 1680–1700, (7) southeastern South Dakota, ca. 1690–1720, (8) near the Omahas, ca. 1720–60, (9) Iowaville, ca. 1760–1823, (10) mouth of the Des Moines River (Lower Iowa Town?), ca. 1760–80, (11–14) return to the Otoes, ca. 1820, (15) Upper Iowa Town, or visit to Saukenuk, ca. 1795–1815, (16 or 17) visit to Peoria, ca. 1811, (18) visit to Kickapoo village, ca. 1811, (19) village at the mouth of the Grand River, 1820s, (20) southeastern Nebraska villages, 1820s–30s. (From Map 821, Central Map File, Records of the Bureau of Indian Affairs, Record Group 75, National Archives, College Park, Md.)

Figure 11.4. George Catlin, *Eagle Dance, Iowa* (1846). Catlin made this painting during a visit to an Iowa camp in the Loess Hills of the Missouri River. While permanent villages were composed primarily of bark lodges, the Iowa used *chehachi* (buffalo-hide lodges) during their buffalo hunts. As the buffalo began to disappear from the prairies east of the Missouri, the Iowa had to travel farther west into the plains, where they were likely to encounter enemy tribes. (National Museum of American Art, Washington, D.C./Art Resource, N.Y.)

Che: The Great One of the Prairies

Today, most Americans associate the buffalo with the Great Plains, rather than with the tall-grass prairies of Iowa and Illinois. But buffalo were definitely important to the Ioway and the tallgrass prairie, too, as proved by archaeological evidence, historical records, and the traditions and language of the Ioway. The Ioway dependence on the buffalo seems to be as old as the tribe itself (Figure 11.4).

At the archaeological sites of the Ioway and our Oneota ancestors are buffalo bones as well as artifacts with buffalo motifs.[23] Archaeologists have also found evidence of long-range communal bison hunts from Iowa into Kansas.[24] During dry periods, when the prairie expanded at the

186

expense of forested areas, the buffalo range also expanded. At the same time, Oneota settlements spread and prospered.[25] With their surplus of buffalo, the Ioway were suppliers of buffalo robes to their relatives the Winnebago (along with that other prairie resource, pipestone from Minnesota).[26] Sites of trading centers have been located along the Mississippi, with hides, artifacts, and dried meat.[27]

In the historic period, trade in bison hides and pipestone between the Ioway and the Winnebago was observed by the French missionary Father André in 1676.[28] Even as late as the early nineteenth century, Lieutenant Stephen Kearny recorded a herd of 5,000 buffalo on the upper Raccoon River.[29]

Culturally, the interdependence of buffalo and Ioway shows up in many more ways. The Ioway had two principal clans, the Bear and the Buffalo, and our stories tell that when the clans of the eastern woodlands, under the leadership of the Bear Clan, met with the Buffalo Clan on the western prairies, the Clans formed one People. While the Bear Clan led the tribe in the fall and winter, the Buffalo Clan led in the spring and summer. The Buffalo Clan name, *Nawo Dayi*, means "Road Maker," referring to the wide buffalo trails worn across the prairies, which were used as roads when moving camp.[30] (These buffalo roads were converted by later Euro-American settlers into wagon roads.[31])

Buffalo Clan traditions also tell how buffalo wallows collected water, which was used by other animals for drinking. Medicinal plants, like the Male Buffalo Bellow Plant, also grew by the wallows, and the buffalo sometimes were seen using these wallows for healing their sick. In 1851, Topomuk, an Ioway Buffalo Doctor, said:

Sometimes when a Buffalo is shot in the breast, he becomes very sick, staggers from one side to the other . . . then two other Buffalo get one on each side, and support it and urge it along, perhaps, and helping it until they get it away. When they doctor it . . . they have a basin of earth [wallow] in which they place the water. This they use in blowing on the wound. If there is no water nigh, one runs off to a stream and drinks water and runs back again and pours it out of his mouth into the basin. They bring the weeds also on their horns and using the water in the basin they blow as we do on the wound.[32]

In hunting buffalo, the Ioway occasionally used the fire-surround method, in which hunters encircled a group of buffalo and fired the prairies around the herd, leaving some areas unburned. At those points, the hunters lay in ambush.[33] Although I have not yet found any traditions of systematically managing the prairie for better game range through fire, Duke Paul Wilhelm of Württemberg did write in 1823 about the intentional firing of prairies by the Ioway: "In the autumn the Indians set the dry prairie on fire and so lay whole forests in ashes, the wind driving the fire on until it reaches the river."[34]

As the botanists tell us today, there was a constant war on the prairie margins between the grasses and the advancing woodlands of bur oak and hawthorne. The firing of prairie grasses and margins, favorable to the deep-rooted grass communities and less favorable to the woody plant communities, ensured that plentiful pastures near favored campsites would encourage the buffalo to remain in the area. Buffalo are notoriously fickle, and their movements are hard to predict. For such a large animal, they are amazing in their ability to be inconspicuous on the landscape, and the scouts often had difficulty finding the herds. Buffalo also stampede, and are notoriously destructive when they do, so precautions had to be taken to keep hunters in line and prevent them from frightening the animals. In pre-horse days, the Ioway, like other

Indians, often stalked buffalo under decoy wolf-skins because wolves commonly prowled the margins of the herds and were paid little attention as long as they did not get too close.

In 1859, Robert White Cloud, an Ioway, was interviewed by the ethnologist Lewis Henry Morgan: "He says they also regard the buffalo as a god. . . . He said the Indian believed the buffalo after being killed and eaten by him had power to cover his bones again with flesh and come to life again, and that he did thus come to life again after being killed."[35]

While the buffalo was the most vital life-giver to the Ioway, many other beings' lives were entwined in the sacred nest of grass, *Tanji*. The elk (*Huma*) supplied meat and hides, and his shoulder blade was used for hoeing corn and beans. The antlers were worked into hide scrapers and quirts. Elk Medicine was powerful for attracting the women, much as when the bull elk bugled, and the cow elk came running. October, as I have said, was known as the Elk Whistling Moon (*Huma Yochinya*).

The wolf (*Shunta*) was loved and respected, not feared. The wolf was the scout, the one that kept watch. My ancestor Mahaska wore a white wolfskin as a cape, which was said to give him the power of invisibility.

White-tailed deer (*Ta*) were hunted along the riverbanks and were a staple. They were so important that special hunting medicines were sometimes used. The skins of unborn fawns were used in the most sacred ceremonies, such as during the tattooing of young girls of high status to bless and protect them.[36] Archaeological evidence indicates greater dependence on buffalo in western prairie sites, and more on deer in eastern wooded sites.[37]

Although the black bear (*Munje*) was not a regular visitor to the prairies, his bad-tempered relative the grizzly (*Mahto*) was occasionally seen. He had a fierce reputation, but *Mahto* also pitied the people and gave them the Grizzly Bear Society, which was complementary to the Buffalo Doctor Society in the healing arts.

There are so many animals of the prairie that were vital in the lives and minds of the people. The meadowlark (*Postinla*) sang about the true nature of approaching strangers. In its nest, the mouse (*Hindunye*) hid ground beans, which might prove invaluable survival food; it was this mouse that raised one of the Hero Twins, who rid the world of monsters and made it safe for people. The gopher (*Mayinye*) shot dangerous medicine at the unwary from its burrows.

There are many more stories that reveal the richness of the prairie landscape and the Ioway intimacy with it. The regathering of them, and their attachment and embodiment in living form and place, is a sacred journey.

Last Thoughts: New Flesh on Dry Bones

In my years in Iowa, looking beneath the blanket of modern agriculture, I have found many connections between the prairie and Ioway customs. For example, the next time you go to a powwow, watch for the Grass Dancers. The yarn and fringe you see hanging from their regalia is a reminder of the old times, when warriors stuffed bunches of tallgrass into their garters and belts or sashes and danced vigorously with low, sweeping motions of the feet, to flatten the prairie grasses and make the dance grounds ready. Among the Ioway, this was a part of the *Herushka*, or *Iroshka*, the primary warriors' society. The warrior dances of the *Iroshka* survive in the deep-voiced Southern Drums of groups like Yellowhammer and in the searching and dignified steps of the Straight Dance.

Whenever I see the Grass Dancers and the Straight Dancers and hear those Southern

Drums, I think about the old tallgrass prairies stretching out like wave upon wave of an endless ocean. And when I think about those prairies, I think about the Old Folks and about the buffalo.

So in April 1997, I decided to visit Walnut Creek (now Neal Smith) National Wildlife Refuge near Prairie City, southeast of Des Moines, because I had heard that a small herd of buffalo had been brought there to graze the restored prairie. I went on a Monday, but to my disappointment, I found that the Prairie Learning Center was not open on Mondays (or Sundays, a word to the wise). Because it was not open, however, I had the refuge almost to myself.

Ironically, the rolling slopes were scarred by the machines being used to replant prairie. Another area was so completely burned that it seemed carved from coal, even though I knew that fire is a necessary tool in establishing and maintaining the health of the prairie. But it was amazing to see the amount and variety of life that was returning. I saw delicately colored birds that I did not recognize, and even a small lizard scooting across the road.

I was there to see the buffalo, though, which are kept in 800 enclosed acres, with a so-called buffalo-proof fence, so I took the road that warned of "Buffalo on the Road." Well, the road went right through the enclosure, but I saw no buffalo. I looked and I looked. I wondered if somehow I was not worthy. While the terrain was rolling and broken, and some portions were wooded, it still amazed me that such large animals could remain so well hidden. I drove through once, turned around, and drove through again. Still nothing.

I was disappointed, and I drove down by the bur oaks, down below the charred slopes. I sat there for a while, listening to the tree frogs peeping near Walnut Creek, and enjoying the smell of growing sweetgrass somewhere nearby.

Then I thought about how the Old Ones be-

lieved that the buffalo could come alive again, by clothing its desiccated bones with a mantle of living flesh. And the thought came to me that this prairie was coming alive in the same way. It had once been killed and the flesh torn away, the soil with its coneflowers and Indian grass, so that the prairie was invisible, nothing left but a sheath of hybrid corn and scattered patches of weeds and scrub. But now the skeleton was again becoming clothed in its old flesh of prairie life—plants, birds, and animals. Like the old stories of the buffalo returning to life, this prairie was returning to life. And somewhere, just over that ridge, unseen as in a great cavern beneath the earth, the buffalo were waiting.

Notes

1. Mildred Mott Wedel, "A Synonymy of Names for the Ioway Indians," *Journal of the Iowa Archeological Society* 25 (1978): 50–77.

2. Ibid.

3. Robert L. Hall, "Relating the Big Fish and the Big Stone: Reconsidering the Archaeological Identity and Habitat of the Winnebago in 1634," in *Oneota Archaeology: Past, Present, and Future,* ed. William Green (Iowa City: University of Iowa, Office of the State Archaeologist, 1995), 9–18.

4. Joseph A. Tiffany, "An Overview of Oneota Sites in Southeastern Iowa: A Perspective from the Ceramic Analysis of the Schmeiser Site, 13DM101, Des Moines County, Iowa," *Proceedings of the Iowa Academy of Sciences* 86 (1979): 89–101.

5. Guy Gibbon, "Cultures of the Upper Mississippi Valley and Adjacent Prairies in Iowa and Minnesota," in *Plains Indians,* A.D. *500–1500: The Archaeological Past of Historic Groups,* ed. Karl H. Schlesier (Norman: University of Oklahoma Press, 1994), 128–48.

6. W. Raymond Wood, "Historic Indians," in *Holocene Human Adaptations in the Missouri Prairie–Timberlands,* ed. W. Raymond Wood, Michael J. O'Brien, Katherine A. Murray, and Jerome C. Rose (Fayetteville: Arkansas Archeological Survey, 1996), 78–87.

7. Lance Foster, *Mayan Jegi: The Ioway Indians and the Lost Landscape of Iowa* (Ames: Native Nations Press, 1997), 18.

8. Lance Foster, "The Ioway and the Lost Landscape of Southeast Iowa," *Journal of the Iowa Archeological Society* 43 (1996): 1–5.

9. Alanson Skinner, "Ethnology of the Ioway Indians," *Bulletin of the Public Museum of the City of Milwaukee* 5 (1926): 181–354.

10. David M. Gradwohl, *Archaeology of the Central Des Moines River Valley: A Preliminary Survey* (St. Paul: Minnesota State Historical Society, 1974), 90–105.

11. Dean F. Straffin, "Iowaville: A Possible Historica Site on the Lower Des Moines River," *Proceedings of the Iowa Academy of Sciences* 79 (1972): 44–46.

12. Alanson Skinner, "Societies of the Iowa, Kansa, and Ponca Indians," *Journal of Anthropology Papers* [American Museum of Natural History] 11 (1915): 488.

13. Foster, *Mayan Jegi,* 14.

14. Ibid., 53.

15. Ibid., 78.

16. For further interpretation of the map, see Mark Warhus, *Another America: Native American Maps and the History of Our Land* (New York: St. Martin's Press, 1997), 37–43.

17. William Green, "Ioway Cartography, Ethnohistory, and Archaeology," MS in preparation.

18. Foster, "Ioway and the Lost Landscape," 2.

19. Martha Royce Blaine, *The Ioway Indians* (Norman: University of Oklahoma Press, 1979), 20.

20. Foster, "Ioway and the Lost Landscape," 2.

21. Mildred Mott Wedel, "Peering at the Ioway Indians Through the Mist of Time: 1650–circa 1700," *Journal of the Iowa Archaeological Society* 33 (1986): 50–77.

22. Mildred Mott, "The Relation of Historic Indian Tribes to Archeological Manifestations in Iowa," *Iowa Journal of History and Politics* 36 (1938): 227–314.

23. Tiffany, "Overview of Oneota Sites."

24. Richard Fishel, *Excavations at the Dixon Site (13WD8): Correctionville Phase Oneota in Northwest Iowa* (Iowa City: University of Iowa, Office of the State Archaeologist, 1995); Brad Logan, "Oneota Far West: The White Rock Phase" (Paper presented at the fifty-fourth annual meeting of the Plains Anthropological Society, Iowa City, 1996).

25. Guy Gibbon, "Cultural Dynamics and the Development of the Oneota Lifeway in Wisconsin," *American Antiquity* 37 (1972): 166–85.

26. Blaine, *Ioway Indians,* 17.

27. Dale R. Henning, "Oneota Evolution and Interactions: A View from the Wever Terrace, Southeast Iowa," in *Oneota Archaeology: Past, Present, and Future,* ed. William Green (Iowa City: University of Iowa, Office of the State Archaeologist, 1995), 65–88; Tiffany, "Overview of Oneota Sites."

28. Mott, "Relation of Historic Indian Tribes," 241.

29. Mildred Mott Wedel, "Indian Villages on the Upper Iowa River," *Palimpsest* 42 (1961): 586.

30. Foster, *Mayan Jegi,* 55.

31. Blaine, *Ioway Indians,* 1979, 22.

32. Quoted ibid., 225.

33. Tom McHugh, *The Time of the Buffalo* (Lincoln: University of Nebraska Press, 1972), 69–70.

34. Paul Wilhelm, Duke of Württenberg, *Travels in North America, 1822–1824,* trans. Robert Nitske, ed. Savoie Lottinville (Norman: University of Oklahoma Press, 1973), 307.

35. Leslie A. White, ed., *Lewis Henry Morgan: The Indian Journals, 1859–62* (Ann Arbor: University of Michigan Press, 1959), 70.

36. Skinner, "Ethnology of the Ioway Indians."

37. Lynn Marie Alex, *Exploring Iowa's Past: A Guide to Prehistoric Archaeology,* 2nd ed. (Iowa City: University of Iowa Press, forthcoming); Joseph A. Tiffany, "The Milford Site (13DK1): A Post-Contact Oneota Village in Northwest Iowa," *Plains Anthropologist* 42 (1993): 205–36.

12 Natural Systems Agriculture: The Truly Radical Alternative

Wes Jackson

Editor's note: This chapter is a slightly edited transcript of Wes Jackson's talk at the symposium on Saturday morning, September 21, 1996. He was the third speaker, and the moderator ended the introduction by calling him a prophet, "even though he has often said that 'there are no gurus in Kansas.'"

I'm glad to be here, although I should say that we don't have any prophets in Kansas either. I tell everybody that I'm the head of a nonprophet organization. I'm generally opposed to such things.

Well, it is a great thing that's going on here, and I've sort of rewritten this talk many times in the past hour. But I'll start this way, because it seems so appropriate. Wendell Berry, in *The Unsettling of America,* said that "we came with vision, but not with sight."[1] We came with visions of former places, but not with sight to see where we are. And later, in a letter, he said, "As we came across the continent, cutting the forests and plowing the prairies, we've never known what we were doing, because we've never known what we were undoing." It took New England 200 years to produce a Thoreau, who would see New England for what it was, rather than through the eyes of the Europeans, and I think what we out on the prairies are doing is beginning to *see* the prairies for the first time.

There have been some voices in the past that have assisted us in our cognition to where we are now, but the cognitive experience is not over, and it will come through vision; it will come through words, it'll come through cognition informing language and language informing the cognition, and so on. Aldo Leopold said in *A Sand County Almanac* that "nothing so important as an ethic is ever 'written.' Only the most superficial student of history supposes that Moses 'wrote' the Decalogue; it evolved in the minds of a thinking community, and Moses wrote a tentative summary of it for a 'seminar.'"[2] And so we are involved as members of that thinking community to try to figure out how to become native to this place. We still have more

191

the mind of the conqueror than we do that of the native.

I want to read from an abstract in a peer-reviewed journal, *Ecological Economics*. There are two authors, one from the Department of Economics at Rensselaer Polytechnic Institute in Troy, New York, the other from the Department of Biology at that university. "The self-organizing principles of markets that have emerged in human cultures over the past 10,000 years are inherently in conflict with the self-organizing principles of ecosystems that have evolved over the past 3.5 billion years."[3] In other words, nature's *economy,* which Don Worster used as the title of his very great book,[4] nature's economy is inherently in conflict with the human economy, or, should we say, the other way around. The rules governing the dynamics of ecosystems within which all human activity takes place are ultimately a function of biological laws, not a function of humanly created economic systems. The conflict between these systems is illustrated by the fact that economic indicators have shown vigorous growth during the past century, while a variety of environmental indicators have exhibited negative trends. The economics go up; the ecological indicators go down. And Aldo Leopold, sitting in Berlin one evening, scribbling on a piece of paper under the general title of "Wilderness," commented about this century and what its contributions might be, thought what a great thing it would be to take the various aspects of human ecology and nature's economy and merge them into one discipline. Well, of course that hasn't happened; it's still in front of us.

Some time in the past century, an invisible line was crossed and now wilderness is an artifact of civilization. What formerly was our source is now primarily an artifact of civilization. But we also see the preservation of the prairie not as mere nostalgia, but as a practical necessity if we're to learn the rules of a natural system with which we must merge because it features material recycling and runs on sunlight. That's the economy of the prairie: it features material recycling and runs on sunlight—a renewable economy. Human economies are extractive economies; they do not feature material recycling. If we could put on some carbon glasses, through which we saw only the flow of carbon, we would be radicalized in an instant, because we would see that what is sponsoring us is the flow of carbon out of extinct floras—fossil fuels that flow through, and that leverage, the contemporary sunlight of forestry, fisheries, and agriculture. So the prairie is not merely a setting or an artifact. It's a practical necessity.

The grass family came onto the scene thirty times longer ago than the Pleistocene lasted. (When I started college, the Pleistocene lasted 1 million years; by the time I was through graduate school, it had lasted 2 million years, and it hasn't gained much since in its longevity.) The Gramineae, or the Poaceae, or what we call the grass family, that group of plants that evolved to invite fires, was put together in such systems as a way of protecting itself from the woody ligneous flora, 65 to 70 million years ago. And recent studies looking at DNA segments of the major crops—the corn, the rice, the sorghums, the barleys, the wheats—show that it's really one big genetic system. The conservation of the germ plasm in big chunks or blocks has been retained, and the difference between them is only a matter of some minor rearrangements. This was learned only in the past five to ten years, looking at the sequence of DNA, comparing, say, the rice map, the map of the rice genome, with that of wheat. Dr. Graham Moore at the John Innes Institute in England found nineteen different segments that were common.[5] He took out his son's Lego set (turning away from the computer) and assigned nineteen different blocks to those nineteen different segments of the rice genome, rearranged them, and got the genome of wheat. Since that time, they have also found this great conservation in the sorghum, and in corn, and so on. Here is this great grass family, and its strategy in evolution has been toward a great conservation of these segments. The further significance of this is that we now have the opportunity to think about making these annual domestic crops *perennial:* corn, sorghum, wheat, and so on.

Now, let's talk about landscaping, and think about the patterns of landscape use that maximize options for future generations. It's getting increasingly wearing, as I go to and fro on my environmental errands, to hear my liberal friends say, "Well, you know, there's a whole bunch of ways to go in the world, you know. I mean, one thing is as good as the other, you know, and we've gotta be open to all sorts of options, you know," and so on. And I can understand the 3 percent of truth in that statement. But the thing that we must start thinking about is: What kind of a standard do we use? If corn and soybeans continue to be *the way* of Iowa, Iowa is doomed! We've lost nearly half the topsoil over much of Iowa; eighteen tons of soil per acre per year in western Iowa going down the tubes. And they hold a conference over here in Dubuque because of the poisoning of the waters in the Gulf of Mexico! Why do they hold it in Dubuque? Because the source is up here, the source of the farm chemicals that are poisoning the Gulf. One of the nuttiest things humans have ever done is to introduce chemicals into the environment that our tissues have no evolutionary experience with, without regarding them as guilty until proved innocent. So one thing is not just as good as another. We don't want "to keep all these options open." And I come back: What did the land look like before the *Entrada?* What did it look like at the end of the Pleistocene, be-

fore the paleo-hunters arrived and found that magnificent fauna? What did it look like before the second *Entrada?* Fossil soils and mollusks of interglacial periods show it was grassland, and that grassland is a product of climate and geology—climate- and geology-determined. In other words, in those interglacial periods, there was a vegetative structure similar to what was seen by Coronado, Lewis and Clark, Long, Pike, and all the rest. And what do we see with corn and soybeans? We see that ecological capital going to the sea.

In thinking about this problem several years ago, I looked at cornfields, soybean fields, and wheat fields, and saw all of them dependent on fossil fuel for traction, dependent on fossil fuel for nitrogen fertility, because natural gas is a feedstock for nitrogen fertilizer, dependent on fossil fuel as a way of controlling the insects, the pathogens, and the weeds, and saw the dumping of alien chemicals, many of which turn out to be endocrine blockers, some of them outright cancer causers (non-Hodgkin's lymphoma is directly related to 2–4-D), and also saw the genetic narrowing of these major crops. In thinking of all these things, I asked: What if we compare those fields with the native prairie? The native prairie runs on sunlight; it sponsors its own nitrogen; it actually *accumulates* ecological capital; and it doesn't feature genetic narrowing, but, in fact, diversity is its key.

And so the fundamental difference: the prairie features perennials grown in mixtures; we feature annuals grown in lawn cultures. So we set out with a research agenda to explore the possibility of an agriculture based on the way the prairie works. I didn't realize at the time that we were asking a far more fundamental question than we first appreciated. We were asking, after all, what nature would have us do. What is nature's standard or measure? The position that has informed agricultural research and, indeed, most human activity on the landscape to the present, is that nature is to be subdued or ignored. That position goes all the way back beyond Bacon; Bacon and Descartes revealed a formalization of sorts. Bacon said, in a letter to King James, something like, "We must bend nature to our will. We must torture her to get truth out of her, even as you, oh king, have been successful in getting the truth out of witches through torture. We've got to do that to nature." Here is a founding father of the modern scientific-technological worldview. Bacon's contemporary Descartes elaborated and implied that we place priority on part over whole by breaking a problem down to the level where there's no ambiguity. Of course, at that point it's totally irrelevant. Ambiguity is essential for relevance.

So it was a system that came into being by narrowing the boundaries of consideration; narrowing the boundaries of causation. And, indeed, like a basketball team that's going up against a team that has a leading scorer who scores half the points, well, you put all five men on the one that's getting half the points. By assuming that our team will keep scoring the same number of points as in the past, we'll win the game. Now nobody believes that, except some agricultural researchers, when it comes to conducting experiments. Not all of them, but enough to create problems. The point is that we have a worldview, now, in which the boundaries of consideration have been too narrowed. It's not just the economist who externalizes the cost to the environment; researchers also externalize these considerations.

At the Land Institute, we set out to answer the question of whether perennialism and high seed-yield can go together (Figure 12.1). Is it in the cards for flowering plants to do that? Warm-season grasses, cool-season grasses, legumes, members of the sunflower family—all angio-

sperms? And the second question is whether a mixture of such plants could outyield a monoculture. And the third is whether the system could adequately manage insects, pathogens, and weeds—whether we could mimic the vegetative structure of a prairie and tweak it to produce seeds for *us,* because humans, if we were given a proper Linnaean description of *Homo sapiens,* it would be *grass-seed-eaters,* primarily. That would be our definition, legume-seed-eaters secondarily. So we had four areas of research: perennialism and high seed yield; polyculturalism rather than monoculturalism; control of insects, pathogens, and weeds; and finding a system to sponsor enough of its own nitrogen.

After some eighteen years of research (and I hope that the literary types here will forgive me for the metaphor here), we've declared a Kitty Hawk and now we're asking for the wind-tunnel phase.

I advertised this talk as "the truly radical alternative, natural systems agriculture." It is more than talking about an agriculture in which soil erosion can cease to be a major problem, because of the perennial roots and because it's the opposite of the way we do agriculture now. Second, the reward goes to the farmer and the landscape, rather than to the supplier of inputs. Third, we're talking about an agriculture in which we have greatly reduced our dependence on fossil fuels and putting chemicals out there with which we haven't evolved. We're talking about an agriculture in which there is something of a repudiation of the worldview of Bacon and Descartes, and an embracing of the worldview of Charles Darwin—an evolutionary, ecological worldview tacked on the modern molecular synthesis.

The reason, I think, that we've had such a hard time getting *out* of that Baconian–Cartesian worldview is they had a 250-year head

Figure 12.1. Terry Evans, "The Land Institute, Experimental Plots, Spring, 1993." (Courtesy of Terry Evans)

start on Darwin. But 137 years without Darwin is long enough, as far as farming and agriculture are concerned. This sort of appreciation for the prairie, expressed through words and visionary art, has the power to change our cognition, the power to move us toward a mindfulness already formalized in Darwin's *On the Origin of Species*. This evolutionary-ecological worldview has grown in the past seventy to ninety years. Modern economics has mostly ignored the implication of *The Origin*. By expanding our boundaries of consideration, because of this worldview, the current way of doing science is challenged. We now have a way to help us move from an extractive to a renewable economy. A more proper balance between a reliance on human cleverness and a reliance on nature's wisdom can result. The human cleverness approach validated by the Enlightenment has yielded some great benefits we would not want to reject, but it needs fine-tuning—and in some important ways.

Descartes said in his *Discourse on Method* that the more he sought to inform himself, the more he realized how ignorant he was. But rather than regard that—his ignorance—as an apt description of the human condition and the very proper result of a good education, Descartes thought our ignorance could be corrected. But by thinking even a little bit, we realize that we're billions of times more ignorant than knowledgeable, and always will be. So rather than a knowledge-based worldview, let's go with our long suit. How about an ignorance-based worldview? Now if we had an ignorance-based worldview, we could ask questions in a different way, and it would be the primordial step toward the necessary humility. Humility coming out of church attendance has been limited. Maybe a humility generated from recognizing how ignorant we are can be formalized. We have ways to begin. By starting with the way the prairie

works, we're not asking to know every little detail that, say, the physiological ecologist might wish to explore. We're merely taking advantage of huge slabs of what works. In other words, by imitating the structures, we can be granted the functions: the retention of the soil; the cycling of the materials; the protection of diversity, which amounts to chemical diversity (thus protecting the system from the epidemic). By taking advantage of the natural integrities inherent within a system, we can embrace this ignorance-based worldview. By acknowledging that we're ignorant, that we're stupid and wicked, a species given to folly—and for a long time to come—we can take it upon ourselves to build a system more resilient to human folly. By declaring that we are ignorant, it doesn't mean we don't try to chip away at our huge boulders of ignorance. De facto, all we've ever done is chip away. We would be featuring the wisdom of nature, meaning the assemblies and processes that have come down through the billions of years of life on this particular planet. That would be a radical departure.

I'm calling for a research agenda over the fifteen- to twenty-five-year period for the wind-tunnel phase. If we had one site with twenty scientists—all the way from the biotechnologists, to the ecologists and the computer modelers, to the environmental historian, to the artist—we could put on this landscape an agriculture that would effectively be the mimic of that old prairie, but still produce grains, and through some of this "Lego-genetics," maybe even get the corn, the wheat, the sorghum, and so on, tweaked into being perennial. At the Land Institute, we have a little less than a hundred acres of never-plowed native prairie featuring warm-season grasses, cool-season grasses, legumes, and members of the sunflower family (Figure 12.2). Jon Piper and students inventoried the ratios at various sites. Next we can elect to imitate that structure

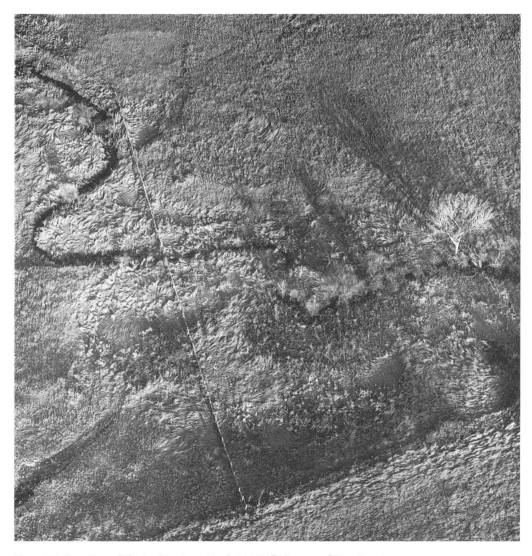

Figure 12.2. Terry Evans, "The Land Institute, March 24, 1993." (Courtesy of Terry Evans)

with analogues of our choice, derived through either the domestication of wild species or the conversion of annual grains into perennials.

Here is the fantasy. In this fifteen- to twenty-five-year period, some twenty Ph.D. level professionals at a cost over a twenty-five-year period of $130 million are at work during this wind-tunnel phase. Even if we had *ten* sites so dedicated, the cost would amount to $1.3 billion. David Pimentel and his group at Cornell, publishing in *Science,* have estimated that soil erosion alone is costing $44 billion per year![6] Even if we were asking for $1.3 billion spread over twenty-five years, that would be peanuts. We're not asking for that; we're asking for only $130 million.

We can begin to think about more than agriculture for grain crops. This same paradigm holds for forestry and for fisheries. Darwin's theory of evolution through natural selection holds in the Arctic and in the Tropics and all places in between. The principles are applicable everywhere. We can begin to think of adjusting these systems to a particular place no matter where we are in the ecological mosaic. We could be creating, in John Todd's words, "elegant solutions predicated upon the uniqueness of place."

We can begin to entertain that vision by thinking of a specific research agenda. I have a great big sheet that outlines this research agenda for a twenty-year period.

If we don't get sustainability in agriculture, forests, and fisheries first, it isn't going to happen. Behind these enterprises stands the science of ecology, which has to do with living things interacting with the nonliving world. There are some well-understood principles, and there is a body of knowledge (admittedly, mostly on the shelf, placed there mostly for its own sake) pertaining to how the world works. Much of it can be applied. The materials sector, the industrial sector of the world, does not have such a body

of knowledge. Darwin brings us back to the reality of the green plant, to the reality expressed by Loren Eiseley: "The human brain—so frail, so fragile, so full of the fondest hopes and dreams and aspirations—burns by the power of the leaf."[7] That's the reality we must keep coming back to.

The barriers? The number-one barrier may be the structure of our consciousness. In our Paleolithic past, any technological innovation likely increased our adaptive value. We've been so successful that technological innovations now may be threatening our adaptive value over a long time. There is the reality, probably also out of our Paleolithic past, that the things once possessed can't be done without. Wallace Stegner talked about this in *Wolf Willow.*[8]

We have to confront what has been built into the meat of us creatures of the Upper Paleolithic. Birth control goes against the grain. Death control goes with the grain. We have to think about how to overcome some of these predispositions, as well as the philosophical problems that come out of Bacon and Descartes. So with that, I'll end, and I certainly thank you for giving me a chance to carry on with senile rapture!

SPECTATOR: In all three wonderful presentations, there are references to the capitalist economy, along with the democracy of diversity, but none seems to be talking about the dominance of a capitalist economy over that diversity. Wes, you didn't really help us see how Archer Daniels Midland and other corporations are part of the emerging global economy, which is becoming more and more dominant all that time, and how powerful those people are. So I guess my question is: Where does the capitalist economy fit into all of this?

WJ: Well, capitalism is an engine of the extractive economy and the industrial mind, and I think a convenient way to frame the issue for me is that if we look at the first major failure of the industrial mind—that is, the breakdown of the Soviet Union—we must say, "Thank God it happened there first, because at least 80 percent of those people are growing their own food." Capitalism and Communism are both just forms of the extractive economy; I mean, whether the individual rips off the environment or the group rips off the environment, it's the same. I think we must address the danger of that mind which has validated extraction. We can say, "Capitalism sucks," but once we've said that a few times, it gets kind of tiresome. So let's start looking at nature's renewable systems, like the prairie. What is the prairie's analogue of currency? What is the analogue of that which features diversity over simplicity in human economies? Check those analogues out, and then the scales will begin to fall from our eyes.

SPECTATOR: Just following up on that, one of the things you suggest is that we integrate those systems, the human economic systems and nature's ecological systems, like the prairie, so as to create a system that is, you say, impervious to human folly. And yet the problem is that the prairie system is clearly not impervious to human folly. It was destroyed by human folly. Is there a little problem with the metaphors here?

WJ: Probably. I lose control of my metaphors all the time. What I mean is that without the plows and overgrazing, the prairie can continue. The problem is this idea that nature can be subdued or ignored. How do we begin to extricate ourselves from that? We want to start a tendency to look to these systems as standards and to measure our progress by how independent of the extractive economy we become. We also want to make our actions the consequence of some degree of mimicry of biological systems. There's a whole field now developing called "biomimesis," where engineering systems are out to imitate bi-

ological systems. This is in its very early stages, but it's got to move all the way to economics; it can't simply be the mechanics of the way a shark moves applied to submarines—which is what they're trying to do so far.

SPECTATOR: The topsoil—will it begin to return, short of the human species becoming extinct? With this perennial idea, will we begin very slowly to restore topsoil?

WJ: Some, yes. Perennials will begin to restore it.

Notes

1. Wendell Berry, *The Unsettling of America* (New York: Avon/Sierra Club Books, 1977).

2. Aldo Leopold, *A Sand County Almanac and Sketches Here and There* (New York: Oxford University Press, 1949), 225.

3. J. M. Gowdy and C. N. McDaniel, "One World, One Experiment: Addressing the Biodiversity–Economics Conflict," *Ecological Economics* 15 (1995): 181–99.

4. Donald Worster, *Nature's Economy: A History of Ecological Ideas,* 2nd ed. (New York: Cambridge University Press, 1994).

5. Graham Moore, "Popular Cereals," *Economist,* 6 May 1995, 80.

6. David Pimentel, C. Harvey, P. Resosudarmo, K. Sinclair, D. Kurz, M. McNair, S. Crist, L. Shpritz, L. Fitton, R. Saffouri, and R. Blair, "Environmental and Economic Costs of Soil Erosion and Conservation Benefits," *Science,* 24 February 1995, 1117–23.

7. Loren Eiseley, *The Immense Journey* (New York: Random House, 1957).

8. Wallace Stegner, *Wolf Willow* (New York: Viking Press, 1962).

13 Sizing Up the Country: Contemporary Artists' Perspectives on the Prairie

Robert F. Sayre

In 1835, when Thomas Cole listed the major elements of "American scenery"—mountains, water, waterfalls, forests, and sky—he left out one-third of the country. The prairies and plains, despite their size, could not be "scenic" or a subject for landscape painters because, as generally viewed, they had only one of these elements: sky. They were, as Cole's contemporaries often called them, the "Great American Desert."

Fortunately, not all artists of Cole's time abided by his strictures. Although Cole has long been called the founder of American landscape painting, he was celebrating only the scenery of the places that he chose to paint and where his patrons lived or went on their vacations—the Catskills, upstate New York, and rural New England. Other artists like George Catlin, Alfred Jacob Miller, Henry George Hine, William Jacob Hays, and William Henry Jackson did paint the prairies and plains, and for that reason their work is all the more important. It provides answers to the great conundrum, composed of two inseparable questions: What did the great center

of the continent look like? How was it represented? Nevertheless, as nineteenth-century landscape artists moved on across the continent, most ignored the prairies, and Cole's concept of "scenery" came to dominate American taste in landscape. Since then, both art historians and the general public have continued to prefer majestic mountains, tranquil lakes, rushing streams, and romantic forests. These have been the focus for most exhibits of landscape art, as they have also been the preferred destinations for most tourists.

As the first major exhibition of prairie landscapes ever assembled, "Plain Pictures: Images of the American Prairie," at the University of Iowa Museum of Art, was therefore a unique opportunity to reconsider American landscape painting and its character and influence. In particular, it seemed a very exciting moment to examine the relationships between how land is seen and how it is valued and used. How had prejudices about the prairie's lack of scenery affected its later history? How had the artists who did paint and photograph it dealt with its aesthetic challenges? What were contemporary artists' responses to it?

The ultimate answers to most of these questions are, of course, in the pictures. They best express how artists see and feel about a landscape, how they deal with it, and even how others might approach it. Even so, viewers enjoy hearing artists talk about their work, and usually see it better as a result. Emily Vermillion, the museum's education curator, therefore invited a number of the artists to give illustrated lectures. Stan Herd discussed his "crop art." Drake Hokanson spoke about his experiences as a prairie author and photographer. And on the first day of the symposium, painters Fred Easker, Keith Jacobshagen, and Genie Patrick, along with photographer Terry Evans, spoke about their work.

Afterward, in order to gather more statements from the contemporary artists whose work was included in the exhibit, I wrote up a short, very unscientific questionnaire that I initially sent to nine of the artists (see the appendix to this chapter). I asked rather simple, factual questions such, as "How long have you painted or photographed the prairie or plains landscape?" "What other kinds of landscapes do you do?" and "What most attracts you—for example, color? form? subject? the natural landscape or the built landscape?" I asked about influences from other artists and writers. And I asked, rather timidly, "What other issues in the prairie, plains, or agricultural landscape most interest you, for example, social and economic issues surrounding farming, sustainable agriculture, conservation, environmental problems?" and whether the artists made a connection between "how land is seen, including how it is represented by artists, and how it is used?" Later mailings asked more contentious questions, such as the relation of art to politics, people's attitudes toward regional-

ism, and the influence of the art market. I had been leery of such questions because I did not want to make "environmental correctness" a standard of taste or to solicit only "environmentally correct" responses. The relationships between landscape and landscape art are complex and problematic, to say the least. Most artists do not want to be propagandists. The romantic landscapist, in the tradition of Cole and the Hudson River School, sought the sublime and picturesque. The efforts to conserve and protect such landscapes came later and generally from others, not the artists. Conversely, realists, broadly speaking, have tried to represent just what they saw, regardless of its meaning. Yet another school of artists and photographers has prized the ordinary and tried to discover beauty in the neglected and even the desolate. The variations among these and other schools are, of course, numerous, and I did not want to direct people into taking polemical positions. It would be much more interesting to see the variety of their positions and to find the heterodoxy in their perspectives, rather than seek an orthodoxy. And yet to elicit such variety, I decided, I had to pose the questions, although I invited the respondents to take complete liberty in the questions they chose to answer and the length of the answers.

What follows are notes on these answers. Some people answered very briefly, while others took three, four, or five pages and enclosed statements or short essays. In all, sixteen (out of twenty) artists responded, revealing a great deal about both their own work and the prairie landscape as they (and others) see it.

Robert Adams, who was represented in the exhibition by a black-and-white photograph, *From the Front Porch of an Abandoned One-Room Schoolhouse, Looking into the Niobrara River Valley* (1978), has been doing prairie landscapes for thirty years and has "loved the prairie from the first time I saw it as a teenager," although he has also photographed urban and suburban landscapes and "what remains of the semi-developed West." He would also photograph other environments: "As Alfred Stieglitz observed, 'wherever there is light, one can photograph.'" As for what attracts him, he answered, "The *form* of *the subject*. Form is the primary metaphor by which pictures speak to us." Willa Cather and William Stafford are the writers who have most influenced him, and in answer to whether he objected to the term "regionalist," he said, "No. As William Stafford observed, *all* art that is worth anything is regional." His answer to the question about politics and art is that art "is not *directly* political. But it *is* socially useful—it helps people *care*." Similarly, he wrote that there should be a relationship between how land is seen by artists and how it is used: "Every artist hopes, certainly, that he or she can help find a way not to kill the earth."

Lee Allen, the oldest living artist in the exhibit, wrote that his "first landscape was painted in 1928" and that "*Corn Country,* now included in the exhibit, [was painted] in 1934." His love of prairie landscape goes back to "automobile trips with my parents through the middle of . . . Iowa. My mind still recalls scenes I thought of painting but which I never got around to paint." As for influences, he mentions Grant Wood and Marvin Cone, both of whom he knew personally. Prairie writers have not influenced him "because my main interest in literature has been world history, biographies, archaeology and natural history." In regard to other issues, he says, "I am a strong conservationist and therefore [am] concerned about loss of our farmland—by encroaching growth of cities and towns." In the 1930s, he painted two post office murals with conservation themes: *Soil Conservation* in Onawa, Iowa, near the Missouri River;

and *Conservation of Wildlife* in Emmetsburg, in northwest Iowa. But he does not care what "political critics think," only wanting people to like landscapes and like his painting. The term "regional" gives him some trouble, because all artists, beginning with cave painters, have "painted those things with which they were familiar" and should continue to. The use of the term by art critics is restricting, although he adds that "Grant [Wood] over reacted" to such critics. Likewise, "the Art Market always worried me," which is why "I accepted a position as an Ophthalmic Illustrator after I married and had a child on the way." He worked in this capacity until 1976, when he resumed painting professionally.

The Chicago painter Roger Brown's *Citizens Surveying the Flat Landscape* (1987) was perhaps the least representational work in the exhibit—a large canvas showing two dwarf-size cars on a straight road lined with evenly spaced small trees, and eight tiny figures, four standing near the road, and four silhouetted on the horizon. Overhead are giant stylized clouds that partially mirror the gentle contours of the land. It is a brilliant seriocomic comment on the banality of the way the land is seen today, through distant interactions not requiring close acquaintance. Still, Brown reported doing prairie landscapes since around 1972, following a trip "out to South Dakota Wyoming Colorado." "Form" is the first attraction, and "then subject. Color for me is generally an exaggerated vision of the natural color." As for regionalism, he said, "I am interested in some artists generally referred to as regionalist. Though I believe Grant Wood & Thomas Hart Benton were as mainstream as you can get in recording and transforming the American scene. I believe that I could not as easily be referred to as regionalist, since my work has a more anonymous air to its subjects & form." "It is important," he continued, in answer to the question about regionalists' connections with land as opposed to city, "to be in an art center such as a city as a young artist before attempting to remove oneself to the country. . . . One needs to develop a strong, unshakable language & belief in oneself before going to the woods." "Any art of mine that dealt with the prairie did so subject by subject or as a basic landscape layout which actually could apply to any part of the country." Finally, on the relationship between visions and uses of land, Brown wrote, "Artists see the land idealistically, if not always presenting it that way. Like most concerned people they are concerned with what is happening to the world environment. I often represent the misuse of land in my work—though finding an appropriate scheme or composition that is largely formed is of the greatest importance."

James D. Butler, currently living in Bloomington, Illinois, says that he "began painting and drawing the midwestern landscape in 1965 . . . influenced by the work of Tom Palmerton, . . . at the University of Nebraska at Omaha, . . . whose work paid homage to Andrew Wyeth." Butler's own work, represented by *Parker's Ridge* (1994), has some of Wyeth's mixture of realism and magic. "My primary interest is in the relationship between man and nature," he says, describing his kind of landscape:

One can find this subject many places, but my exploration of this topic comes from the area of this country that I know. For me to choose to paint a particular site, many things must attract me. Certainly the subject would be of primary concern, but a particular light and the ability to build an interesting composition are also important considerations.

Continuing to define his work, he says,

I am interested in artists who have found ways to carry personal responses to their surroundings back into their art in profound ways. It has nothing to do with illustrating an idea, rather with a heart felt and intellectual response to who they are, where they come from and how their audience might connect to those feelings. These ideas cut across time and geography and do not necessarily result in realist work. For example, I find inspiration in the work and thoughts of such diverse artists as Terry Allen, Wayne Thiebaud, Edwin Dickinson and Antonio Lopez-Garcia. Probably none of these artists would be classified as regionalists and yet in many ways they are. The reason why I dislike the term "regionalist" is that in the past it was used to define the *limits* of certain artists' work.

As for the question about politics and aesthetics, he writes, "I do have strong feelings about the environment, the use of the land and what we are doing to ourselves through various pollutants. However, the struggle to make good paintings is always the central issue for me."

Fred Easker of Cedar Rapids, Iowa, expresses similar feelings about politics, art, and the environment, although his work is distinctly different from that of Butler. His work in the show was *Morning on Springville Road* (1995), a long, low painting (17 × 90 inches) showing a rural road cutting straight across the foreground and then gently curving off to the left horizon. "I've been painting the Iowa landscape for about six years," he says; and this is definitely an Iowa scene. Just previously, he had been doing a lot of commuting, while taking a writing course, and thus driving over the landscape. Then "I saw an exhibit of the work of Frederic Church, an artist I have always admired, at the National Gallery":

In Church's work I recognized that beyond the great technical facility, there seemed to be something of substance. . . . In my writing, I came to understand how important a sense of space was to me personally which seemed connected to a lot of early childhood experiences on the farm of grandparent-like family friends as well as to adventures in the undeveloped areas around my boyhood home. As I commuted, I began to formulate in my mind what kind of landscape paintings I would be interested in creating. I recognized the difficulty of making what at times seems featureless terrain into something visually interesting and took it as a challenge. I chose familiar places as a place to start.

Describing those places further, he says,

I am most interested in the wonderful abstract forms of the subtle Iowa terrain which are revealed by the farmer's plows, fences, roads and by the light of the sun in the early morning or late afternoon when it produces brilliant and sparkling colors. What is most important in my work is how these elements suggest the energy that exists below the quiet surface.

Thus Easker readily accepts regionalism and the works of Grant Wood and Marvin Cone, which he knows well, having worked for nearly four years at the Cedar Rapids Museum of Art. He objects only to its seeming to be "limiting" and its having "in some minds a pejorative connotation." Accepting Wood's notion of "painting what you know," Easker goes on to say, "Art is really about the artist." And yet in his answer to the question about the influences of art on how land is seen, he says,

A number of people who have been interested in my work tell me that they often see Iowa through my eyes, which means to me that how they see their environment has been changed by their experience with my work. That seems powerful, and it would be great if their experience with art would affect their decision making processes concerned with the environment. However, I don't think painters have much impact on society today.

Terry Evans began photographing the prairie in 1978, and the variety of her perspectives is suggested by her four works in the exhibition. One is the black-and-white aerial view *Rosehill Cemetery, Saline County, Kansas* (1991), showing a tiny, square, tree-rimmed rural cemetery completely surrounded by smoothly cultivated fields. Another is a color triptych of fields of grass: *Chase County, South of Matfield Green, Kansas* (1993). The third, also taken at eye-level, is *Fairy Ring, Fent's Prairie* (1979), while the fourth is the ground-level, or root-level, color picture *Prairie Roots and Big Bluestem and Other Grasses, Konza Prairie* (1979). The reasons for such multiple perspectives are given in a short statement that she sent:

My photography is an exploration of prairie from its native state to its use, abandonment, and restoration, from both ground and aerial perspectives. My purpose always is to tell the prairies' stories, past and present through the visible facts of the landscape. In order to see the prairie whole, it is vitally important to look continually at both the complexity of local place and people and the broader geographic context of ecological, agricultural, and cultural patterns. My best prairie pictures weave together history and memory, ecology and beauty and thus suggest a story of a place, a particular place.

The artists she listed as having had most influence on her were George Catlin, Grant Wood, Alexander Hogue, and Wright Morris. The writers were Wright Morris (again), Willa Cather, Wes Jackson, Donald Worster, Wallace Stegner, Sharon Butala, and John Neihardt. In answer to the long question, "What other issues in the prairie, plains, or agricultural landscape most interest you, for example, social and economic issues surrounding farming, sustainable agriculture, conservation, environmental problems?" she simply penned in, "All of the above." In answer to the question about how land is seen by artists and how it is used, she wrote again at length:

I would like for land to be used by artists, farmers, residents, industrialists, and the military according to the natural ecology and structure of the land itself. Your question implies that artists "see" the land properly & should thus influence other land users. We all need to see with attention, honor, & respect for land. We artists do not necessarily see it better than anyone else although at least we start with the intention of seeing it. We still bring out own assumptions, values, & preconceptions with our vision.

Consistent with these statements, she further wrote, "Aesthetic issues are all bound together with environmental, political, social, & conservation issues." And on the matter of regionalism she wrote, "After living in the heart of rural prairie, in central Kansas for 26 years, I moved to Chicago a few years ago. I thought the move would destroy my artistic identity, but it has instead expanded my vision & allowed me to see my own work more clearly." In Chicago, one of her projects is photographing the 25,000-acre Joliet arsenal plant, which is being abandoned by the army and converted into a prairie park.

Harold Gregor of Bloomington, Illinois, also responded at length, saying that the questions helped him "to shift my gears from making and writing about art to the somewhat neglected consideration of my own motives and aims." Recalling that when he moved to Illinois from California in 1970, op art, pop art, and abstract expressionism were the dominant styles and landscape painting was "considered to be a completely retrogressive enterprise." He nevertheless "decided to attempt the rural landscape," beginning with "large scale realistic depictions of the dramatic corn cribs that stand like sentinels on the prairie." These were accepted by galleries and sold. But by 1973, he was ready for something else: "I came upon a corn meal bag imprinted with a 4-color silk screen image of an aerial view of a prairie farm. I painted a 5 × 5.5 foot enlargement of this image, and after studying it for awhile, began a long series of color-formed paintings, trying to fuse color with descriptive imagery, within a flat space format." These "flatscapes," as he called them, continue

to attract him. One of them, *Illinois Flatscape #56* (1994), a big, close-up aerial view of a complex farmstead, painted in bright oil and acrylic, is one of his three pictures in the exhibit. He has also experimented with long panoramas, which relate to how the prairie appears from a moving car, and "'trail' paintings," which emphasize "the light, trees, and atmosphere discoverable on our local walking trail." He has even "made a series of dramatic tornado drawings," but jokes that the film *Twister* "used up the subject for a while."

As these accounts show, Gregor is definitely interested in the formal issues and challenges in prairie picturing, taking them on with a combination of careful persistence and inventive spontaneity. Yet he has also given a lot of thought to both spiritual and environmental issues: "I try to picture what I feel is true of this area: that the farmers hereabouts truly try to exist in an ecological harmony with the land. The farmers I talk to are all very aware of the ecological imperatives that dictate their farming procedures. Most of them really respect, love, and consider their position in the wider scheme." The aesthetic and ecological perspectives come together for him because, "anything that inspires an aesthetic reward becomes more valued." Although "not a preacher," he says at one point that he would "feel very good if my paintings ... announce a plea for ecological balance similar to Wes Jackson's thoughts." He seems to like all things prairie, and has, he writes, ever since, while in the service in World War II, he drove from Detroit to Texas: "Passing through Illinois at sunset" and "driving for what seemed like forever into the slowly altering color atmosphere" was "an Emersonian sublime moment!" He notes, however, that the experience meant so much because he had grown up in Detroit, "a city boy." "Because I had no investment in the landscape as such, I was able to derive from it a pure aesthetic or spiritual moment denied any-one whose interests were already focused." This is his answer to whether regionalists should spend time elsewhere. He adds that in 1974, he "came close to buying a loft in New York City." His midwestern landscapes had been selling very well. But "I knew I could not live in the city and paint prairie landscapes." So he rehabili-tated an old Bloomington theater to live in and bought part of a downtown building for a stu-dio: "Spectacular farm scenery comes into view only a couple of miles away in all directions." "I have become an artistic prairie-addict!"

Walter Hatke is a painter who grew up on the Kansas prairie but now lives in Schenectady, New York, where his subject has become the landscapes of the Mohawk Valley and its sur-roundings. Yet his working methods still em-phasize a very careful study of whatever country he paints and a personal and familial engage-ment with it. "It is my conviction," he writes,

that the best landscapes are those where the artists . . . have had firsthand acquaintance with the very land-scape they are addressing. One must walk across the land, touch it, note the crunch underfoot, breathe the air, literally smell and taste the atmosphere. I take notes, jot down details and thoughts. One must know the subject inside and out; there is absolutely no sub-stitute for direct experience.

In preparing for a painting, he will even "tramp around to the other side of buildings I know won't be visibly included in a work." His paint-ing *River Fields* (1983) was started when he was living on a farm near Lawrence, Kansas, "in an area I knew from my youth, where I'd hunted fossils, canoed on the adjacent river, camped nearby, and visited intriguing old native stone homesteads, drawn and painted on occasion." But the painting was finished a year later when he was teaching in Pennsylvania. This was con-sistent with his method of doing most of his ac-

tual painting in his studio and working "a great deal from memory." All this gives his work a profound personal and ideological content, even though he steers clear of politics per se. While in Iowa as a graduate student, he says, he "loved the Amana Colonies," and he still feels drawn to "areas developed by utopian/millen-nialist societies." He likes the way their land-scapes create "a palpable sense of peace" and sat-isfy "both esthetic and pragmatic visions." Such agrarian values are much on his mind and highly visible in his work.

A native Nebraskan, Harold Holoun left for the Far West at age twenty-two, "saying I'd NEVER come back," but returned in 1970 and "was so overwhelmed by the primal earth/sky relation . . . that I had to deal with it in some way (though my first attempts were essentially abstract)." He is thus another artist initially very influenced by abstract expressionism who has both used it and gone beyond it. He confesses to having been "really pissed by seeing Mark Rothko's paintings, because I felt that he'd ze-roed in on a kind of ultimate American land-scape," and he remains very attracted to "formal relationships" and "earth forms and masses weighed against sky space and sky forms." He also reports a concern for the land as land that a pure formalist might not have:

I see a great disparity in how land is seen, and how it is used. In the past thirty or so years, I've seen efforts by state and local groups in various prairie states be-gin to view their regions as areas of pride, be it es-thetic, historic, whatever. But these are pockets of "sanity" in what I see is still a wrenching misuse (or should I say overuse) of a fragile kind of land(scape) that isn't able to sustain itself well in the face of this kind of onslaught.

To him, the overuse of pesticides and fertilizers, the spread of center-pivot irrigation, and the cutting up of the Loess Hills of Iowa and Nebraska are both aesthetic and ecological out-rages. Although he does not consciously think about these things in selecting subjects, disliking political art, he admits that they may affect him subconsciously. Guardedly optimistic about the survival of the prairie environment, he con-cludes "that the prairie artists, writers, and poets have had, and will have, some influence in mak-ing that happen."

Keith Jacobshagen, who lives in Lincoln, Ne-braska, is also, in his own words, "not interested in directing my work politically." His personal feelings about "the land, pollution and conser-vation could play an unconscious part in the way I make images, but [that] is not the reason I make images." "I have a need to express some-thing deep inside . . . to get it out, to scratch the itch and say something about this small but spa-cious world." His attachment to the plains began when he was a child and spent his weekends "at a small grass country airport where my father taught flying." He often flew with his father and so had a special perspective on the land, sky, and clouds. But he also enjoyed just "hanging out in the countryside . . . , taking in the light, space and agra life of south central Kansas." Regarding the present attractions of the plains landscape, he writes, "The first response is emotional, straight from the heart. But very quickly the mind's eye is taken up with space, light, the sub-tleness of forms, proportions, color and how these things react on the imagination. . . . There is enchantment in light, it is the great sensualist of emotion and meaning to me."

The excitement of painting for him is the bringing together of light, the change of seasons, weather, and "our agrarian, urban, suburban culture." Suggestively referring to all these forces as our "connections to living," he goes on to say that he believes that "the eye functions in a close symbiosis with the fears, needs, desires, con-cepts and representations we carry within us."

Such a prolonged, close, and generally beneficial relationship among different organisms—land-scape, eye, and feelings—seems to have become, for Jacobshagen, a kind of dependence, for in answer to the question about what he would do if he moved to a new area, he answers simply, "I have no idea." He not only feels "deeply about this place that I live," but clearly feels *through* or *by* this place. Such a symbiosis also makes his work a kind of autobiography. At the sympo-sium, he showed slides of pictures from a com-bination sketchbook and journal.

Jacobshagen does not call himself a regional-ist, however, because he feels that his work "is informed as much by what is outside of this place as it is by what is here" and that the outside issues and ideas are important. The "dogged in-sistence" of the regionalists of the 1930s that "they did not have to pay attention to what was going on in New York, London and Paris" often made their work "narrow, unexpansive and down right bloodless." Fortunately, "cyber space and the sophistication of publication" now make it possible for people to stay informed and to keep an "intellectual and emotional balance."

Illinois photographer Gary Irving seems to feel equally dependent on the land, but more protective toward it. "We protect the landscape for which we have an aesthetic attachment," he says. "If we don't develop an appreciation for the prairie, both natural and cultivated, I suspect it will continue to be subjected to pressures it can-not sustain." Irving's views are doubly interest-ing because he also describes his work as "less documentary" than that of many other photog-raphers and "more inclined towards the Roman-tic. My work is less about the place depicted [than] it is about a state of grace that I find in myself as I view the scene." His photographs made with a panoramic camera, often taken in the light of early dawn, with rich colors and deep shadows, vividly illustrate this. A new book of his, depicting not only prairies but the midwestern forests and wetlands, is in fact entitled *Places of Grace,* and he says in answer to the question about literary influences that "the writer that best describes how I view the world is . . . C. S. Lewis." This paradoxical attachment to the midwestern landscape and the religious and spiritual literature of an Oxford don is striking, to say the least, although Irving also names the work of Wright Morris and David Plowden, particularly Plowden's *The Floor of the Sky,* as important artistic influences. What may explain the paradox is his attraction to *light:* "Light is the dominant attraction for me. Because the transforming early light washing over the spare landscape provides, for me, the visual context I need to convey what I feel, the minimal landscape offers more to work with than, for example, an area like the Sierras, which seem to stir little interest." Or, as he says in answer to the question about regionalism, affirming the need to experience different places, "I do find that returning to the Midwest from, say, New England does energize me. It is like being able to breathe again, to really stretch out and see everything. I don't find desolation here; I receive consolation."

Iowa photographer Drake Hokanson takes a more political position than Irving. "Looking at dry shrinking towns on the plains," where much of his recent work has been done, "I wonder about sustainable human culture, not just sustainable agriculture. We've yet to come to grips with the limits and opportunities of the plains—we refuse to understand or care about the region, and refuse to care much about those who live there." He goes on to say that "land is a lot more complicated than art" and that no photograph can possibly suggest all the influences, natural and cultural, that go into making it look the way it does. It is exactly this "uneasy marriage between the natural and human made

landscapes" that Hokanson is attracted to, however, and his photograph in *Plain Pictures—Big Bluestem, Peterson Township, July, 1990—*is a very affecting example. It shows a lone, surviving clump of native big bluestem waving its distinctive seed head between a gravel road and a vast cultivated field; and he writes, "I'm just as happy, maybe happier, when somebody looks at one of my photographs, ignores the artistic stuff, and identifies the same grasses I did when I made the photograph." But just as he believes that land is more complicated than art, he also believes that "art is more complicated than politics," explaining that as an artist he might not "see an eroded field as ugly" and might photograph a Wal-mart "and not make it ugly." For related reasons, perhaps, he has enjoyed the stimulation he has received from other places, such as New York ("a city I love") and the dairy land and woods of Wisconsin, where he now lives. The artists that most influenced him are "Karl Bodmer, Wright Morris, Hiroshige, Thomas Moran, the FSA [Farm Security Administration] photographers, Gauguin—I respond to lots of people's work." Like many photographers, then (Walker Evans and David Plowden also come to mind), Hokanson seems to follow a fine line between the political and the artistic, between work that is documentary and work that is individualistic and creative. Yet his photographs reflect his deep knowledge of prairie and plains history.

David Plowden himself, it might be observed, while combining the documentary and the aesthetic, also works in both the desolate and the heroic. His photograph in the exhibition was the stark *Nuclear Generating Station, Sillman Valley, Illinois* (1981), showing just the squat, sinister cooling tower, with noxious-looking clouds above it. In his popular and, it now seems, very culturally influential book, *The Hand of Man in America* (1971), Plowden said he began by wanting to document "our magnificent creations," but then felt "an urgent necessity to photograph the country as it was being transformed and our increasingly dismal condition which we seem to accept so easily." He wanted, he wrote, "to express my deep distress over our appalling indifference and our misplaced priorities." In the text to his photograph of a Great Northern Railroad train west of Havre, Montana, he criticizes travelers and vacationers for regarding the plains as "only a speedway" and having "eyes and mind set on some distant place." He also makes the thoughtful comment that the "plains may give the illusion of space, of being still the frontier; but that even in the empty land, hundreds of miles from the nearest town or human being, on the horizon there are the lines; wires, roads, rails, all leading beyond to some distant place were a body of men dwell." Equally stunning is his defense of the Homestead Act (now, it seems, more mentioned for its failures than its success), which is printed opposite the picture of a desolate and abandoned, but once proud *Homestead near Piqua, Ohio*. Plowden's perspective on the plains and prairies, on Chicago and the Great Lakes, on railroads and small towns unites a sense of the plain and noble Lincolnian past and the often desensitized present.

Stuart Klipper, not surprisingly, lists some of the same photographic ancestors as must have influenced Plowden: "19th Century America Exploration Photographers; Weston, Walker Evans, Atget." He also acknowledges the influences of "Willa Cather, Mari Sandoz, Ole Rölvaag, Barry Lopez, Paul Gruchow, Kathleen Norris, etc." Yet he is clearly his own man. In answer to the question "How do you think of your work as different from these other artists?" he succinctly says, "It just is." And his work in the exhibition, *Cornfields off Highway 169, North of Fort Dodge, Webster County, Iowa* (1992), "just is" different.

Showing the enormous cornfields across three-quarters of the picture space, with a storage bin and a few trees on the far right, it seemingly tells several stories at once. It tells of huge, imposing corn crops—"bin busters"—and overburdened storage facilities. It tells, in the abandoned windbreak, of a house and farmstead that are no more. And so it captures the ironies of poverty amid plenty, victory for a few and defeat for many, which are the ironies of the American prairies today, in their present condition as the "farm belt." Nevertheless, Klipper expresses no strong political opinions or preference for prairie landscapes over others. He has also photographed many other landscapes: "polar, ocean, mountain, desert, urban, wetland, etc., etc.—just about every of our planet's physical terrains & cultural geographies." He looks for "placement, presence, ambiance, numenousness, artifact, etc." But underlying all these quests is his motto: "Know where you are, be where you're at." "That's photography for me," he crisply says. Thus on the relationships between how land is seen and how it is used, he writes, "The world needs to be seen clearly to contend with it most honestly. Ideally, this is the function artists can play in a society. Artists, as per Jefferson, thus should be more intimately integrated into the systems & processes that determine how we do what we do with what we have, be it the land or our homeplaces."

A major interest in form returns in the answers given by Genie Patrick, who lives in Iowa City and Oaxaca, Mexico. It was in the latter city that she began painting landscapes in 1978: "an immersion in nature, its moods and forces" moved her to paint and draw "nature's forms . . . seeking to learn the lessons that this activity can teach." What further attracts her, she says, is "color, light, form, the interaction of weather, seasonal changes, patterns of clouds in the sky, all related to the visual characteristics of the landscape, [including] the effects of agricultural processes." The painters and paintings that have most influenced her, she goes on, are "Gauguin, Persian miniatures, Italian Renaissance panel paintings, and American artists such as Arthur G. Dove, Edward Hopper, and Marsden Hartley." They constitute what she calls her "form memory." Regionalists have not influenced her, nor have midwestern writers, and she is not interested in the relations or arguments between art and politics. Even so, she hopes that her work "gives the observer a symbolic and intense experience with the land, nature, and ecology." Like a number of the other artists whose work was in the exhibition, Patrick is "rewarded to hear from people who have looked carefully at my landscape paintings that they now see the real landscape in a new way." Therefore, she hopes that "they may become concerned for its fate and active defenders of its continuance." Underscoring this attachment to Iowa and Mexican landscapes is her answer to whether regionalist art depends on "deep, lived experience with the land [or] the opposite." "I grew up in the Deep South," she says, "where I found no forms in the landscape which had aesthetic value for me. The soft and diffused light, the overgrown qualities which obscure the edges and clarity of forms were anathema to me as subjects of contemplation for my art." By contrast, forms in the Iowa landscape clearly do appeal to her, and she has studied them meticulously, as perhaps only a painter does, and as a statement she wrote for the exhibit symposium makes carefully explicit. "My work has always been involved with shapes and linear rhythms," she began.

My earlier paintings were comprised of flat shapes emphasizing the picture plane. At first these paintings were abstractions; later they were landscapes, painted from drawings which addressed the particulars of interlocking puzzle pieces characteristic of that landscape. I consciously sought out scenes which had clear and distinct shape patterns, making it easier to translate them into my composition of painted flat shapes. Texture and color differentiations in nature made patterns clear to me for abstracting into a rhythmic field of shapes.

This is, unfortunately, only a fraction of her "Artist Statement," but it gives an idea of how she looks at the prairie. The formalist is often accused of not really looking at the object, only its form. Patrick's devotion to form makes her look at the landscape all the more clearly. If she is selective—and who is not?—she is also exquisitely appreciative.

The final respondent to this unscientific survey is James Winn, born in Hannibal, Missouri, and now living in Sycamore, Illinois, a prairie town near De Kalb. "I have spent all my adult life trying to be visual," he wrote in an accompanying letter, "and believe that it is my only articulate expression. Nevertheless, here are my attempts to answer your questions." The note reminds us again that the artists' pictures are the ultimate expression of their visions and that the words "vision" and "perspective," as used here, are metaphors from the arts of painting, drawing, and photography. And yet Winn's thoughtful answers add to an understanding of his work and to seeing the prairies better, as they are seen through his work. A former student of Harold Gregor, Winn is like Gary Irving, James Butler, Harold Holoun, and others in finding the prairie sublime:

What I am most interested in is how open, flat, and vast the prairies are. I am most keenly aware of this when returning from the city (Chicago) or from a forested or hilly area. Spaces like those seem almost an indoor affair. . . . When I stand alone (but not totally alone, I do not like that, there are twenty farms in sight) under the constantly changing sky, it is often for me a sublime experience. I sense order, purpose, transcendence: Presence. That is what I am trying to picture. The prairie with its varied skies is a great vehicle for the aesthetic of the sublime.

Quite understandably, he cites the Luminists as his greatest influence, defining them not as "regionalists" (a term he, too, believes is just an art critics' "pigeon-hole"), but as part of an international early-nineteenth-century movement, found in northern Europe and Russia as well as America. Like many of the Luminists, his interest is also in "the mundane and overlooked commonplace." One of his other subjects is "Midwestern small town back yards or front porches." He likes them in "raking evening sunlight. It creates strong value patterns of contrasting lights and darks, and the colors are bright and saturated." But the backyards and front porches seem not to affect him the way the prairies do. This emotion is described powerfully in his brief statement:

I would like to in some measure share with the viewer that uplifting spiritual presence I sense residing in the land. I am trying to address the aesthetic of the sublime, a glimpse of the Orderer in His order. More than to inform, I want the viewer to be moved emotionally. Therefore in my pictures the compositional elements, especially value, color and line are adjusted to embrace the harmonic sense of transcendent purpose in nature. I want to paint scenes of a place where you think you might hear ". . . the Lord God walking in the garden in the cool of the day" (Genesis 3:8).

With such a variety of responses, there is no way to summarize all these artists' perspectives on the prairie. Some, like Fred Easker and Genie Patrick, are drawn to the formal shapes and patterns in the carefully tended fields, roads, and pastures that cover the rolling earth. Others, while attracted by these features, are more moved by the prairies' sublimity: the vastness of the space, the intensity of the light, the magnificence of the skies. Harold Gregor, however,

who responds to both these qualities, seems to have been further intrigued by the technical challenges that the prairie presents to the artist. With their "flatscapes," aerial views, root-level perspectives, panoramas, elongated picture frames, and other devices, prairie artists have had to be just as resourceful and inventive, I am tempted to say, as the inventors of rakes and plows and washing machines. Still other prairie artists today take a deep and complex historical perspective. Robert Adams, Terry Evans, and David Plowden, for instance, are in the tradition of Willa Cather and Wright Morris in noting and suggesting prairie history. But their differences demonstrate that there is not just one historical perspective. There are many. There are the vast environmental changes, the human suffering and achievements, the political hopes and defeats, the technological creations, and the great economic forces that have swept across the prairie and left their indelible marks.

Then there are these artists' various degrees of engagement with environmental issues, a question that is of both current and long-term interest. Whether they intended to or not, the artists in the Hudson River School tradition, like Albert Bierstadt and Thomas Moran, have had a lasting impact on the country. By helping create the American taste for mountainous terrain as "wilderness scenery," they contributed to the setting aside of national parks and the preservation of land that was once considered "worthless." Twentieth-century photographers like Ansel Adams and Eliot Porter have had an even greater impact. With their work promoted by the Sierra Club and other environmental groups, and printed in coffee-table books and on posters, they not only have popularized the Sierras and the desert, but have made parts of them into national monuments, sacred icons, that are off-limits to mining, logging, and dam construction. The prairies and the plains, though, have not been similarly represented. Valued instead as farmland, or as "only" farmland, infinite and featureless, they have been exploited at will. Indeed, in places they have been exploited to extinction. As almost all the contemporary prairie artists quoted here attest, there is definitely a relationship between how land is seen and how it is valued and used. As Robert Adams so simply puts it, art "helps people care."

But Adams's few, plain words may also hide the relationship's complexity—its many varieties and dimensions. Lee Allen's post office murals, *Soil Conservation* and *Conservation of Wildlife,* are examples of the propagandistic realism encouraged by the Works Progress Administration in the 1930s. Although later scorned by abstractionists and high modernists, such art now has both historical interest and an affectionate and critical following. Across the plains and prairies, especially in small towns and cities, people seek out the surviving examples of it. Roger Brown's *Citizens Surveying the Flat Landscape* takes a more sardonic perspective. It does not apply specifically to prairies. It also does not celebrate the landscape or promote conservation as much as it ridicules the "Citizens." With the painters and photographers of contemporary rural Illinois, Iowa, and Nebraska, who do celebrate the landscape, a question then arises: What landscape are they actually celebrating? A cornfield may be attractive for its order and symmetry, but also be an example of sickening chemical agriculture and a site of erosion and exploitation. Prairie monoculture bitterly proves that the vast and sublime are not necessarily healthy. Making the modern farm look good in photographs and calendar art has for too long been the goal of the farm-equipment and chemical advertisers. To guard against such deceptions, an artist must know his or her subject intimately. Walter Hatke advocates this

when he says, "One must walk across the land, touch it, note the crunch underfoot, breathe the air, literally smell and taste the atmosphere." Even look at the back of every building. But this kind of familiarity takes time, study, and experience.

Having this knowledge should be a goal of the true regionalist, however "limiting" or "pejorative" the term is. Knowledge such as Hatke advocates is what can make regionalism ultimately very positive. Yet the testimony of these artists, Hatke included, is that one's understanding of one's region is definitely enhanced by travel, study, and living somewhere else. Harold Gregor and Harold Holoun studied in the West. Stuart Klipper, Gary Irving, and most of the prairie photographers have done work in many other places. Even Terry Evans of Kansas found that Chicago did not "destroy my artistic identity." Rather, it "allowed me to see my own work more clearly." Nevertheless, there are not universal prescriptions on this point. Evans benefited by going to Chicago. Gregor decided not to go to New York. Such choices are, quite rightly, extremely personal.

The number of these prairie artists and the diversity of their interests, techniques, working methods, and perspectives demonstrate, finally, the great complexity of the prairies today. Despite the monotonous uniformity that the prairies continue to have for many viewers, these artists have found what can justly be called a new continent, filled with complex forms, intense and subtle light, slices of social and national history, environmental change, political conflict, and the interweaving of all these forces. The artists are, in turn, helping others to see this new and renewed landscape, aware, as Gary Irving says, that "if we don't develop an appreciation for the prairie, both natural and cultivated, I suspect it will continue to be subjected to pressures it cannot sustain." At the same time, as Terry Evans humbly says, artists don't necessarily see better than other people: "We all need to see with attention, honor, & respect for land."

Appendix

These ten questions were asked in the final version of the questionnaire:

1. How long have you painted or photographed the prairie or plains landscape? How did you become interested in doing it?

2. What other kinds of landscapes do you do?

3. What most attracts you—for example, color? form? subject? the natural landscape or built landscape?

4. Do you feel your work has been affected by a specific artistic tradition? Is that tradition "regionalist" in your view? If so, and if you can separate the chicken from the egg, what drew you to that tradition? Do you object to the term "regionalist"?

5. What prairie or midwestern writers have most influenced you?

6. Political activists have often had a double relation to art. On the one hand they love to have artists represent their cause somehow—in the prairie tradition, for instance, some of the painters in the thirties were loved by the left—and on the other hand politicos often dislike what they see as "aestheticizing," deflecting people from the political into the aesthetic realm. Where do you see your own work in relation to such issues generally, and to more specific issues like soil conservation, prairie restoration, pollution, and the like?

7. Some people claim that regionalist art is made possible by a deep, lived experience with the land, and others have suggested the opposite. Kathleen Norris, who writes about the plains, has said that regionalist writers have in every case spent some important time elsewhere (very often it is New York), and it is perhaps this distance that makes their art possible, and gives it its specific shape, when they return. How do you feel this applies to you and your work?

8. To what extent do you feel the art market rewards or provides a disincentive for the work that you do?

9. If for some reason you had to move to a new area, what would become of your prairie art? Would you transfer your attention to your new environment?

10. Do you see a relationship between how land is seen, including how it is represented by artists, and how it is used? What would you like that relationship to be?

I would like to thank Joni Kinsey and Tom Lutz for suggesting some of these questions and for helping revise others.

CONTRIBUTORS
INDEX

CONTRIBUTORS

Pauline Drobney is Refuge Biologist at the Neal Smith National Wildlife Refuge and Prairie Learning Center, the 8,654-acre prairie–savanna restoration south of Prairie City, Iowa. Previously, she ran a natural areas consulting company, Compass Plant Consultants, in Cedar Falls, Iowa. She is a graduate of the University of Northern Iowa, and has B.A.s in both biology and art, and an M.A. in biology. She was also a co-founder and the first president of the Iowa Prairie Network.

Ed Folsom is the F. Wendell Miller Distinguished Professor of English at the University of Iowa. Editor of the *Walt Whitman Quarterly Review* for fifteen years, he is the author of *Walt Whitman's Native Representations* (1994), editor of *Walt Whitman: The Centennial Essays* (1994), and co-editor of *Walt Whitman and the World* (1995) and *Walt Whitman: The Measure of His Song* (1981, 1998). He has also co-edited *Major Authors on CD-ROM: Walt Whitman* (1997) and, with Kenneth Price, directs the "Walt Whitman Hypertext Archive," a World Wide Web–based teaching and research tool.

Lance M. Foster is an enrolled member of the Iowa Tribe of Kansas and Nebraska, a member of the Bear Clan, and a descendent of White Cloud, an Iowa chief, through his grandmother, Esteline Murphy Foster. He was raised in Helena, Montana, the son of Gary and Rita Foster. He maintains that he owes his accomplishments and knowledge of traditional teachings to the love and support of his family and to relatives and family friends, especially the family of Herman Bear Comes Out, of the Northern Cheyenne, and the family of Pete Fee, of the Iowa. Foster has B.A.s in anthropology and Native American studies from the University of Montana, and attended the Institute of American Indian Arts in Santa Fe, New Mexico. He received his M.A. in anthropology and his M.L.A. in landscape architecture from Iowa State University. He is the author of several articles, including the article on Iowa for *The Encyclopedia of Native Americans in the Twentieth Century* (1994). He has served as a consultant on cultural sites for the Iowa Office of the State Archaeologist and the Minnesota State Historical Society. As a visual artist, he has won several awards for his paintings of Iowa subjects. He also owns and operates a website and a publishing company, Native Nations Press. He recently moved to Santa Fe, New Mexico, to be with love Lisa Nelmida, of Hawaii, who serves as a continuing inspiration and supporter.

Robert E. Grese is interested in landscape design and management that preserves the unique qualities of a place. He has studied Jens Jensen as a primary exemplar of such work and elaborated on Jensen's thought and design in *Jens Jensen: Maker of Natural Parks and Gardens* (1992). He teaches in the School of Natural Resources and Environment at the University of

Michigan, where his courses include topics in landscape architecture and ecological restoration. He is active in helping organize a volunteer stewardship effort to preserve and restore special natural areas in the Huron River Valley and leads prairie and savanna restoration efforts in Nichols Arboretum at the University of Michigan.

Wes Jackson founded the Land Institute in Salina, Kansas. His books include *New Roots for Agriculture* (1985), *Altars of Unhewn Stone* (1987), and *Becoming Native to This Place* (1996).

Joni L. Kinsey is associate professor of American art at the University of Iowa. She is the author of *Plain Pictures: Images of the American Prairie* (1996), which won the Eugene M. Kayden National Book Award for 1996. She was also the curator for the exhibition "Plain Pictures: Images of the American Prairie," held in 1996 to 1997. Her other publications include *Thomas Moran and the Surveying of the American West* (1992) and numerous articles and chapters about American landscape art and imagery of the West and Middle West.

Aldo Leopold was born in Burlington, Iowa, in 1887, graduated from the Yale Forest School in 1909, and worked for many years for the U.S. Forest Service, mainly in the Southwest. In 1933, he became professor of game management at the University of Wisconsin. He died in 1948 of a heart attack, while fighting a brush fire near his "Shack" property in central Wisconsin. *A Sand County Almanac* (1949), although still unknown to many Americans, is a classic of environmental literature.

Tom Lutz is a cosmopolitan, living half the year in Los Angeles and half in Iowa City. He is the author of *American Nervousness, 1903: An Anecdotal History* (1991) and *Crying: A Natural and Cultural History of Tears* (1999), and an editor of *These "Colored" United States* (1996). Having spent years living the good life, raising his own organic food and harvesting his own woodlot for fuel, he is now living the good life, commuting in and out of Hollywood and hobnobbing with the glam. He is working on a screenplay that may or may not have a scene involving prairie restoration.

Curt Meine is a conservation biologist, writer, and historian. He works with the Crane Specialist Group of the World Conservation Union (IUCN) and the International Crane Foundation in Baraboo, Wisconsin, as coordinator of the IUCN Action Plan for Cranes. He is the author of *Aldo Leopold: His Life and Work* (1988), editor of *Wallace Stegner and the Continental Vision: Essays on Literature, History, and Landscape* (1997), and co-editor of *The Essential Aldo Leopold: Quotations and Commentaries* (1999). Curt resides in Prairie du Sac, Wisconsin, where he is active in efforts to restore the former Sauk prairie.

Rebecca Roberts is an associate professor of geography at the University of Iowa whose research explores the knife-edge between natural and social constructions of the environment. Her recent research, published in *Economic Geography, Environment and Planning, Annals of the Association of American Geographers,* and *Journal of Rural Studies,* has focused on agriculture, water, and sustainability in the central United States.

Robert F. Sayre is editor of *Take This Exit: Rediscovering the Iowa Landscape* (1989), called by J. B. Jackson "the book about rural America that we have been waiting for: one that tells us how the everyday landscape works." He is also an authority on Thoreau and on American autobiography and is the editor of *American Lives* (1994). "Landscape is a culture's autobiography," he says, "where greed and love and all its many other secret, unspoken designs are carved in the earth. The prairie reveals the U.S.A. like an open book."

Jane E. Simonsen, a doctoral student in American studies at the University of Iowa, grew up in Wisconsin wooded country but considers the midwestern open country her second home. As an undergraduate in English at Gustavus Adolphus College in St. Peter, Minnesota, she cultivated an interest in researching the social meanings of western landscapes as well as a penchant for cycling county roads through the Minnesota prairie, both of which entail an appreciation of level grounds. Her graduate work has included research on homestead legislation and western women's literature, and she is especially interested in literary, legal, and photographic representations of landscapes. "I hope," she says, "that as more abandoned rail lines are converted into bike trails, Alexander Gardner's visions of the prairie will be revived."

Shelton Stromquist teaches labor and social history of the United States at the University of Iowa. He is the author of *A Generations of Boomers: The Pattern of Railroad Labor Conflict in Nineteenth-Century America* (1987), *Solidarity and Survival: An Oral History of Iowa Labor in the Twentieth Century* (1993), and *Unionizing the Jungles: Labor and Community in the Twentieth-Century Meatpacking Industry* (1997). His interest in "prairie politics" grows out of a larger, ongoing project dealing with the politics of progressive reform. He has just completed a new book, *Reinventing a "People": The Progressive Movement and the Class Question,* and is working on another that focuses on urban working-class politics in the Progressive Era.

INDEX

Abstract Expressionism, 205, 206

Adams, Ansel, 211

Adams, Robert, 201–2, 212

Addams, Jane, 8, 110, 116, 117, 122n40, 126, 127

Aerial views, 38, 46n47, 174, 205

Aesthetics: of abstraction, 67; classical (sublime, beautiful, picturesque), 9–10, 17–18, 19, 20, 62–63, 64, 65, 201; and conservation, 131–39; and cosmopolitanism, 94–95; and economics, 4; modernist, 18; of prospect painting, 5, 15–16; of regionalism, 88, 92–93, 102; Romantic, 207–8; traditional, in landscape architecture, 126–27; traditional, in western photography, 65; of wilderness protection, 154. *See also* Abstract Expressionism; Architecture; Art and politics; Form; Prairie aesthetics; Prospect

African Americans, 54–56, 77. *See also* Exodusters

Agriculture: agricultural chemicals, 193, 206; agroindustrial capitalism, 29, 40. *See also* Corn; Prairie, breaking and plowing of; Prairie aesthetics, as garden; Prairie plants

Allen, Lee, 202, 212

Allison, William B., 29

Anderson, Sherwood, 33, 102

Architecture, 8, 33; landscape architecture (*see* Jensen, Jens); Prairie School, 33. *See also* University of Wisconsin Arboretum

Art and politics, 202, 203, 204–5, 206–7, 208–9, 211–12

Art market, influence of, 202

Atget, Eugène, 209

Atwood, David, 28

Bacon, Francis, 194, 198

Bears, and Ioway culture, 188

Bell, William A., 66, 73

Benton, Thomas Hart, 21, 202; *Open Country, 23*

Berry, Wendell, 87, 92, 95, 102, 103, 191

Betz, Robert, 174

Bierstadt, Albert, 211

Bodmer, Karl, 208

Boime, Albert, 17

Brady, Mathew, 63

Brodhead, Richard, 88, 92, 94, 101

Brown, Roger, 202–3

Bryan, William Jennings, 6, 8, 108, 109, 145

Bryant, William Cullen, 26

Buffalo (bison), 149, 154, 166, 170; in Ioway culture, 186–89; and ragweed, 162; in Whitman's poetry, 54

Butala, Sharon, 204

Butcher, Solomon, 20; *Using All the Farm for Crops, Plowing Corn in the Dooryard, Custer County Nebraska, 21*

Butler, James D., 203

Capitalism, 4, 6, 28–32, 87, 198–99; capitalists, 27–29, 32; and corporate power, 109–10; ecological capital, 192–93. *See also* Prospect

Carver, Jonathan, 161–62

Cather, Willa, 4, 6, 34, 39, 202, 204, 209; *My Ántonia,* 93, 94; *O Pioneers!,* 94, 98–101; and regionalism, 86–87, 101–2

Catlin, George, 17, 204; *Eagle Dance, Iowa, 186; Nishnabottana Bluffs, Upper Missouri, 18*

Chardon, Francis, 26

Chicago: architects, 129; and the *Midland,* 88; as midwestern trade center, 28, 29, 111–12; parks and landscaping, 125–27, 129–31; and progressivism, 116–17; Renaissance, 33. *See also* Chicago Wilderness Project; Jensen, Jens; Joliet arsenal

Chicago, Burlington and Quincy Railroad, 112–13

regionalism, 91–92. *See also* Cosmopolitanism; Regionalism
Loess hills, 169, 183, 185, 206
Long, Steven, 16
Lopez, Barry, 209
Luminists, 211

Magazines, 27–29, 88, 95–96
Manifest Destiny, 6, 61, 74
Mart, Vincent, 38
Masters, Edgar Lee, 108, 109, 111
Maynard, Fredelle, 57
McCrea, Samuel H., 29
Melville, Herman, 26, 103
Middle West (and Midwest), 7, 107–8, 111–12; and architecture (*see* Jensen, Jens); ecology (*see* Leopold, Aldo); ecosystem, 176–77; "Middle Place" and Oneota culture, 179; place names, 55–56, 170; plants, 124; politics, 107–19; and regional exceptionalism, 111; and women readers, 88. *See also* Local-color movement; Plains; Prairie democracy; Prairie ecosystems; Prospect; Regionalism
Midland, 88
Miller, Alfred Jacob, 200
Minnesota, 107–8; Nonpartisan League, 114; progressivism, 115; roadside restoration, 176
Missouri: Exodusters, 54; Prairie Foundation, 176; St. Louis, 62
Moran, Thomas, 208, 211
Morris, Wright, 22, 204, 208; *Abandoned Farm, 25*

Natural Resource Conservation Service, 153
Natural Systems Agriculture, 4–5, 193–94, 196, 197. *See also* Agriculture; Jackson, Wes; Land Institute
Neal Smith National Wildlife Refuge (Walnut Creek NWR), 9, 175, 189
Nebraska, strikes in, 113. *See also* Cather, Willa; Weaver, John E.
Neihardt, John G., 204
No Heart of Fear, 183–85; map by, *184*
Nonpartisan League, 113, 114
Norris, Frank, 93, 111
Norris, Kathleen, 87, 93–94, 209
North Dakota, 110; Nonpartisan League, 114
Nye, Russel, 107, 111–12, 114

O'Brien County, Iowa, 5, 35–43
Ogden, William B., 28
Oklahoma Green Corn Rebellion, 114
Oneota Idians, 179, 181
Open Spaces Act, 34, 41
O'Sullivan, Timothy, 64, 65

Packard, Stephen, 176
Palmer, William Jackson, 65, 66, 71–72
Patrick, Genie Hudson, vii, 25, 201, 209–10; *A Season Turning, 26*
Paullina, Iowa, 41. *See also* O'Brien County, Iowa
Pike, Zebulon, 16
"Plain Pictures" exhibit, vii, 89, 200–201
Plains: as artistic subject, 207–8, 209; and buffalo, 186; as desert, 16; lack of artistic representation, 212; and leveling by rail, 71–72; in Whitman's poetry, 53. *See also* Landscape; Prairie aesthetics
Plowden, David, 208–9
Pocahontas County, Iowa, 9, 164, 170
Poetry and politics, 108–9, 117–19. *See also* Whitman, Walt
Populist movement, 8, 113–14
Populist Party, 110. *See also* Middle West, politics; Populist movement
Portage, Wisconsin: Agency House, 9, 161–62; landscape, 161–62
Porter, Eliot, 211
Prairie, breaking and plowing of, 4, 5, 32–34, 167, 169–70. *See also* Agriculture; Corn; Homestead Act
Prairie, tallgrass, 146, 173, 176; and agriculture, 169; demise of, 149, 169, 177; and Ioway Indians, 181, 188; as metaphor for democracy, 48–50. *See also* Prairie ecosystems
Prairie aesthetics, 5, 15–16, 61; complexity, 204, 209, 212; and democracy, 73–78; elements of, in landscape architecture, 124, 129–31, 137; flatness, 63, 65–67, 78–84, 205; as garden, 16, 28, 37, 50–52; and identity formation, 35–43; lack of traditional aesthetics, 19; 26–27; metaphors, 28, 29, 33–34; paradoxes in, 34–35; and politics of preservation, 34–43; tabula rasa or blank, 15, 26, 29, 38, 62–63; in Whitman's poetry (*see* Whitman, Walt). *See also* Aesthetics; Landscape; Prospect